Albino Luciani

POPE JOHN PAUL I

A Passionate Adventure

Living the Catholic Faith Today

Second Revised Edition

Translated with an Introduction

by Lori Pieper, OFS

Preface by Justin Cardinal Rigali

New York

TAU CROSS BOOKS AND MEDIA

2014

Library of Congress Control Number: 2014950106

ISBN:

978-0-9796688-8-3 (Paperback)
978-0-9907756-0-7 (EPUB)
978-0-9796688-9-0 (Kindle)

The texts translated here come from the following work and are used with permission:

Opera Omnia di Albino Luciani, Giovanni Paolo I
© P.P.F.M.C. Messaggero Di S. Antonio-Editrice
Basilica del Santo, Via Orto Botanico 11, 35123 Padova, Italy
www.edizionimessaggero.it

Cover Design by Lori Pieper.
Front Cover photo courtesy of *L'Osservatore Romano*.
Back Cover photo of Cardinal Luciani in 1973 is in the public domain

Contents

The Church

The Pope

Catholic Social Teaching

Living the Christian Life

Evangelization and Catechesis

The Tough Questions

Faith and Culture

Prayers

Acknowledgments

Because the hoping and planning for the publication of this work have stretched over many years, it would be impossible to thank all the people who helped me in my labors. But I am grateful to all of them, named and unnamed.

First of all, my thanks are due to Ray and Lauretta Seabeck with whom I have collaborated since 1990 publishing the English-language edition of *Humilitas,* for their support and friendship and their cooperation in reprinting translations that first appeared in this journal.

To Don Francesco Taffarel and Msgr. Ausilio da Rif for their help with questions about Luciani's writings, and Don Diego Lorenzi and the late Msgr. Mario Senigaglia, for their help and insight.

To the late Edoardo and Antonietta Luciani, who aided me in my research many years ago, and to Pia Luciani, Stefania Falasca, Loris Serafini, Paul Spackman, Nancy Fusillo and Mo Guernon for their present help and support.

My delighted thanks to Justin Cardinal Rigali for agreeing to write the preface, and for so beautifully capturing the spirit of John Paul I as we all knew him.

To Bill Kalush of the Conjuring Arts Research Center, for his great patience in disruptions in my work;

And, as always, to my parents, John and Betty Pieper, for their constant love and support.

Abbreviations

The Documents of Vatican II

AA   *Apostolicam Actuositatem* — Decree on the Apostolate of the Laity

AG   *Ad Gentes* — Decree on the Mission Activity of the Church

CD   *Christus Dominus* — Decree on the Pastoral Office of Bishops

DH   *Dignitatis Humanae* — Declaration on Religious Liberty

DV   *Dei Verbum* — Constitution on Divine Revelation

GS   *Gaudium et Spes* — Constitution on the Church in the Modern World

GE   *Gravissimum Educationis* — Declaration on Christian Education

IM   *Inter Mirifica* — Decree on the Means of Social Communication

LG   *Lumen Gentium* — Constitution on the Church

NA   *Nostra Aetate* — Declaration on the Church's Relation to Non-Christian Religions

OE   *Orientalem Ecclesiarum* — Decree on Eastern Catholic Churches

OT   *Optatem Totius* — Decree on Priestly Training

PC   *Perfectae Caritatis* — Decree on the Adaptation and Renewal of Religious Life

PO   *Presbyterium Ordinis* — Decree on the Ministry and Life of Priests

SC   *Sacrosanctum Concilium* — Constitution on the Liturgy

UR   *Unitatis Redintegratio* — Decree on Ecumenism

Other Works

AAS   *Acta Apostolicae Sedis*

EN   *Evangelii Nuntiandi*

MC   *Marialis Cultus*

MM   *Mater et Magistra*

Opera Albino Luciani — Giovanni Paolo I, *Opera Omnia.*
           (Padua: Edizioni Messaggero 1988-89. 9 vols).

OR   *L'Osservatore Romano*

PL   Migne, *Patrologia Latina*

PT   *Pacem in Terris*

RD   *Rivista diocesana del patriarcato di Venezia*

A special note about Luciani's citations of the best-known works of St. Francis de Sales, without doubt his favorite writer: he almost always calls *An Introduction to the Devout Life* by the title *Filotea*, after the original addressee, the devout woman who is a "friend of God"; likewise he cites *A Treatise on the Love of God* as *Teotimo* for similar reasons; the addressee is "God-fearing." The citations preserve these versions of the titles when they occur.

Preface

With great devotion to the memory of Pope John Paul I, Lori Pieper, OFS introduces us to his person and his teaching. In *A Passionate Adventure, Living the Catholic Faith Today*, she presents in her English-language translation a significant collection of the pastoral writings of Albino Luciani before his election to the See of Peter.

The content of this book confirms the accuracy of the image that the world received of John Paul I, at the time of his election, as a joyful and gentle Pope whose own life was totally centered on the Person of Jesus Christ, the Chief Pastor of the Church.

From Pope John Paul I's own words, there emerges a clear expression of how he exercised his pastoral office, how he loved his people, and how he proclaimed to them the Word of God in all its purity and integrity and with all its demands. We meet a Pope rich in humanity, exemplary in showing kindness and compassion, calling us to Jesus and inviting us to pray.

This book leads up to encounter John Paul I in so many different situations of his pastoral ministry. Hence we come to understand how, despite the shortness of his pontificate, his legacy of faith and love endures in the Church. The publication of this volume is a welcome contribution for those who wish to understand the papacy as it has been exercised in recent times. This book offers a splendid opportunity to encounter an outstanding disciple of Jesus Christ in the person of John Paul I.

August 15, 2014
Solemnity of the Assumption of the Blessed Virgin Mary

† Justin Cardin Rigali
Archbishop Emeritus of Philadelphia

Foreword to the Revised Edition

From the moment that Pope Francis first stepped onto the balcony of St. Peter's Basilica on March 13, 2013, the world was captivated by his smile, his humility and the simplicity of his speech. And those of us who recall the papal elections of 1978 found ourselves unexpectedly saying, "He's just like John Paul I!"

That smile, those homely metaphors, the enchanting wit and humor, the brushing aside of protocol and ceremony, the closeness to the poor, the insistence that the papacy is service—all those characteristics of Pope Francis are strikingly similar to those of the last Italian Pope. Unfortunately, too many people in the English-speaking world still don't know about John Paul I and the gifts he brought to the Church all those years ago.

It has been my dream for more than 35 years that people should know more about Albino Luciani. As a college student, I was captivated by him at his election on August 26, 1978, and mourned when he died suddenly barely a month later, on September 28.

As time went by, and everyone else seemed to have forgotten him, I was collecting information about him. I sent to Italy for his published writings and read them, teaching myself Italian in the process. I dreamed of someday writing a full biography of him. I also wanted to make his writings available in English to celebrate not just his holiness and wisdom as a priest and bishop, but his skill as a gifted writer as well.

After the appearance of the sensational book *In God's Name* by David Yallop in 1984, I knew I had to start work on an accurate account of Luciani's life and death right away. I traveled to Italy, meeting his family and collecting information for a biography.

Even after all the sensationalism and sales raised by Yallop's book and by John Cornwell's *A Thief in the Night,* published in 1989,

I could not find a publisher for my work, which was deemed "not controversial enough" by major publishers. I had no idea then that it would be twenty-five years after his death before Ray and Lauretta Seabeck and I and a lovely Carmelite nun were able to put together *The Smiling Pope: the Life and Teaching of John Paul I* (Our Sunday Visitor, 2004).

Since then, I have longed to expand on the small number of Luciani's pre-papal works in that volume, and especially to give the complete text of some of his writings that had sparked controversy. Some of these had even been misunderstood and misquoted, such as his interview on the first "test-tube baby" in 1978 and his pastoral letter on birth control after the release of *Humanae Vitae.*

At length I was able to fulfill my dream. The first edition of this book was planned thematically to go along with the Year of Faith in 2013. For several reasons, the work had to be done in haste. Now that I am publishing a new edition to coincide with the completion and consignment of the *Positio* for John Paul I's canonization process in September 2014, I am taking advantage of the opportunity to update and revise my Foreword and correct a few things that were overlooked in the original. The revised edition is also completed by a new preface by Justin Cardinal Rigali.

So many things have changed in the Church in the decades since these writings were first published in Italian in the 1960's and 70's. But open this book to the first section and you will be hit with their contemporary relevance.

In 1967-68, Luciani was the bishop of Vittorio Veneto, and his diocese, along with the rest of the world, was celebrating the original Year of Faith called for by Pope Paul VI in the wake of the Second Vatican Council. The themes of Luciani's writings sound quite familiar to our ears: the challenge of evangelization amid controversy over the proper interpretation of the Council, theological dissent, the existence of mythological elements in Scripture, the rise of relativism, the relationship between faith and science and the growing influence of atheism.

During the Year of Faith just past, and still today, the faith is again being attacked on all sides by doubt, skepticism and the dissent of many theologians. We are again trying to find a way to preserve the faith without the Church being ripped apart by controversy.

Luciani's writings are a product of their time, of course, but many of the answers he gave to these questions are perennial ones, still sound and useful, and are conveyed by a master teacher. Especially important is his frequent admonition that dissent and questions of interpretation of the Council must not be allowed to take over the whole discussion on faith. The Year of Faith, he said, "is a clear testimony, a translation of inner faith into virtuous outward actions and an active Christian life." ("Something Less than a Syllabus"). In the same way, Pope Benedict XVI hoped that the recent Year of Faith would be "a time of grace and commitment to an ever fuller conversion to God, to reinforce our faith in Him and to proclaim Him with joy to the men of our time."[1]

The most recent Year of Faith was timed to coincide with the 50th anniversary of the opening of the Second Vatican Council. The themes of Luciani's writings sound in harmony with the themes of the Council and of the New Evangelization in a way that can be seen as prophetic in regard to the papacies of his successors, John Paul II, Benedict and now Francis: the universal call to holiness, the apostolate of the laity in the world, the continued need for evangelization and the ongoing reform of the Church.

But in order to share our faith, we need to understand and live deeply the mysteries of our faith. Luciani applied himself daily in his episcopal ministry to helping people do this. He wrote beautifully on the faith, because he was a man of faith. His whole approach can be summed up in this passage from one of the selections in this book ("How Jesus Returns at Christmas"):

Paul sums up the whole Gospel well when he says, *dilexit me et tradidit semetipsum pro me* (Gal. 2:20): "He loved me and gave himself for me." But

St. Paul was not content with summing up; he drew some practical conclusions. That love, he said, is only the first love; now must come the second, mine. Christ has written the first page of the book; now I must write the second. The immense love that Christ has for me leaves me no peace, it compels me, it cries out to me: "Get moving, Paul, and do something for him in return" (cf. 2 Cor 5:14).

And he really got moving: he set out to follow Christ as though on an impassioned and passion-inspiring adventure.

Faith, Luciani said, is a "yes" to God with our whole being. Faith is allowing ourselves to be "seized" or captured by God, so that we can be given the ability to follow him and grasp hold of him. Philippians 3:12 and the surrounding verses—judging by the number of times he quoted them—must have been one of Luciani's very favorite passages of Scripture. This reflects his understanding that faith is not a passive thing. We ourselves must run that race, like St. Paul, for the eternal prize, which, he recognized clearly, is Jesus himself.

Luciani was a master in aiding his readers or hearers in understanding the truths of the faith, whether through poetry or homely metaphors. All of these truths are explored in this book. But he stressed most of all two things: first, God's love and mercy are infinite, famously expressed in his words as Pope: "God . . . is Papa, even more a mother";[2] and second, faith is a journey, an adventure, and love of God is its driving force. In his dialogue with a young boy named Daniele, he said:

> The Lord has given us this strong desire to make progress. Look. We began by living in caves, in lake dwellings, then in huts, then we put up houses, then palaces, now there are skyscrapers. Always

advancing. At first we went on foot, then on horseback, on camels, then in carriages, then by train, now by airplane. Always advancing. This is the law of progress . . . the love of God is a kind of journey. We must make progress here too. "Lord, make me love you more and more." Never stop. The Lord has said to all Christians: "You are the light of the world," "You are the salt of the earth," "Become perfect as your Heavenly Father is perfect" . . . never stop.[3]

He readily admits that in the modern secular age, staying on course is difficult, but possible, and he stresses that God can reach even the most lost ("Light in Our Darkness"). He also knew that love of God is the secret of faith, when he said, citing St. Francis de Sales: "In the wind (of temptation), the great fires (of love of God) grow larger, while the little ones go out!"[4]

The same ardor blazes on almost every page of this book. "The truths of faith are not cold, inert things," Luciani insists, "but incandescent fire, one that urges us on, makes us restless, a fire bursting with energy, that compels us to take eager and passionate action" ("Faith and Conversion").

Luciani, himself such a passionate believer, one wholly committed to following Jesus, urges us to "go and do likewise" (Lk 10:37). My prayer is that this book will help us all to do just this.

Lori Pieper

August 26, 2014
36th Anniversary of the Election of John Paul I

Notes

[1] Pope Benedict XVI, Holy Mass for the New Evangelization, October 16, 2011. Translation from the Vatican web site: www. Vatican.va.

[2] There is an English translation on the Vatican web site.

[3] General Wednesday audience of September 27, 1978. The Pope substituted the dialogue for a passage he had originally written.

[4] "The Ship of God," letter to St. Francis de Sales; *Illustrissimi*, in *Opera* 1:310.

A Note on the Translation

All translations from the Latin and other languages of the work of the saints and Church Fathers are my own, unless otherwise noted. For the works of Popes and Councils, I follow those by the Holy See (available on the Vatican web site).

Scripture citations present a special difficulty; Luciani of course usually used the common Italian translation of Scripture, but at times, it seems that he translated according to the sense of either the Latin Vulgate or the Greek text. At time he even paraphrased Scripture to give a livelier impression to his readers. For this reason, in translating I have done my best to adhere to his original wording or at least his original sense in these passages. Therefore while at times, where possible, for the better comprehension of readers, I have conformed the wording to the best known American English Catholic edition, the New American Bible, I did not and could not follow any particular translation strictly.

Introduction

Man of Faith: The Life of Albino Luciani

In writing this short biography, I do not intend to give anything like a complete account of Albino Luciani's life or thought. But since English-speaking readers know so little about his life, some background is needed for reading his works, and fortunately it is not difficult to give people information they don't have about him. I want to give enough detail to allow readers to understand Luciani's family and the world he grew up in, what motivated him and the general shape of his thought. I also want to correct some erroneous impressions that have arisen and give some context—in regard to both happenings in the Church and Luciani's own life—to some of the selections from his writings, especially because they belong to another historical era.

A POOR CHILDHOOD

Albino Luciani was born on October 17, 1912, in Canale D'Agordo, a little village in the Dolomite mountains in northern Italy. Because of the bad economic situation in the area, both his parents had been forced to leave Italy to look for work elsewhere very early in their lives.

Albino's father, Giovanni Luciani, left home at the age of eleven to work as a bricklayer in Germany and Switzerland, and later at the glassblowing factories in Venice. His mother, Bortola Tancon, had left school at the age of fourteen to work and help her family. In 1911, after various jobs, she was working in the kitchen at the hospital of S. Giovanni e Paolo in Venice, and considering a religious vocation, when she met Giovanni, then a widower with two daughters who were deaf and in need of a mother. The sisters advised Bortola to marry him which she did happily. Giovanni had joined a socialist labor union in Germany, and though he left the Church in his youth, his devout wife brought him back to the faith.

They returned to live in Canale d'Agordo, but to support his family, Giovanni had to work a good part of the year in France or Germany, where work was available. He was absent at the time of the birth of his first child Albino, who was named for a friend of his killed in an accident at work. Later, in addition to Pia and Amalia, the daughters of his first marriage, came Federico (b. 1915), who died in infancy, Edoardo (1917-2008) and Antonia (1920-2009). Just before World War I, Giovanni went to Argentina, where there were many Italian emigrants, hoping to establish himself there and send for his family. This plan was abandoned when Italy entered the war and Giovanni came home to join his country's military reserves. So John Paul I just barely missed becoming the first Argentinian Pope.

Albino suffered from hunger during his childhood, especially when the village was invaded by Austrian troops during the war. He and his sister Pia even had to go and beg for food. But life was not always harsh. "Our family had very, very little money," Edoardo recalled in an interview, "but . . . all of us always had smiles on our lips and we knew the most joyous and carefree childhood. My father, when he was working at home, used to whistle from morning till night."[1]

The family's example of a profound Catholic faith was also important to Albino. His mother taught the catechism to her children herself, and the family always said the Rosary around the brick stove. Many years later, he wrote that on entering the village church as a child in poor clothes, "I had the impression that the organ was greeting me and my little playmates . . . as though we were so many princes. From this came the first vague intuition . . . that the Catholic Church not only is something great, but also something that makes the poor and the little ones great, honoring and uplifting them."[2]

Albino was always lively as a boy; he also got into more than a little mischief at school. At the age of ten, however, deeply struck by a holy Capuchin friar who came to preach the Lenten sermons in his parish, he felt the call to become a priest. He wrote to ask permission from his father who was then working in France. Giovanni answered yes, and added "I hope that when you become a priest you will be on the side of the workers, for Christ himself would have been on their side."[3] All his life, Albino was to follow his father's advice.

SEMINARY AND PRIESTHOOD

At the minor seminary in Feltre for the *ginnasio*, which consisted of four years of humanistic and classical studies. Albino, who had loved to read since his earliest childhood, delighted most in literature and history. Don Giulio Gaio, his Italian literature professor in the fourth year, discovered that he not only loved to read, but could write as well. When the students put together a mock newspaper during a lesson, Don Giulio made Albino the editor. This fueled a life-long love for journalism in the boy. He often said that if he hadn't become a priest, he would have become a journalist.

Don Filippo Carli, his parish priest, offered Albino some even more crucial help with his writing. When he moved to the major seminary in Feltre, for his two years of *liceo* and later his theological studies, Don Filippo began assigning him articles to write for the parish bulletin. When Albino brought him his first effort, he read it, then said: "It's well written, but it smacks of a sermon, and it's too long and too difficult. Remember that the little old woman, (do you know her?), who lives at the edge of the village, will have to read it too. Can you imagine her, poor old woman, with her eyeglasses on her nose, and her trembling hands, faced with these words bristling with *isms* you've put in, and with such long sentences? Try again!"[4]

Albino took his advice and always sought simplicity in his sermons after he was ordained. Most people who remember Pope John Paul I at all think of the breezy style of *Illustrissimi*; in fact, he was able to write in a wide variety of styles from the professorial (he was a theology professor for many years) to the most popular style of comic dialogue. (For an example of his "professorial" style, though leavened with his typical humor and pastoral sensitivity and clarity, see "Something Less than a Syllabus").

After Don Albino's ordination in July 1935, he served the parish in his native village and then in the nearby town of Agordo, where he also taught religion classes to the young men in the technical mining institute. The area was very poor, and Don Albino aided the miners who were out of work, and the rest of the poor population as best he could; he became known for his charity, even though he had little himself. Edoardo Luciani recalled this vividly: "I remember one poor woman. She was Polish, and she married a man from Agordo . . . They had a lot of little girls, all blond. When this woman used to visit my mother . . . she would cry as she described what Albino was doing for her in Agordo."[5]

In 1937 Don Albino was appointed professor and vice-rector of the diocesan seminary in Belluno. It was an unusual appointment, because he was just 25 and did not yet even have the qualifying licentiate in theology. In fact, Don Albino was just the type of gifted young man dioceses typically send to Rome for study. And the bishop, Giosué Cattarossi, and the seminary rector were anxious to do just this. But the diocese had a shortage of priests, and because they lacked a qualified professor to replace him, they didn't want to let Don Albino leave his teaching duties to attend classes at a university.

The problem was finally solved in 1941 when the Gregorian, the Jesuit university in Rome, agreed to let Don Albino earn his doctorate there without having to attend classes. So he started his university studies on his own while teaching. In October 1942, he passed the exams for his licentiate (roughly equivalent to a master's degree) in theology which was awarded *magna cum laude*. He then began studies for his doctorate.

At various times, Don Albino taught classes not only in theology but in patristics and canon law as well as art history and sacred art. His pupils later remembered his humility—especially remarkable since he had a really brilliant intellect—and the clarity and simplicity with which he explained even complex ideas.

The progress of Don Albino's studies was interrupted by the Nazi invasion of Northern Italy in 1943. Mgr. Ausilio da Rif of Belluno recalled for me how Don Albino helped his family financially after the Germans had destroyed his home and even gave him his own coat to wear. Luciani also showed real courage in teaching his students to reject Fascist and Nazi ideology and, along with other members of his family, aiding members of the Resistance. He began to form with some other priests, a "social school," involving talks and spiritual direction, which would help form young men in Catholic social teaching, one that would prepare them to take part in social and political reconstruction after the war was over.[5]

When peace returned, Don Albino turned to completing his doctorate by writing his dissertation, on "The Origin of the Human Soul According to Antonio Rosmini." Rosmini, a priest and religious founder, was a leading nineteenth-century Church reformer. But some of his theological propositions had been condemned. Rosimini accepted the correction humbly, but the controversy remained alive. Luciani's dissertation was on one of these propositions: that the human soul grew or developed from the soul of the parents, rather than being created directly by God. Ever since Thomas Aquinas, direct creation was held to by almost all theologians, and other solutions condemned. Rosimini held what might be considered a middle position. He suggested that the "sensitive" or animal soul grows from the parents' souls, but while in the womb, God "illuminates" the soul so that it becomes rational. Luciani loved Rosimini's works, and hoped to clear his name in the dissertation. But as he worked on it, he had to admit that theologically his idea did not hold up, and in his final version he said so.

Luciani often worked far into the night at his research and writing after his day's work was done. He successfully defended his dissertation at the Gregorian in February 1947. Almost immediately on his return, however, stressed and worn out, he fell seriously ill with what was at first suspected to be tuberculosis. It turned out to be viral pneumonia, but he was ill for several months. After he recovered, the new bishop of Belluno, Girolamo Bortignon, wanting to relieve him of his his grueling schedule as vice-rector, made him pro-vicar general of the diocese. He was appointed to direct the diocesan Catechetical Office in 1949. He took part in the project to write a regional catechism for the Triveneto. Out of that experience also came his first book *Catechetica in Briociole* [Catechetics made Easy], a manual for catechism teachers. In it he showed his love for children and understanding of how they learn. He officially became Vicar General in 1954. During all this time, he continued to teach at the seminary.

During the 1940s and 1950s, Don Albino fulfilled his love for journalism by writing many articles for the diocesan paper in Belluno, *L'Amico del Popolo*; he wrote a number of articles refuting the claims of the socialists and championing the Church's social teaching. In 1946, he contemplated the effort it would take to reconstruct society after the war:

> For how many people these days does Christ hold out his arms in vain?
>
> Directly, over this world persuaded by hatred and discord, he preaches love. Over the ruins, over the destruction of what once was, he cries, "I, I alone am the Resurrection and the Life. Come!"
>
> But how many will come? How many will reconcile themselves with him, making a firm pact of friendship? The Easter pact? How many, on the other hand, will pass by him without recognizing him?

They will look for reconstruction in a political party,
in a man, in a program, in everything except in Him.

This is the tremendous drama that is
experienced especially at Easter: People who live in
the midst of Christianity, but without living
Christianity and without knowing it![7]

Luciani saw that the traditional faith of the people in the
Veneto often lacked serious roots. Only too often it was mere
convention, not based on a life-giving relationship with Jesus Christ.
He could see that the world was becoming secular and that there was
a need for evangelizing Christians themselves.

BISHOP

Cardinal Angelo Roncalli, the Patriarch of Venice, knew and
admired Luciani. In October 1958 Roncalli was elected Pope John
XXIII; very shortly after his election he appointed Luciani bishop of
Vittorio Veneto, and consecrated him himself in St. Peter's Basilica
on December 27, 1958. Six days before the consecration, Luciani
had a long private audience with Pope John that indelibly marked
his understanding of his episcopate, and later his papacy, especially
in regard to humility and service ("Pope John XXIII").

In his first sermon in his new diocese on Jan 11, 1959,
Luciani told his people: "I would like to be a bishop who is a teacher
and a servant."[8] Even then, in line with Pope John, he anticipated
one of the great themes of the Second Vatican Council: that the
Church should be at the service of the world.

Barely two weeks after Luciani entered his new diocese,
Pope John XXIII announced that he would convene an Ecumenical
Council for the Church. As part of the preparatory phase of the
Council, all the bishops of the world were asked to submit their *vota*
to the preparatory commission, indicating the subjects they wanted
the Council to treat. Luciani wrote that the Council should stress "the
theme of Christian optimism . . . against the widespread pessimism,

hence: against the relativists the validity of human reason for arriving at truth and certainty; against individualists and subjectivists, the capacity of free will to predominate over somewhat obscure psychological forces."9 He had a very clear understanding of what ideas lay under the malaise of society, and of the cure: they were to be met with the joy and optimism of the good news of Christ. He also asked that the Council devote some space to discussing the role of the laity in political and social action.

Luciani was defined by one of his friends, Cardinal Hyancinthe Thiandoum, the Archbishop of Dakar, as a "spiritual son of Pope John XXIII" because of his capacity to see far and look to the future of the Church.10

Luciani delighted the people of his diocese of Vittorio Veneto by his fascinating sermons, which often contained very simple stories, but were full of wisdom. He often mentioned the local art works from the Middle Ages to make his points. One of Luciani's more pleasant duties was to oversee the opening of the diocesan process for Fra Claudio Granzotto, O.F.M, a talented sculptor. In his homily celebrating a Catholic artist, he expressed his ideas about the spirituality and temptations of artists ("Fra Claudio Granzotto").

Luciani took part in all four sessions of the Council in Rome, beginning in 1962. Even though he never spoke on the Council floor, and made just one written intervention, he did take a serious role behind the scenes convincing many of his fellow Italian bishops that the Council was a good idea. He was very enthusiastic about the ongoing process in the Church, and kept in constant contact with his diocese, with Catholic Action groups, and especially his seminarians, about what was happening. He guided the seminarians to an understanding of being a priest in a changing world ("On the Way to the Priesthood").

Luciani later said that he had been criticized before the Council for his insistence on the Word of God as well as the sacraments. "Some people had judged me an innovator (perhaps a dangerous one)," he said, "but the Council, with *Dei Verbum*, showed that I was right." He explained that it is the word of God, when heard and assimilated, that generates and strengthens faith, and it is faith makes reception of the sacrament effective and fruitful.[11] (See also "The Bible and the Laity").

One of the Council's most important documents, the Decree on Religious Liberty, was passed on November 19, 1964. At the time of his election as Pope, there was talk that Luciani was opposed to religious liberty. In fact, in January 1965, he told the priests of the Veneto region that the decree was "very timely and of very great importance," and called the day it was passed "the most tremendous day of the Council."[12]

Luciani once told a reporter that one of the most important moments at the Council for him had been hearing a layman describe the great gap in wealth between the industrialized nations and the Third World. Intensely engaged with the Church's social teachings, he welcomed the issuing of Pope Paul VI's *Populorum Progressio* in 1967, and in subsequent years frequently spoke about the encyclical ("*Populorum Progressio* Ten Years Later").

He showed his love for the people in poor countries and devotion to the Church's missionary impulse by lending a number of priests from his own diocese to the missions in Brazil and Africa, and visiting his diocesan mission in Africa in 1966. Again anticipating the New Evangelization, in 1968, as bishop of Vittorio Veneto, he wrote about two different mission territories, Africa and Italy, the "new frontier" and the "newer frontier" ("Homily for the Close of the Year of Faith").

Luciani had the Council and its proper interpretation always in mind; people who knew him said he had practically memorized the Council documents. His perspective on Vatican II was remarkably like that of Pope Benedict XVI: a hermeneutic of reform in continuity.

In 1967, Pope Paul VI opened the Year of Faith, marking the 1900th anniversary of the martyrdom of Saints Peter and Paul. At that time, the first rumblings of dissent on both the left and right could already be heard. Some in the traditionalist wing of the Church began to denounce as heresy everything that came from the Council or from the new theology, without discrimination.

Luciani gave a conference in private for the bishops of the Veneto on some current theological controversies, which was reported in the newspapers as being directed against "some errors contrary to the Faith." It was then that he found out that some of his priests had been influenced by the scare tactics of the emerging reaction to the Council, because they immediately wrote to him to ask for details about these errors. In order to combat this exaggerated alarmism while giving his priests the proper information on the theological controversies, Luciani wrote a little treatise in the diocesan bulletin, entitled with his typical humor, "Something Less than a Syllabus."

Some months later, a revised edition of the work came out, called, almost inevitably *The Little Syllabus,* which was a bit less hopeful in its tone.[13] By this time, the post-conciliar situation was already starting to heat up.

In the 1960's Luciani had hoped the Pope would decide that some form of artificial birth control might be allowed. In 1967, when Pope Paul VI was dissatisfied with the results of the papal commission on birth control, which had recommended a change, he asked the bishops of Lombardy and the Veneto to supply him with a report of their own. Out of these deliberations, Luciani wrote the document for the Pope, which is widely rumored to have been "liberal" in tone. Its content has never been published. But there is one intriguing clue, in that Paul VI relied on this text in writing the final part of *Humanae Vitae*, addressed to scientists, in which he said:

> . . . medical science should by the study of natural rhythms succeed in determining a sufficiently secure basis for the chaste limitation of offspring. In this way scientists, especially those who are Catholics,

will by their research establish the truth of the Church's claim that "there can be no contradiction between two divine laws—that which governs the transmitting of life and that which governs the fostering of married love" (GS no. 51).[14]

This confirms that Luciani did not want to do away with Church teaching in this area, but to ascertain what methods might be used in accordance with Church teaching; he may have thought that the hormones proposed for contraceptive use could help regulate a woman's cycle.

Though many rejected the encyclical, Luciani wrote to the people of his diocese, asking them to join him in a "sincere adherence to the papal teaching" ("On Reading the Encyclical").

PATRIARCH AND CARDINAL

Pope Paul had become aware of Luciani's theological acumen from his report on birth control, and appointed him Patriarch of Venice in December 1969. He also chose him as one of his personal appointments to the 1971 Synod of Bishops. Speaking at the Synod, Luciani suggested that dioceses in the industrialized countries should send 1% of all their income to the Third World, to be given "not as alms, but something that is owed" and urged practical means to make people aware of their duties to their poor brothers and sisters ("The Brothers' Portion").

Luciani was greatly loved by the common people of Venice because of his simplicity and availability. He often put his bishop's pectoral cross and the scarlet zucchetto in his pocket, and walked through the narrow streets or *calle*, talking with people. When he had to travel across the Grand Canal, he would take the steamboat bus or *vaporetto* with the rest of the people, rather than a private motor launch. Nothing at all changed in his simple manner after he received his cardinal's hat from Pope Paul VI at the concistory in March 1973.

Luciani maintained an open relationship with cultural figures, artists and filmmakers. He found himself having to comment on controversial works offered at the Venice Film Festival. He established the Diocesan Museum of Sacred Art at the old monastery of Sant'Apollonia in Venice, which has ever since attracted great interest in its exhibitions.

He was also happy to continue his journalistic efforts by writing pieces for the daily newspaper of Venice, *Il Gazzettino* ("On Wings of Hope"). The first of the letters that became *Illustrissimi* were published there; later the editor of the *Messaggero di San Antonio* asked the cardinal to continue the series. It was published as a book in 1976 and attracted considerable notice even before he became Pope.

The period of serious dissent against Church teaching was already beginning, and had affected a number of younger priests and university students. The question of pluralism in the Church arose. Weren't differences in interpreting the faith legitimate? Luciani answered in a homily ("A Healthy Pluralism").

Some younger Catholics accepted the fashionable ideas of liberation theology. This brand of theology was not a distant concern related only to Latin America. Groups of young radicals in Western Europe, including the "Christians for Socialism," were also adopting the ideas, and carrying them to extremes. For some Catholics in Italy, this meant using Marxist analysis to not only call for a revolution in society, but to declare the hierarchy of the Church a class enemy. Luciani replied with an analysis of why their works were departing from the faith. ("Marx and the Theologians"). Luciani was widely criticized because of his insistence on obedience to Church teaching and to the Pope.

He was also at the center of controversy over the liturgy, because he was careful to correct abuses while teaching the Council's plan for liturgical renewal ("Participating in the Liturgy"). Even the Rosary was "contested" by some who saw it as a form of prayer fit only for a superstitious age and uneducated believers.

Luciani, who said the Rosary daily, mounted a spirited defense of it ("Is the Rosary Outdated?"). I learned from family members that the Feast of the Holy Rosary was his favorite Marian observance; it was always celebrated with great devotion in Canale D'Agordo.

Other clashes took place over "women's issues," to which Luciani often devoted attention. He admitted the societal injustices against women that the Church had often accepted in the past, while addressing modern concerns about women's ordination ("Women in the Church and in Society"); he supported feminist advances, but maintained his fidelity to the faith when he led the fight in Italy against abortion ("Thou Shalt not Kill!").

Luciani was deeply concerned about problems of the workers, and set up a special diocesan commission to help them with their problems, saying: "Workers suffer when their Catholic brothers and sisters refuse to recognize that capitalism has serious faults and they . . . very superficially call every worker who fights for the recognition of his rights a 'Communist.'"[15] Msgr. Mario Senigaglia, who was Luciani's secretary at the time, told me that Luciani had often intervened personally in labor disputes, and his efforts once kept a factory from closing, saving many workers' jobs.[16]

There was much discussion in the mid-seventies over the inclusion of "human advancement" as a component of evangelization. Luciani spoke often about this issue, and he was insistent that human advancement was a part of evangelization, but added cautions to help avoid distortions; this was evident in his intervention at the 1974 Synod of Bishops ("Evangelization in Our Time"). The ideas of the Synod were taken up by Pope Paul VI in *Evangelii Nuntiandi.* The encyclical certainly contained a much broader vision of evangelization, but much of the talk was about this aspect. In speaking to young people on evangelization after the encyclical, Luciani took the broader road; he urged them to escape "Christian convention" and live in such a way as to make the Gospel attractive ("Not Convention, but Conviction").

"The little ones," the imprisoned, the poor and the suffering were always foremost in Luciani's thought. In 1976, he sold the expensive gold pectoral cross that had been given to him by John XXIII, and another offered to Venice by Paul VI and used the proceeds to aid a home for handicapped children. From then on, he wore a very simple metal and blue enamel crucifix around his neck; he also wore it as Pope.

Luciani became very well known among the cardinals in Europe and the Third World. African cardinals Bernardin Gantin and Hyacinthe Thiandoum visited him in Venice, and he met with Cardinal Aloisio Lorscheider and the Brazilian bishops' conference in Brazil in 1975, where he also visited the colonies of poor Italian emigrants.

Throughout his time in Venice, Luciani took part in ecumenical gatherings. Msgr. Senigaglia, his secretary, recalled that he took part in services for the Week of Prayer for Christian Unity every year in Venice ("Meditation at an Ecumentical Prayer Service").[17] He also hosted meetings of ARCIC (joint commission of Anglicans and Catholics), and addressed a gathering commemorating the Holocaust in 1975.

A means to faith that Luciani saw as necessary and vital is proper catechesis, something he constantly promoted throughout his life as a bishop and sought to update wisely. He commented very incisively on how to update catechesis in his intervention at the 1977 Synod ("Catechesis and Christian Commitment").

CONCLAVE AND PAPACY

When Pope Paul VI died in August 1978, Luciani paid tribute to him and defended him against his critics on the left and right ("Pope Paul VI"). The ensuing conclave seemed to be shaping up to be one of the most difficult in recent history. Never had the Church been so divided as it was then, between traditionalists on the right and dissenters on the left, and secularism exerting an almost irresistible undertow. Luciani himself was certain the time had arrived for a non-Italian Pope, and indicated his desire to vote for the Brazilian Cardinal Lorscheider.

At the end of July, Luciani had given an interview for an Italian magazine about the birth of Louise Brown, the world's first "test-tube baby." (The term used now is "in vitro fertilization" or IVF). The interview reached the press after Pope Paul's death, and Luciani's name began to make waves. Too many of the press quoted the interview selectively, and ever since then, the public has often had the false impression that Luciani was indifferent to or supported IVF.[18] But reading the whole, Luciani's prophetic intuition about the harm that IVF would lead to is clear ("Test-tube Babies").

Latin American, Asian and African cardinals played a large part in determining the election, and they were for Luciani. He was elected by an overwhelming majority of the cardinals on the first day of the conclave. He amazed the world at his first appearance on the balcony of St. Peter's to give his blessing by his smile, which radiated the love of God. He took the first double papal name in history, and was the first Pope qualified to put a "First" in front of his name in a thousand years.

In his address to the cardinals in the Sistine Chapel the morning after his election, John Paul I said: "We want to recall to the entire Church that her first duty is still evangelization . . . if all the sons and daughters of the Church know how to be tireless missionaries of the Gospel, a new flowering of holiness and renewal will burst forth in a world thirsting for love and truth."[19] He seemed to be anticipating the "new springtime" of hope in the Church he successor spoke about and its strong connection with New Evangelization.

He broke another millennium-long tradition by beginning his reign not with the imposition of the traditional triple tiara, but with a simple Mass and clothing in the pallium, the band of lambs' wool that is the symbol of a shepherd.

For four unforgettable weeks, he gave the world his enchanting catechesis on humility faith, hope and love. On

September 23, as he took possession of his cathedral of St. John Lateran, he told the people of Rome: "The poor, as St. Lawrence said, are the real treasures of the Church, and so they should be helped, by those who can do so, to have more and to be more."[20] The whole world loved his evangelical style. Then on September 28, 1978, he died suddenly in the night and left the Church plunged into grief.

Nothing could have been more astonishing—except for what happened next: the election of the first non-Italian Pope in 400 years.

Time often passes more quickly than we can imagine; it hardly seems possible that the titanic reign of John Paul II is now history, and that two more Popes have succeeded John Paul I, just as it hardly seems possible that we at last have the Latin American Pope he desired.

But John Paul I has not been forgotten. Over the years, working with the Seabecks, publishing *Humilitas* and participating in the conference in Queens in October 2012 that marked the centenary of his birth, I have come across many people for whom John Paul I was been a deep and permanent influence in their lives. I know people who were brought back to the faith by him, or discovered their vocations because of him.

Just before the centenary conference, a priest named Fr. Peter Conley from the diocese of Birmingham, England wrote to tell me that he is doing everything possible to spread the catechetical insights of Luciani as a part of the New Evangelization, and compared his simple and captivating style to the one used in the YouCat for teens. "If there was ever a prophet of the New Evangelization, it is him!" he said.

Today we need such a prophet more than ever. I pray that the hopes of many will be fulfilled and that, in harmony with the rumors coming from the Church in heaven, one day soon the Church on earth will proclaim and celebrate Albino Luciani, Pope John Paul I, by another great and fitting title.

In other words: *Santo subito*!

Notes

1 "Interview du frère de Jean-Paul Ier," *La Documentation Catholique*, September 25, 1978, p. 810.

2 *Su questa polvere il Signore ha scritto: testi autobiografici di Albino Luciani* (Belluno: Istituto bellunesi di ricerche sociali e culturali, 1979), p. 15.

3 Antonia Luciani and Stefania Falasca, *Mio fratello Albino: ricordi e memorie della sorella di Papa Luciani* (Italy: Trenta Giorni Soc. Coop, 2003), p. 19.

4 From a spiritual retreat to the clergy of Venice on fostering vocations; *Opera*, 8:135-36.

5 Edoardo Luciani, letter to the author, February 15, 1985.

6 Patrizia Luciani, *Un prete di montagna* (Padua: EMP, 2003), p. 286.

7 *Amico del Popolo*, May 4, 1946, p. 2; the article is unsigned, but according to Don Ausilio Da Rif, Luciani's teaching colleague, it is *senz'altro* (certainly) his; personal communication to the author, October, 1985.

8 The whole of this sermon is printed in Ray and Lauretta Seabeck, *The Smiling Pope* (Huntingdon, IN: Our Sunday Visitor, 2004), pp, 194-98. Some points come directly from the notes he made directly after his meeting with Pope John; see Stefania Falasca, "Croce liscia, per 'distendersi sopra,'" *L'Avvenire*, June 5, 2013, p. A03.

9 *Acta et Documenta Concilio Oecumenico Vaticano II* Series 1, vol. 2, pt. 3 (Vatican City: Typis Polyglottis Vaticanis, 1960), pp. 747-48.

10 "Chi era Giovanni Paolo I," *Gente Veneta*, no. 35 (September 16, 1978), p. 5.

11 Fr. Venanzio Renier da Chioggia, a Capuchin friar, wrote of his conversations with Luciani on this subject, see *Humilitas*, Italian ed. (April 1997), pp. 3-5, 12.

[12] *Il Buon Samaritano: Corso di esercizi spirituali* (Padua: Edizioni Messaggero, 1980), p. 239.

[13] The revised version appeared in *Il dono della chiarezza* (Rome: Edizioni Logos, 1979). My thanks to Don Francesco Taffarel, Luciani's secretary in Vittorio Veneto, for details about the history of this work.

[14] This has been confirmed by Luciani's friend, Fr. Francesco Saverio Pancheri: see his *Il breve sorriso di Papa Luciani* (Rome: Ripetta 124, 1979), pp. 31-32.

[15] RD 57 (November 1972), p. 103.

[16] Mario Senigaglia, interview with author, November 2, 1985.

[17] Mario Senigaglia, interview, November 2, 1985.

[18] For instance, from a recent article in *The Tablet*: "Luciani . . . was asked about the morality of the in vitro fertilisation . . . He replied that he had no idea, but he shared the joy of the parents" (October 9, 2010).

[19] Translation from the Latin mine. There is also a translation on the Vatican web site.

[20] Translation mine. There is also a translation on the Vatican web site.

The Year of Faith 1967-68

Something Less Than A Syllabus

Letter to the Priests of Vittorio Veneto[1]

My dear priests,

Some of you have said to me, "We see from the press that you have reported on 'Some errors against the Faith.' Couldn't we also avail ourselves of your report in view of the 'Year of Faith' now in progress?"

I replied: The Year of Faith is something else. It is a positive thing, not a Syllabus of Errors. It is an open profession of faith, individual as well as collective, which benefits us as well as others. It is a clear testimony, a translation of inner faith into virtuous outward actions and an active Christian life. Listen to me: try to have your faithful live the "Year of Faith" by speaking to them with enthusiasm about the Word of God, Jesus, and the Church more than about errors. And don't be satisfied when your listeners are convinced: once they are convinced, they must act, they must act! Like Paul, strive so that "the word of God may make progress and be hailed by many others" (2 Thes. 3:1). Show by ardent words and actions, with a pure and charitable life, that you are "racing to grasp Christ since you have been grasped by Him" (cf. Phil. 3;12). When you talk about the Church, say that Christ loved her and "handed himself over for her . . . . to sanctify her . . . in order to present to himself the Church in splendor, without spot or wrinkle . . . that she might be holy and without blemish" (cf. Eph. 5:25-27).

The Year of Faith also means shedding light on the faith. Now, faith is saying "yes" to God, clinging to Him with our whole spiritual being and making our own the truths that He has revealed to us and set before us by means of the Magisterium of the Church. Explain it to the faithful: this "yes" is an act of loving trust in God

29

and at the same time an acceptance of His truths. We don't believe because we like these truths or because they are convenient to us, or because they are in agreement with scientific data or the fashion of the day, but because they have been revealed by Him who loves us and neither can nor will deceive us. If it were not for Him, we would not believe.

The Apostles and their successors, Pope and bishops, willed by Christ as official teachers of the Faith, are not in that position as masters, but simply as servants of the Word of God; they safeguard it and explain it without adding or taking away anything from it. Accepting and venerating their teaching is the means ordinarily necessary to arrive at the true Faith and the best way to be members of the Church.

Returning to the report that was asked of me, I have no trouble in agreeing to give it, but I will offer only some excerpts, only in the doctrinal sector, and with some adaptation. Excerpts, let me make it very clear, that are "reserved" to you. If exposed to the faithful, they might be counterproductive. In the second part, inasmuch as they are a review of some erroneous tendencies, they will seem to be almost a "Syllabus" in form, while in fact they aim only at arousing interest and giving information, as well as some elements of evaluation. Not, therefore, a Syllabus that fills you with the passion of a heresy-hunter, who looks for error so he can hurl anathemas at it, or a Crusader at war with the infidels, or an exorcist on a witch hunt! It will be a Syllabus which, by putting you face to face with error, which sometimes exists, will enamor you of the truth, and will lead you to spread that truth in the most suitable and persuasive way! So if you come face to face with error in the parish or the school, try and see if, instead of uprooting and throwing it down, it might be possible to trim and prune it patiently, bringing to light the core of goodness and truth which is often not lacking even in erroneous opinions. The truth, when presented properly, is persuasive all by itself. A person who is in error almost always fears being defeated. For him, "convinced" means the same thing as "conquered."

A LITTLE ETIOLOGY ...

It cannot be denied that in the Church today there are serious problems and even errors against the faith. Often it is a question not so much of formal errors, as tendencies, uncertainties, and situations of discomfort and restlessness, which means that, along with dangerous confusion, there is also good faith or illusion or ingenuousness or a sincere seeking of the truth.

One explanation of the phenomenon may be that it is part of a very vast change now taking place, which affects not only religion, but all of civilization.

A profound change, the Council calls it: in "patriarchal families, tribes, clans and villages,"[2] in industry, which now prevails over agriculture; in urbanization;[3] in emigration which makes people change "their manner of life,"[4] in the family, which has taken on a new face, not only because it has been reduced from the large circle of grandparents, uncles and aunts, brothers and sisters-in-law and sons and daughters-in-law to the triangle of father, mother and children, but more, because of the conflicts that are manifested there; "Young people . . . indeed become rebels in their distress . . . Parents . . . frequently experience greater difficulties day by day in discharging their tasks."[5]

We are dealing with a "new way of thinking." Human reason is the same as always, but the attitudes it is taking toward God, neighbor and the world are new. Until a short time ago, the lion's share in "intellectual formation" was taken by philosophical culture and literary humanism; now it is "increasingly based on the mathematical and natural sciences and those dealing with man himself, while in the practical order technology . . . takes on mounting importance."[6] Until a short time ago, man was afraid of nature, felt it to be an enemy, and felt himself dominated by its forces. Now "the conviction grows not only that humanity can and should increasingly consolidate its control over creation, but even more that it devolves on humanity to establish a political, moral, social, and economic order which will to an ever better extent serve man and help individuals as well as groups to affirm and develop the dignity proper to them."7 "The human race is giving ever increasing thought to forecasting and regulating its own population growth."8 It wishes to dominate the cosmos, by resolving "to master outer space,"9 it dominates "the past by means of historical knowledge. . . the future by the art of projecting and by planning."10 "Hence many benefits once looked for, especially from heavenly powers, man has now enterprisingly procured for himself."11

Hence, the consequences in religious life: "On the one hand a more critical ability to distinguish religion from a magical view of the world and from the superstitions which still circulate purifies religion and exacts day by a more personal and explicit adherence to faith . . . On the other hand, growing numbers of people are abandoning religion in practice."12 This refers to "religious life" in non-Christian religions, Christianity, and the Catholic Church itself. The last is experiencing, in addition, its own particular difficulties.

To remedy this situation, it seems, we are more than ever compelled by duty to proclaim the truths of faith, but we should prefer a positive, documented exposition, insist most on what is essential, present the truths in such a way that they are intelligible to the men and women of our time,13 and remain in contact with modern culture. We should also take this into account in the renovation of studies in the seminaries.

It seems then, that people take the wrong attitude when they *systematically* ignore and attribute little value to certain new aspects of science, theology and pastoral work, and refuse to admit that when faced with new situations, the *unchangeable* revelation can be expounded and applied in a new way. There is more danger, however, in those who take the opposite attitude, and want to resolve the new questions with *completely* new solutions, which bypass or willfully ignore elements of tradition that are part of the faith itself.

For you priests, the popular press, which often sets forth and solves difficult problems without the necessary depth, competence, and prudence, is one of the causes of confusion. For this reason, I urge you to put several question marks beside some of these news reports, with their simplistic theology, which propose and resolve difficult questions in a few lines. It is better to tackle, in a committed way, the study of some serious reviews with a medium or high degree of popularization, which in turn depend on works of scholarly research. Better yet, attend the announced meetings of the Diocesan Commission for Priestly Culture. And read, and study! But do it, I beg you, with a little bit of critical sense! Today, in fact, Italian theological publication consists largely of translations from French, German and English, and it happens that some works brought into Italy from abroad risk being badly digested and absorbed by us or even becoming harmful, when the reader acquires them blindly and without taking into account the diversity in cultural environment, intellectual categories, and religious conditions.

The mass of the faithful, on the other hand, is influenced by the press and other means of communication, which "muddle" minds on religious and moral problems so effectively and to such an extent, when they oppose our work, blow by blow, that we would become discouraged, if we did not have the help of God and the inner power of the truth to rely on. Can we also have confidence in the faithful themselves? Solid and united in their choices, they could influence movies, newspapers and television. But it seems that we are still far from this goal.

It is also necessary to avoid exaggerated alarmism in pointing out and reporting possible errors. To make a scandal of a scandal is also a scandal. Nor is it permissible, even when done to make a healthy impression, to exaggerate and generalize cases that are isolated or of limited scope and offend against truth or charity.14

The danger was noted by Maritain himself. While admitting that at the moment the *"Moutons de Panurge"* (progressives) outnumber the *"Ruminants de la Saint Alliance"* (conservatives), he writes that the latter, instead of serving the pure truth, strive to "bar the way to threatening dangers, to lock doors, to throw up barriers," and meanwhile, "the great mass of the Christian people," caught between the claims of the Christian left and right, ". . . is troubled and unhappy."[15]

AN INFORMATIVE AND ORIENTATIVE REVIEW

1. In regard to *Sacred Scripture*, I point out the fascination exercised on the younger generation by the so-called "demythologization" (it's the fashionable word). There is a radical "demythologization" that goes so far as to deny every dogma and allows only a religion made up of pure evangelical charity, even this conceived in a strange and unusual way. There is a partial "demythologization," which is being presented as though it were a *salvage operation* (!) for a Christianity in danger. "Either we demythologize," some say, "copiously pruning from the Old as well as the New Testament, and then the people will accept 'Essential' Christianity; or we do not demythologize, and then all of Christianity will appear to modern people as a mythology, as a fable, and it will only be accepted as a fable!" Some Catholic scholars have imprudently come close to this demythologization, and because of this vigilance by the Magisterium is imperative. The firmness of this vigilance, however, must go hand-in-hand with serenity, and must not impede the difficult work of Catholic exegetes, whom the Council has encouraged, exhorting Biblical scholars "to continue energetically with the work they have so well begun, with a constant renewal of vigor, and loyalty to the mind of the Church."[16]

Divino Afflante Spiritu, for example, gave full rights in exegesis to the distinction of literary forms[17] for the difficult passages of the Old Testament. The Council has extended the application of the same literary forms to all of Scripture. The latest decrees of the Biblical Commission are in the same direction. The decrees of the beginning of the century, on the other hand, convey the opposite meaning. What happens? Some people appeal to the old documents to give a restrictive interpretation to the new ones: on the other hand, others more wisely appeal to the latest documents to say that the old ones, which were suitable at that time, since the problems were then put in other terms, are to be taken with moderation and that certain conclusions, now widely admitted, can be serenely accepted. It seems good that the Magisterium has supported, or at least not discouraged, these latest biblical scholars, as long as they remain within the limits of honest research, though warning that literary forms are still sensitive matters and difficult to handle.

2. *Mistrust of human reason* is spreading. It is said to pursue truth without ever arriving at it; even if it were to arrive at it, it would lack adequate means to express it as it really is; it is more in conformity with the "human tragedy" to seek truth than it is to find it. To Pirandello (*Right You Are if You Think You Are*), truth is not something fixed, but says to the one who searches for it: "I am what you think I am!" not what really is. With idealism, there had been an exaggerated rationalism: thought claimed to be everything, and the world was presented as a projection of thought. Now the reaction is in the opposite direction: thought has capitulated and now is saying: I am worth very little, life and feeling are worth more than me. Why pursue the essence of things? Let us stop with the things that exist; what interests us is that which does not repeat itself and which exists, here and now. Hence the tendency to abandon technical terms in theology, relativism and existentialism in philosophy, the exaggeration of the influence with which history and conscience, changing with the times, are supposed to operate on the truth, going so far as to change even the objective meaning of revealed truths.

It is needless to say that the capacity of human reason is an undeniable essential; reason can come to know and to express certain and immutable truth; it even penetrates, and fruitfully, faith tells us, into the partial knowledge of mysteries, in themselves as well as in the harmony that binds them together.

Maritain is right, in a sense, when he warns against the two dangerous modern attitudes of "chronolatry" and "logophobia." Many people today, in fact, are chronolators, they adore the theories of the passing moment, meteor-ideas, full of fear of appearing out of date. Many are suffering from "logophobia," that is, they are afraid of philosophy, common sense, and even first principles. In place of Truth they put Verification; in place of Reality, the Sign; they are allergic to Reason and to reasoning, giving importance only to what profits and pays.[18]

As for the influence of history on revealed truth, we must conform to the traditional doctrine of the development of dogma: the truth remains the same as always but it is like St. Patrick's well; it can always be better understood by us and the formulas that express it can be improved, perfected, and made more accessible to modern men and women.

In expounding this traditional doctrine, the Council has specified the causes of the development of dogma, which are: the action of the Holy Spirit, *in primis* [first], but also the reflection and study of the faithful, the inner knowledge of spiritual things and the preaching of the hierarchy.[19] From this it seems that we can deduce that the path of logical development is not the only means for the development of dogma: the emotive-sensible factor can be admitted to complement it, if it is true that the object of belief is not only the revealed truths, but God Himself, God the Person, who gives Himself to humanity. Loving Him more can mean knowing Him better.

As for theological terminology, this is useful, and should be retained, though without exaggeration and abuses. Those who use this terminology in speaking to the faithful, supposing they are well acquainted with it, when in fact it is almost completely unknown to them, are actually abusing it. It thus happens very often that the people, instead of encountering the adorable person of Jesus, encounter dry and difficult formulas.

Papini said to theologians (though with some exaggeration): "Every age has its own language, its own desires, its own dreams, its own problems; you have stopped the clock of history at the fourteenth century and continue to dish out the same everlasting gruel to docile students for the priesthood, without caring about the Christians who are outside the closed doors and who by now are used to more tasty and appetizing fare . . . Go out into the fresh air now and then, listen to the voices coming from souls that hunger for certainty, don't disdain to learn something even from non-theologians. I spoke before about the poets: you will be great theologians if you do not disdain some poetic virtues. When you want to go on high, the spinning of dialectics is not enough. The two Testaments, which are also the source and foundation of your doctrine, are brimming over with poetry. Saint Augustine, a theologian, was a poet, just as Dante, a poet, was a theologian. But you are horrified before the daring, the beauty, and the music of thought. Art and imagination are unbearable scandals to you. You construct the highest towers with the most refined rationalistic engineering, but you stop up every crack from which you might be able to glimpse a mountain peak, the thin line of the sea, a wild flower, or the face of a child. You discourse on creation without deigning to give a glance to the concreteness of creation; you talk of mysteries without perceiving the everlasting divine mystery that is in the palest berry on the hedge as well as in the giant pale galaxy speeding toward the ends of the universe; you theorize on the human soul and you don't realize that there are souls close to you that pant and throb, souls that perhaps are waiting for only one word from you in order to climb higher than you on the ladder rising to the eternal."[20]

3. The *historicity of the Gospels* is doubted or denied, especially by applying the theory of "form criticism." I will give a prolonged notice about this, out of consideration for the oldest priests.

More than forty years ago the Protestant Rudolf Bultmann and his followers reasoned: it is impossible to understand the value of Gospels, without first studying them and determining how they were formed and out of what elements they were formed, and without first tracing the history of these elements. This history then, is as follows: There were at first many different fragments ("forms") told out loud or even put into writing about Jesus Christ: those fragments had their "cradle" in the various Christian communities of Palestine. Some of these resembled little sermons with illustrative stories and sayings (the socalled "*Kerygma*" with Paradigms and Apophthegms); others had the form of clusters of sayings (*Logia*); others, a little at a time, assumed almost the form of stories or fables, because told by those who loved to give a picturesque coloring to their own speech; others later took the form of myths, actually making Jesus into a god.

At this point came the Evangelists; they gathered the various scattered materials, stitched together the various "forms" and gave us the Gospels, which, therefore, are mythologized stories. They do permit us to know what stories the first Christian communities told *about* Jesus, but tell us nothing or almost nothing, *of* Jesus and the preaching *of* Jesus. The result is a paradoxical situation: Bultmann, believing and pious, venerates Jesus, but is not completely certain that Jesus existed, or if he existed, precisely who and what he was!

Bultmann's conclusions were disastrous; was the point of departure just as disastrous? Those "forms," that is, those elements in that "cradle" of the first communities, are they to be taken seriously? Did they exist before the written Gospels or not? Some Catholics thought that it was possible to admit it hypothetically and see if that led to good results. Did Bultmann abuse "form criticism"?

Anything can be abused, and it does seem to be true that our Gospels were told aloud before being written down; that along with the common data in the three Synoptic Gospels, there were different data, and the same common elements were regrouped in different ways; and it seems that stories, sayings, parables and instructions can be distinguished in them. Of course the primitive Christian community did not create the Good News, but only received and preserved it: and it is a Good News directed from on high by the Holy Spirit and controlled in its transmission by Apostles vested with authority and closely attentive to its immutable fidelity; the collection and transcription were made by men who were "the original eyewitnesses and ministers of the word" (Lk. 1:2). All this remaining firm, why couldn't we search and excavate on the terrain of the "forms" and their history?

Some Catholic scholars tried to do it in moderation and with prudence, arriving at the following conclusions: it seem that, when speaking to the first Christians, the Apostles narrated the episodes and the teachings of Jesus that they considered best suited for arousing faith in Him, being concerned with making the fulfillment of prophecies stand out in the events of his life, while they were sparing with details that would have satisfied the curiosity of their hearers. The "Life of Jesus" was repeated in this form in the community, and it was in this form that it was taken up and written down by the Evangelists. But the Evangelists were inspired by the Holy Spirit and did not limit themselves to "stitching together" as Bultmann says. They did not have the concern with chronology of modern historians, who are closely attentive to detail, chronology and the psychology of the characters; rather they were especially intent on including in their writings whatever concerned "salvation history" (incarnation and birth, baptism and public life, death and resurrection). As for style or literary genre, they sometimes sketched out their stories in the expressive forms of the Old Testament.[21] In this way, their Gospels, as literary genres, turned out to be something original: not ordinary history, not pure theology, but sacred history.

This type of conclusion seemed too close to the Bultmannian school of "form criticism" and at the time of the Council some asked that it be disapproved. The Council limited itself instead to the following words: "The Evangelists wrote the four Gospels, selecting some things from the many which had been handed on in voice or in writing: reducing some of them to a synthesis, explicating some things in view of the situation of their churches, and preserving the form of a proclamation, but always in such fashion that they reported on Jesus with honesty and truth."22 In this prudent line, it seems, we should seek the defense and the remedy. The form theory is to be renounced in its exaggerated form; some of its elements may be used. We must affirm, therefore, that the Gospels contain true history, even if it seems appropriate to add that it is a special type of history, sacred history, which is always tied to "salvation," which is sometimes mixed with theological reflection, and is written by authors who had faith in Jesus as Messiah and Son of God.

Bultmann's followers suppose that it was the faith that existed in the Christian community and in the sacred writers that compelled them to "mythologize."

From the Gospels, it appears rather the contrary: faith actually impelled the narration of the words and deeds of Jesus as they really happened. Matthew and Luke, for example, narrated the miraculous events of the Infancy with a discretion and sobriety that are truly significant for those who compare them with the exaggerations of the apocryphal Gospels or even with certain medieval biographies of saints. "The Gospels," said de Grandmaison, "are not so much apologies as epiphanies." In fact, they were not concerned with avoiding apparent contradictions, and with polishing and touching up the portraits of the Apostles. The portrait and doctrine of Christ in the Gospels themselves present difficulties that a "mythologist" could have removed from the text with little difficulty. The account of the passion and death of Jesus is the reverse of mythologization.

Science, in turn, should take care not to wander from its own field. It does not control all of history, but only the scientifically verifiable in history. It may be that on this or that point science can say absolutely nothing; it does not follow that the point is not true history and that the believer does not possess another source—the inspired sacred writer—for knowing that the point is true history.

Concerning the Resurrection of Christ, for example, science can ascertain that the Apostles were sure that they saw the risen Christ. Believers, accepting the testimony of the Apostles, go further: they have full certainty that the Resurrection actually took place.

Again, it is supposed that the historicity of the events recounted by the Synoptics would be compromised if the same events appear to be in harmony with the salvific design of God, or are mixed with frequent allusions to the Old Testament.

Examination of the documents, however, leads rather to the conclusion that it was not the primitive Church that invented the harmony and allusions to justify its own existence, but that it was the person of Christ himself and his ministry which demanded the said harmony and allusions and that the events that took place in Palestine under Pontius Pilate were truly guided from on high by a redemptive mind and will.

Let's admit, then, that the three Synoptic Gospels were derived from antecedent sources, written or oral, or—as the method of form criticism has it—from collections of the miracles, parables, and aphorisms of Jesus. Well then, the miracles, as narrated, always have the task of proving that the Kingdom of God awaited by the Jews had come. The parables appear to be not only a system for illustrating simple truths of the moral order, but often aim at explaining the salvific significance of certain events in the life of Jesus. As for the aphorisms, they were pronounced by Jesus with absolutely extraordinary authority and were accompanied by the announcement of the judgment of God on those who reject the Good News. The constitutive elements of the Synoptics seem completely saturated with Christology. It is not clear how a critic can "prove" that the christological interpretation is an after-the-fact invention that was stuck onto these events by the primitive Church.

It is especially necessary to call attention to three points:

a) There is an unfathomable difference between the Resurrection of Christ as presented by the Gospels and the various "resurrections" in the myths of the Hellenistic-Oriental religions.

The latter are reduced to vague things, vaguely mentioned, with no indication of time and place; the former is resurrection in the true sense, a historical fact, historically verified by the Apostles. The Apostles testify to it in a hundred ways: in season and out of season, they make the Resurrection the center of the "Good News of salvation", the theme and basis of the Christian *kerygma*; they are personally transformed by the Resurrection into different men; completely convinced, they are, at the same time, so convincing that they cause numerous churches to spring up from preaching based on the Resurrection, even in the Greek atmosphere, which was completely allergic to the idea of resurrection. (cf. Acts 17).

The Resurrection of Christ, then, has been from the beginning the subject of theological reflection and St. Paul states that the Resurrection 1) makes sense of the Passion; 2) affirms that Jesus is the Christ; 3) makes Jesus the Lord; 4) is the first fruits and pledge of our future resurrection; and 5) is a symbol of what happens to the believer at his baptism. Such affirmations cannot be understood, they remain things founded on air, if the Resurrection is not a historical fact.

b) As for the *miracles*, it seems that it must be conceded that in whoever admits them as proof of the true religion, religious and moral dispositions of the soul are necessary, and that the use of reason alone is not enough.

And indeed: if the miracle is a "sign of credibility," then from the beginning it is a tangible event, capable of attracting attention and provoking admiration for a person or a doctrine.

That, however, is not enough to give the spectator assurance that the event is actually beyond the power of nature and to make him understand its religious value.

Jesus performed great miracles, but the spectators were not agreed in interpreting them. St. Thomas says that the greatness of the miracles would not be enough to make the disbelief of the spectators inexcusable, unless the miracles themselves were accompanied by an illuminating grace.[23]

42

Supernatural grace? Here:

— *Everyone* admits that some natural dispositions are required ("I am disposed to receive truth from outside, as soon as it appears as such to me").

— A number of people add: it is also necessary for the soul to have experienced on one hand, its own personal need, and on the other, to perceive that revealed religion is able to satisfy this need.

— Some require a previous *lumen fidei* [light of faith], or supernatural grace. It is not enough, in fact, to understand the miraculous event; it is necessary to perceive at the same time the revealed truth to which it is bound. With a single act, the mind must see in the miracle the sign and the divine-supernatural truth signified; to see the latter, a supernatural "*lumen fidei*" is required.

Fideism? A vicious circle (to believe, it is necessary to understand the miracle, and to understand the miracle it is necessary to believe)? It does not seem so, because a double and reciprocal priority of reason is at work. It is true that I do not perceive the credibility unless the *lumen fidei* exists first; but it is also true that adhesion to faith is impossible for me, unless it is first preceded by the judgment of credibility.

c) For the *virginal conception of Christ,* we respond to the obvious Scriptural difficulties with the traditional answers.

If the Apostolic writings, aside from Matthew and Luke, do not speak of such a conception, that is due to the fact that the *kerygma* was limited at the beginning to presenting the words and deeds of the Lord from the Baptism of Christ to His Resurrection; interest in the events of His infancy emerged later on with the increase in the veneration surrounding Jesus.

As for the texts of Luke and Matthew, it is impossible to empty them of their historical truth by resorting to the hypothesis of a special literary genre, unless we confine ourselves (as Laurentin does for St. Luke alone) to the hypothesis of the *midrash*, a literary genre, which is equivalent to "meditated history." This seems to mean that in the Infancy Gospels there is true history and more than history.

4. There is a tendency to deny *the divinity of Christ*, making Him into only a great religious personage or hero, who little by little acquires a consciousness of his mission, and who, after uncertainties, decides to be a religious and not a political Messiah, etc.

The tendency is due a little to the intense interest which it is customary today to bring to psychological and anthropological questions; a little to the Biblical studies centered on "salvation history," which have focused attention on the humanity of Christ; a little to an irenism which strips Christ of his divine dimensions in order to make his sublime teachings acceptable to larger circles of souls; a little to a far from praiseworthy tactic that admits the divinity of Christ, but suggests that we should not proclaim it to those of other religions and to nonbelievers. Now for us to stress that Jesus was made like one of us is useful for ascetical and pastoral theology. We must, however, continue to firmly believe and openly proclaim that he possessed, in addition to a human nature, a divine nature as well; that in the historical Christ, the two natures not only were not opposed to each other, and did not block the work of redemption, but that the Word made use of human nature assumed as an instrument in order to communicate His gifts to men.

As for Messianic consciousness, the Gospel shows Christ invested with a full consciousness of His Messianic dignity right at the beginning of his ministry. Already at twelve years of age, in His response in the Temple, He appears conscious of His divine sonship and vocation. The Epistle to the Hebrews shows Him to us in the act of offering Himself to the Father in body and soul from his first entrance into the world. Certain events, such as the Baptism in the Jordan and the Transfiguration, did not increase in Jesus the consciousness of his own mission, but only officially manifested the ministry of Jesus to others. In any case, the dogma of the hypostatic union postulates that in the humanity of Christ there was from the beginning a full consciousness of His relationship with God and of His mission in regard to men.

5. There is a tendency to exaggerate the importance of the charismatic gifts at the expense of the hierarchy and the social organisms, in the name of a "spiritual Church" and a "human messianism."

This is because people have ideas that are not very clear and Vatican II has been misinterpreted and not fully absorbed. It is true, of course, that the Council has spoken broadly of charismatic gifts, admitting that they exist[24] and affirming that those who possess them have "the right and the duty to use them . . . for the upbuilding of the Church."[25] But it has also said that the Pastors have the duty to "make a judgment about the true nature and proper use of these gifts."[26] That if the charismatic gifts are gifts distributed by the Spirit, "among these gifts stands out the grace given to the Apostles. To their authority, the Spirit Himself subjected even those who were endowed with charisms."[27] As a remedy, the faithful are to be properly instructed in the exact doctrine: the Holy Spirit "furnishes and directs (the Church) with various gifts, both hierarchical and charismatic."[28]

The "hierarchical gifts" are: the primacy of the Pope, the episcopate, the priesthood, and the diaconate, with the relative powers of jurisdiction and order, which are always at work. With the "charismatic gifts," God, through mysterious channels, reserves it to Himself to act if and when he thinks right–as a rule, infrequently–directly on souls for the benefit of the Church whether they are souls of pastors or of simple faithful.

6. The value of the Magisterium, especially the ordinary Magisterium of the Pope, is at times not appreciated; some seem to maintain that it is simply a "recorder" (bishops = notaries of the *aggiornamento* in progress), which gathers together and makes known though authoritatively everything that is gradually taking

place in the religious consciousness of the community. Some judge it to be a "nuisance" to stay as far away from as possible, while they exalt, on the other hand, in comparison to this, the "charismatic gifts" of theologians, or else a "unity", which is not to be uniformity but "a pluralism in the Church or of the Churches."

Today it is necessary to insist strongly on the sincere and inner respect that everyone owes to the acts of the authentic Magisterium, even when not infallible, which is the *"regula proxima fidei."* And the adjective "authentic" should be clearly stressed. It means that the Pope and the bishops do not simply set forth truths, but do so with authority, creating in the faithful the obligation of accepting them. At the same time, we should also stay with the Council, which says: "Theologians are invited to seek continually for more suitable ways of communicating doctrine to the men of their times. For the deposit of faith or revealed truths are one thing; the manner in which they are formulated without violence to their meaning and significance is another"[29] ". . . let it be recognized that all the faithful, clerical and lay, possess a lawful freedom of inquiry and of thought, and the freedom to express their minds humbly and courageously about those matters in which they enjoy competence."[30] Two passages should be stressed here, and they are: "humbly" and "about those matters in which they enjoy competence." We might add, in regard to "expressing": "at suitable times and places."

The "charism" of theologians should not be overrated, but appreciated within its just limits. If theologians are not actually part of the hierarchy, and do not exercise the authentic Magisterium, nevertheless they carry out an important task for the benefit of the Church. They are the experts who study the revealed truths in the light of reason enlightened by faith in order to obtain a more profound knowledge of them. They can have from God, through research carried out in a spirit of humble service and paying close attention to the indications of the Magisterium, gifts of true competence to place in the service of the Magisterium itself.

It is understood that the theologian is often simply a "postman" between the Magisterium and the faithful: he brings the word of the Magisterium to the people, adapting it to the various capacities of the hearers. Often he is the "expert" who explains the motives for magisterial documents that have already been issued. But often he is the "researcher"; on his own initiative, he tackles the study of new problems anticipating the Magisterium, preparing solutions. It is important, in this case, that his researches be made in the light of revelation and that he be disposed to accept, in his conclusions, the judgment of the Magisterium itself. And then theology proceeds "not without some light form the Holy Spirit, to which the theologian must be attentive and docile."[31] But this procedure is not easy today, for the theologian must reconcile unchangeable truths with a changed philosophical and scientific climate, a changed interpretation of Scripture and the changed mentality of his hearers. Like the Biblical scholar, he deserves understanding and encouragement.

As for pluralism or pluriformity or healthy unity in the Church, they are all things admitted by the Council. There are a very few people, however, who tend to wear out the concept, steeping it in Rome-or Curiaphobia, while projecting fantasies of local Churches as self-governing or provoking the "atomization" of particular churches endowed with an exaggerated autonomy. The correct way seems to be: individual churches furnished with reasonable personality of their own, but solidly united to Peter, who is the center and cause of unity.

7. Concerning *the dignity of man*, there is a double tendency; some overvalue natural dignity, advocating an exaggerated autonomy; others insist unilaterally on supernatural dignity and fall into a pseudo-spiritualism which cuts the faithful off from real life, preventing them from becoming part of earthly reality, from being able to persuade others and from spreading the right kind of "propaganda" for the Church. A well-balanced pastoral approach

should, on one hand, show man dependent on nature, on the other, it should commit him to a constant effort to dominate nature; in one aspect, a servant of God, in another a brother of Christ. On one hand, repeating with the Bible: "O man, you are a little less than the angels"; on the other, observing with the Council: That happens because he is created in the image of God! Because he has been placed by God over all earthly creatures.[32] Christ has given man divine sonship, but he has, in addition, increased human perfection!

8. *The Angels* are the "great unknowns" in these times of tendential cosmolatry. Some have insinuated the doubt that they are not persons; many do not speak of them. It would be fitting to recall them more often as ministers of Providence in the government of the world and of humanity, and to try to live in familiarity with them, as did the saints from Augustine to Newman.

There is also not much talk of *the Devil*. In the Middle Ages, there had been some exaggerations. "It is enough to read Peter the Venerable's *De Miraculis* [on Miracles] in order to understand the power of imagination when applied to the havoc wrought by Satan. He it is who comes to torment faithful souls, his fury proportioned to their virtue; he it is who, in hideous or alluring guise, prowls about the monasteries. As incubus, he forces virgins to his will, and procreates foul offspring in their wombs. As succubus, he tempts men vowed to God. Could one doubt the truth of this when St. Augustine (*De Civitate Dei*, XV, 23) said that it is so? Representations of the Devil are numerous. In churches he grimaces from the capitals or assists with his fell legions at the day of doom; he appears in frescoes, in miniatures and even on the stage. He is everywhere! . . . Superstition, a degraded form of supernatural faith, can have dire consequences, by perpetuating the practice of witchcraft and exploiting cowardice. This is where demonology joined hands with age-long magical beliefs which the Church has never managed to completely eradicate. Strange as it may appear, trust in the efficacy of these rites took on a new lease of life instead of decaying between the 12th and 14th centuries. Witch, sorceress, and poisoner were never out of work. It was firmly maintained that one could direct the powers of hell against the enemy by making a small wax image in his likeness and running it through with a bodkin; the practice is called 'imitative magic.' There were also stories of men changing themselves into beasts and running about the countryside intent on every sort of crime; such were lycanthropes and werewolves. Finally, it was thought that old hags flew by night to assist at Satan's Sabbath!"[33]

These exaggerated medieval beliefs have been replaced by modern reactions that are so exaggerated that they led Charles Baudelaire to say: "The Devil's most successful trick is this: convincing us that he doesn't exist!" The Devil, that is, gets men to deny him in order to lead them to repeat the revolt against God that was already his. The modern theologian should maintain whatever the Magisterium has said officially, remaining reserved and prudent as to the rest and especially in judging alleged extraordinary events. As for the general influence of the Devil on humanity, it is necessary to admit it, but greatly attenuated and re-dimensioned by the victory that Christ has won over him. On the cross, Christ seemed to be defeated, when he was actually the victor over the Devil. We are in the same line; in temptation, in pain, but sustained by the grace of Christ, victors with Christ!

Leon Bloy wrote: "When we do not speak to God or for God, it is to the demon that we speak and he listens to us in a formidable silence!" This and similar statements are paradoxes; they do not encourage religion, but rather discredit it.

9. There are various attempts to harmonize *original sin* with the hypothesis of an evolution of beings that, guided by God, branched out into polygenism.

Some explain that they do not mean "originating" sin committed by a first man: they admit only "originated" sin, the sin "in us," equivalent to the actual sins of human beings added together, or else reduced to a symbol of human destiny—meaning that human beings are indeed going to lift themselves up and will finally be able to give themselves to God, but that they begin from a position of harmful egoism.

Others present "original" sin in a new manner; a) a collective sin by which the first human beings, as they emerged from the pre-human state, refused to take the will of God as the rule for their lives, thus introducing, little by little, the reign of sin into the world; b) for Teilhard de Chardin, "originating" sin is only the distance which existed at the beginning of humanity between the human condition of that time and the perfection that humanity is called to achieve; c) Fathers Flick and Alszeghy admit—as a hypothesis—a personal and actual sin by the first among the pre-humans who reached the human goal. Such a sin insures that God does not grant to him the preternatural gifts that he had prepared for him; the other pre-humans, as they reach human maturation, and all the human beings who come afterwards, are deprived of the same gifts, not because they descend from the first man, but because they are one with him, and he, in some way, epitomizes them. The two Fathers try to explain how that "first man" can epitomize all the others. The same divine influence, they say, regulates their ascending from inferior to superior forms. "Salvation" is also prepared by God in mass for an entire people of God and not for individuals taken one by one. Then too there is the so-called "corporate personality" recently brought to light by Biblical scholars: that is, God is accustomed to choosing a few men, who act in the name of the collective group and determine the position of the entire community toward God (see Abraham as "father of all believers," Moses, David, etc). On the strength of these considerations, the act done by Adam is not only the first of a series of similar acts performed by the human beings who will come afterward; it is an act of super-individual value, as though collective, by the whole human community.

These opinions—excepting, perhaps, that of Flick and Alszeghy[34]—are in conflict with the classic texts on original sin;

Genesis 2-3, Romans 5:12-23, the Tridentine Decree and *Humani Generis*. Now Paul VI's discourse of July 11, 1966 has been added.

One the strength of these documents, in fact, it is a matter of faith that original sin exists in each one of us, that it is true sin (although called thus analogically in comparison to actual sin); that it entails unhappy consequences for body and soul, and that it was the prevarication of Adam, the "first man," that caused these unhappy consequences. These truths, because they are matters of faith, are to be stated and repeated as clearly as possible.

We recognize, however, that it is difficult to state them clearly, and to respond to all the difficulties that arise. The Magisterium, after enunciating them, leaves to the theologians the task of thoroughly researching their various aspects and trying to explain them.

10. Concerning *moral theology* some have gone to such extremes as to deny that outside of us objective moral laws exist, capable of binding us, or that there exists a natural law. They even resort to situation ethics, in practice made up of laws that each personal fabricates for himself case by case, according to the circumstances, in the name of the so-called "spontaneous sincerity," which seems to them to be preferable to the imperative of the very commandments of God. On this side of these true errors, there are positions that are more nuanced and of a practical significance. That is, some doubt that some less obvious precepts are "natural laws." Some find it difficult to reconcile obedience to "nature" with the domination of man over nature which is growing stronger every day. Some think that certain laws, as proposed by the Church, are not applicable in practice, and that the Church is asking that they be observed without taking into account, for example, the dimensions of conjugal life, the demographic problem, etc. The sense of sin has also been greatly weakened. Now, we can concede, standing on the researches made by modern moralists and psychologists, that human actions are conditioned much more than was once believed by

environment, the collective pressure of social life, temperament, etc. We can hope that there will be more thorough research in moral theology, and that some elements in it that are not founded on revelation will be dropped. We can also justify the appeal to individual conscience, when a person is first provided with an upright, well-formed conscience. But the existence of an objective moral law always remains unshaken; sin is still sin, that is, an offense to God, and a misfortune for the sinner; and the problem of freedom and responsibility does not change in substance. We also must not forget that the grace of God is still the essential factor in the human struggle.

11. On the subject of the *Eucharist*, the words "transfinalization" and "transignification" are used instead of "transubstantiation". The reasons they adopted are: 1) The term "transubstantiation" is used for "things," while Christ is a "person." 2) Transubstantiation is a term of scholastic, essentialist theology; today we must think and speak instead in terms of existentialism, and existentialism tries, above all, to answer these questions: "Of what use is it? What good does it bring to others?" 3) The liturgy has made us reflect on the community aspect of the Mass and has brought to light that there are a number of ways in which Christ can be present among us.

Therefore, in the Eucharistic celebration the Risen Christ is truly present. He is like the father of a family who issues an invitation to dinner, and we are the invited children. The bread and wine are means by which He signifies His love to us and communicates His gifts to us. Thus it is said that Christ is present; but that the bread and wine, offered to us by Christ, do not change, are not converted into the pre-existing body of Christ. They are only a special bread and wine, invested with a holy purpose, immersed in a holy action.

Paul VI, in *Mysterium fidei*, did not call this opinion heresy or error, but put the faithful on guard against it because it was scandalizing the faithful and it was abandoning lightly the venerated and untouchable formula of "transubstantiation." In reality, the opinion seems to deny two dogmas: the Real Presence and transubstantiation. It is true that the aim of the Eucharist is to signify and communicate the supernatural life of the believer and the community, achieved by means of the Real Presence of Christ: in this we are in agreement. The Dutch theologians however, seem to be saying: signifying and communicating the supernatural life of the believer and the community is what the Real Presence consists of! If so, we cannot be in agreement.

On the other hand, we can admit that today people are inclined to confuse "substance", a word which indicates a profundity that escapes all chemical-physical analysis, with the "non-profound" physical-chemical elements.

Today more effort and patience is required to make it clear how we should conceive of the indivisible mutation or succession of two substances, under appearances that remain identical and visibly identical.

12. Concerning *Penance*, it seems we should recognize attitudes rather than actual errors:

1) This sacrament is respected less and less frequently received than at one time. There have been reports of experiments where children have been admitted to First Communion without previous Confession (at seven they are incapable of committing mortal sin, we must eradicate from their minds the idea that Communion and Confession are inseparable);

2) The required and proper "sense of sin" becomes in some subjects a pathological and depressing "guilt complex";

3) Some see confession more as a magic means for placating the distress of their souls than as a conversion and renewal of their lives.

4) Local traditions, where the sacrament is received as a matter of convention, not infrequently lead to a formalism disliked by modern people, who demand spontaneity and conviction.

5) Many do not perceive that a person who lives in mortal sin is almost a parasite on the Church; the aspect of the reconciliation of the believer with the community in confession escapes them.

6) Others, on the other hand, seem to exalt the reconciliation with the Church too much, to the detriment of the complete auricular confession of sins.

All of this requires effort and commitment to giving better instruction from catechists, educators, theologians and liturgists, with special emphasis on sorrow for sins and on the mercy of the Lord, which is expressed through the Church.

As for children's confessions, it has not been clearly demonstrated that they cannot commit mortal sins. But it is certain, on the other hand, that they can fulfill the "substance" of the sacrament: confession, sorrow, restitution, and that as members of the Church they have a right to be admitted to this sacrament.

13. Little is said, in general about *the end times*. Some exaggerate in insisting on points of doctrine that are not certain; some like to stress only the dread of the end times, while St. Paul and the early believers wanted the coming of Christ and the end of the world to happen quickly! Others, finally, confess their repugnance at treating the subject, because of the difficulties that they find in speaking of it in a way that conforms to revelation and at the same time is adapted to the modern mentality. Here too, there is an urgent need for good work by theologians in the areas of research and popularization.

The Council's enumeration of the ten different classes of *atheists* seems valid. It is composed—as the speaker said in the hall—in such a way that an atheist reading it would find nothing there that is not true, and he will also hear the cry of a Church cruelly grieved by the oppression of her children, and by the mutilation of man without God. And yet he will know and feel that he is loved by the Church with a true and invincible love. In practice, the ten classes can be reduced to two: *theoretical atheists*, who reject the idea of God and do not wish to hear any talk of Him, and *practical atheists*, who are so immersed in their affairs that they live in the practical sense without God. Along with the theoretical atheists, there are recent philosophies which cast doubt on all ways of knowing God. Hence the necessity of philosophical and theological research concerning the validity of arguments that prove the existence of God and a serious commitment to introducing God once more into vast sectors of modern thought. However, it seems to be a true observation that atheism almost always presents itself as more of an affirmation of man than a denial of God; that is, religion is rejected because it is considered *alienation*; the "death of God" is required so that man can live in the fullness of liberty and well-being.

Two old thoughts of John XXIII also seem good: a) distinguishing atheism (deadly and pestiferous) from the atheist, a human person worthy of consideration and respect; b) the atheistic-Marxist doctrines remain what they are and as they appear printed in the book; the social movements that have emerged from these doctrines, on the other hand, are in turn entering, though slowly, into the general evolution of the world. So we will have to know how to wait with patience and at the same time do whatever is in our power to present the true doctrine properly, and to persuade them— especially by our life and actions—that there is a Christian humanism that is infinitely superior to Marxist humanism.

The lack of Christians and lived Christianity, is perhaps the cause of the paradoxical atheism which has risen very recently, and was not recorded by the Council: *Christian atheism*!

In an early version, it means: "Enough of speeches about God! Let's find God in works! Let's experience Him without words and dogmas!" Clearly, there is a spirit of truth here, but united with a very grave danger: religion without dogmas, at least explicitly formulated.[35]

In a second meaning, more frequent among Christians, there is the idea that atheism does some good, because it stimulates and awakens sleeping Christians. Here too there is some truth, but we fall into dangerous paradoxes.

I will cite some of them. For Simone Weil, for example, of two people who do not know God, the one who is closer to God is the one who denies him! She begs the believer not to combat atheism, unless he has first used it to his advantage.

For Father Liegé, "a vaccine of atheism would not hurt the mass of churchgoers; it will purify their sense of God." For Pierre Crozon, "Atheism, by denying and criticizing, has the task of purifying the sense of God in humanity!" For Stephen Barne, if on one hand, atheism is a scandal for reason and faith, on the other, it is necessary for the progress of reason and the deepening of faith.

I repeat: exciting and stimulating, but paradoxical expressions. To purify our religious sense, we need not atheism, but faith!

*****

My dear priests! Here you are at the end of this review, which in the spirit that animates it, is anything but a Syllabus.

Don't let the list of more or less erroneous tendencies impress you. There have always been errors in the Church. Think of what Paul (Colossians, Galatians) and John (Revelation) wrote about the heresies of the first centuries, and of the heretical movements of various kinds that existed throughout the whole Christian Middle Ages.

Don't let it pass through your minds that these new tendencies are the fruit of the post-conciliar period. *Humani Generis* and some of the speeches of Pius XII already spoke of a good part of them.

Don't believe either that "theological research" in and of itself leads to certain dangerous conclusions. Only the research of isolated and reckless theologians, who fortunately, are not the best theologians in existence, is exposed to serious dangers.

Nor should you want to throw stones at "research" itself or at debate. "If they debate, it is a sign that they do not have faith," one of you has said to me. But I know many people who debate precisely because they have faith, and they would like their faith, which is somewhat crusted over with debatable human opinions to be cleaned and purified! And think too, of the undeniable thirst for God and religious truth that large sectors of young people and humanity in general reveal today.

It is that humanity for which Our Lord died, about which he is concerned as the head of his Church, and for which the Holy Spirit is constantly at work in the Church. We must have faith in the destiny of this humanity, and we must work as hard as we can at our posts to make it happen!

Vittorio Veneto, September 8, 1967, the feast of the Nativity of Our Lady.

+ Albino, Bishop

Notes

1 *Opera* 4:56-82.

2 GS, no. 6 (1332).

3 Ibid., no. 6 (1333).

4 Ibid., no. 6 (1134).

5 Ibid., no. 7 (1338).

6 Ibid., no. 5 (1329).

7 Ibid., no. 9 (1346).

8 Ibid., no. 5 (1330).

9 Ibid., no. 5 (1329).

10 Ibid., no. 5 (1330).

11 Ibid., no. 33 (1423).

12 Ibid., no. 7 (1340).

13 "Our duty is not only to guard this precious treasure, as if we were concerned only with antiquity, but to dedicate ourselves with an earnest will and without fear to that work which our era demands of us, pursuing thus the path which the Church has followed for twenty centuries" (John XXIII, Opening address at the Second Vatican Council, October 11, 1963).

14 *I cite some examples, from among the most recent:*

a) In an article subtitled "A Contribution to the 'Post Council,'" *Palestra del Clero* (1967, pp. 880 ff) speaks of "enormous heresies" on account of which "God alone knows the scandal that arises when they are vigorously maintained by the best of Catholics, or those who are deemed as such"; among them, "the denial of the primacy of the Roman Pontiff, placed in competition with the sovereignty of the Apostolic College, which is the greatest heresy of the 'diarchy' of the Church." . . . There is also "the devastating plunder of Sacred Scripture, by which, in the name of science, or so-called science, a veil of suspicion is cast over the entire Book of God; entire chapters of it are arbitrarily removed; an interpretation lacking in supernatural understanding and wisdom is given to those passages that have not been successfully harmonized with a scientific knowledge which, when not also arbitrary, has its own, always limited, way of seeing things, which must produce caution on one side and the other."

b) A book *Perchè il Concilio non ha condannato il comunismo* [Why the Council Did not Condemn Communism] (published in Rome on July 13, 1967), says, "It was no secret to anyone that international Communism, through a thousand channels, a thousand pressures, and a thousand equivocations, paraded with great learning by a conforming, obsequious and myopic press–often even by the so called free and independent press, and often even by the tottering, frightened and conformist Catholic press, (and valid for everyone is the example of the reporting in the Catholic daily of Bologna *L'Avvenire d'Italia*)–it was no secret to anyone, as we have said, that international Communism has exploited and politicized the Council for its own expansionist ends." (p. 10)

"And all the *dialogues*, the *encounters*, the *agreements* that took place before and afterward – which are intensifying and multiplying today at a deafening and frenetic pace – prove this truth. Today there is even a fear of saying the word "Communism," and everything is censored, betraying history, the daily news, and the truth. Even Our Lady is censored" (p. 11).

"The new conciliar spirit, as the new progressive laity and priests live and defend it, is nothing but an unhoped-for water flowing into the Communist garden" (p. 12). "The painful and scandalous examples, inside and outside Italy, are innumerable, they are known to everyone, and they are multiplying at a tragic geometrical ratio" (p. 12).

c) *Renovatio* (no. 3, p. 501) writes: "On the plane of editorializing and opinion, we find ourselves face to face with a phenomenon of infiltration and conquest of power on the part of a small group, supported by a richness of means and a quite notable consensus. Theology now seems to be a domain reserved to Frs. Rahner, Schillebecx, Chenu, Congar, etc. Is it possible that there are no longer any theologians of a different bent? . . . The literature of theological *aggiornamento* is in fact in the hands of a pressure group which behaves like one and which has succeeded in creating an orientation in its favor among the editors and public."

d) The *Dizionario di teologia biblica*, translated and published by the Morcelliana publishing house, in a good three articles ("Virgin Birth," "Brothers of Jesus," and "Virginity,") solidly defends the dogma of the virginity of Mary, though stating that she "chose perpetual virginity for herself *after* having conceived, as a virgin, the Holy Child" (p. 1509). Therefore, one of these articles was cited unfairly, in *Crisi nel giovane clero* p. 18, in order to prove that there is a crisis of faith in the clergy, and the author, Bauer, was unjustly accused of not making "any reference to the desire or intention [of Mary] to remain a virgin." The virginity of the Most Blessed Virgin Mary *ante, in et post partum* is indeed an article of faith, but that Our Lady expressed her intention of perpetual chastity *before* the Annunciation is only the most common interpretation.

15 *Le paysan de la Garonne*, (Paris, 1966, p. 46. [Eng.: *The Peasant of the Garonne*, tr. by Michael Cuddihy and Elizabeth Hughes (NY: Holt, Rinehart and Winston, 1968), pp. 25-26].

16 DV, 23 (906).

17 The books of the Bible are truly the word of God, because, written through the inspiration of the Holy Spirit, they have God for their author and they teach with certainty, faithfully and without error, the truth which God, for our salvation, decided should be deposited in the Sacred Writings. But who determines their exact meaning? The final decision rests with the Magisterium, which has the task of authentically interpreting the law of God. Prior data for a mature judgment, however, are often supplied to the Magisterium by the studies of exegetes or private interpreters. The latter, in reading the Bible, will have to search with great care for what the sacred writers intended to say. To this end, they will keep in mind the whole content of Scripture, the tradition of the Church, but also the so called "literary forms." It might be a history, it might be a poem, it might be a teaching, it might be something else, but a form, a category there must be. Every form has a great variety of subforms: a narrative, for example, can be a fable, a fairy tale, a short story, or a novel; a novel can be a love story, a historical novel, a psychological novel, an adventure novel, a detective novel, a science fiction novel, etc. Every one of these forms, however, operates by fixed laws or rules; the writer must submit to them, and anyone who studies the book scientifically, even at a distance of centuries, must discover these rules. Anyone who wants to properly understand an ancient tragedy, for example, must know that the authors of that time were subject to the law of the "three unities" of action, time and place: that is, to recount a single event of violent passion, to have all its characters act in the space of 24 hours and all in the same place. Those who study the *Orlando Furioso* must know the laws of the verse form used; they know that it consists of eight-line stanzas, of hendecasyllabic lines with alternate lines rhyming, and with the two last rhymes "kissing," that is, next to each other. In the same way, those who study the Bible must try to find what the sacred writer wanted to express, and in reality did express, in the circumstances in which he lived, in the conditions of that time and that culture, by means of literary genres, means of understanding and narrating then in use. And this is because, as the Council said, God has

used in speaking to us, an admirable condescension ; his words have been made like to the words of men, just as the Son of God made himself like to man, assuming the weaknesses of human nature.

18 *Le paysan de la Garonne*, pp. 26, 28, 37. 19 DV, no. 8. 20 G. Papini, *Lettere di Papa Celestino VI* (Milan: Mondadori), 1960, pp. 412, 415. [*Letters of Pope Celestine VI to All Mankind*, trans by Loretta Murnane (New York: Dutton, 1948). Giovanni Papini (18811956), was a Italian journalist, literary critic, poet and novelist, who spent a number of years as a Modernist skeptic until a dramatic reversion to Catholicism in 1921. – Trans].

21 Cf. R. Laurentin, *Structure et theologie de Luc I-II* (Paris: Gabaldo, 1957).

22 DV, no. 19, 101.

23 *In ev. Jo. XV, lect. 5, n. 4.*

24 AA 3 (921).

25 Ibid.

26 *Lumen Gentium*, no. 7.

27 Ibid., no. 4.

28 GS, 62.

29 Ibid.

30 Ibid.

31 Paul VI in *L'Osservatore Romano*, October 2, 1966.

32 GS, no. 12.

33 Henri Daniel-Rops, *La chiesa delle cattredrale*, Torino, 1954, pp. 51-52 [Eng. trans.: *Cathedral and Crusade: Studies of the Medieval Church, 1050-1350* (New York: E. P. Dutton, Inc., 1957), pp. 38-40].

34 It should be noted: 1) the two Fathers wrote only by way of a hypothesis (*if* tomorrow polygenism were proved, how might it be reconciled with original sin?); 2) Their manner of exposition does not contradict the Tridentine phrase *"propagatione, non imitatione, transfusum inest"* [transfused into (everyone) by propagation, not

imitation], nor the phrase of the saint of Carthage: *"ut in eis (parvulis) regeneratione mundetur quod generatione* (it is possible to translate 'at the moment of generation' instead of 'through the means of generation') *traxerunt"* [and what they (young children) acquired at at the moment of generation is cleansed in them through regeneration]; 3) Paul VI (in the discourse cited) seems to be speaking more against those who use polygenism to deny original sin than against polygenism; (4) the Pope's discourse was delivered to a selected, qualified commission of 13 people; two of these were Flick and Alszeghy themselves; it seems unlikely that the Pope condemned their attempt in their presence. It is difficult, however, to admit with them that the first man was "deprived" of gifts that had only been prepared, that potentially existed, but which he did not yet possess.

35 This form of atheism has not yet arrived over here, but in England and America they are already talking about the "God is dead theology," which some jokingly and polemically call "Mini-Theology" or "Pop Theology." For some the God who "dies" is only the false idea of God that some people have made for themselves: the God falsely conceived as being against freedom, well-being, science, people. And up to this point, this atheism is no great harm. But for others the true God is "dead." Jesus the Christ-God is no longer present in the world; present instead is His Word, which continues to have an influence on humanity. Thus Christ finds himself on the same level as Homer, Dante and Mohammed, still living today through the influence that their writings have. For still others the God who concerns himself with humanity does not exist, but a Christian will have some practical advantages if he imitates the life of Jesus. Others, finally, and more radically, say: the principal thing taught by Christ is freedom: in the name of this "Christian" freedom we must come out of the "ghetto of the Church" and immerse ourselves in the full reality of modern life in order to lend a hand in the construction of the new world. They reach all these fine conclusions starting from the most opposite points: from *structuralism*, for example, a philosophy which is concerned with language ("We must read the Gospel in a new way"); even from *psychoanalysis* ("We must overcome the *Oedipus complex*: the children—that is we—must consider the religion of our fathers outdated"). We are, therefore, face-to-face with an atheism which calls itself "Christian", because its advocates paradoxically profess themselves to be Christians; its content, however, is as *anti-Christian* as ever!

Letter to the Diocese of Vittorio Veneto

For the Close of the Year of Faith[1]

Dear people of the diocese,

On the evening of the feast of Pentecost, in the cathedral, we officially concluded the Year of Faith. The Pope had called it for the occasion of the nineteenth centenary of the martyrdom of the holy Apostles Peter and Paul.

1. Talk on the Faith

To the faithful who packed the church, I spoke as follows.

You have come for the Year of Faith: therefore you believe; therefore the following four fundamental points must be firmly fixed for you: 1) God exists, 2) God has spoken, 3) God has sent his word on a journey intact from Adam down to you, 4) You are saying yes to his word!

1. *God exists.* Distinct from us, infinitely more good and infinitely greater than us! Without him we would not be. Before him only one attitude is possible for us: "You are holy, you alone are the Lord, You alone are the Most High!" As Abraham said, "Before you. Lord, we are dust and ashes!" (Gen. 18:27)

2. *God has spoken.* In speaking, he has told us something of himself and what he has done and intends to do for us. "I love you," he has said, "I have always loved you and I want to see you safe and happy. A magnificent plan of salvation has been conceived for you in heaven. At a specific moment, the plan began to be realized and

went into action on earth, and I have intervened in your favor from the first human being down to now, once, twice, a thousand times, millions of times and I am intervening still. These interventions of mine, placed one after another, through so many centuries, make a very long line, which is called salvation history. Each of you has been inserted in it one by one. At its center, however, is my Son, Jesus Christ. Through him everything was created. In order to save you he became man, conceived by the Holy Spirit, and born virginally of Mary ever virgin, he suffered under Pontius Pilate and died on the cross for your sins. Risen on the third day from the dead, and glorified with the Father, he sent the Holy Spirit to his Church to sanctify her. He was also made your judge, to assign, according to your merits, eternal reward or punishment. He is the Savior, because he wants the salvation of everyone, because he never tires of calling souls, running after those who are fleeing and offering forgiveness, so that he might redeem humanity and the world marked by the first and universal fall of original sin." This is, in essence, what God has said. It is a word, but in the rich sense: that is, not a mere movement of the lips, which expresses the thought of the mind, but a dynamic and creative decision of the divine will. It is a call, because it calls us to work and cooperate with him. It is a message, because it is a kind of loving and urgent letter that urges us and expects a reply from us.

3. *The word of God is on a journey.* That is its destiny. "Go and make disciples of all nations . . . I am with you always until the end of the world" (Mt. 28:19) Christ said to the apostles and, by means of the apostles, to us. The Church is wholly missionary. "Every disciple of Christ has the duty to spread the faith as much as possible."[2] We talk of a "Church in dialogue." We should talk about it above all in this sense: Those who have received the word should not keep it to themselves, but must pass it on, through dialogue, to others and these people to still others, ensuring that it continues on its journey through space and time.

On its journey, however, the word must not change in its contents. So that it might not change, Christ has furnished his church with suitable gifts. All believers, "from the bishops down to the last of the faithful,"[3] are endowed with a kind of supernatural sense, called the "*sensus fidei*," that helps them to recognize what God has truly revealed. The hierarchy alone, on the other hand, has been given "the office of authentically interpreting the word."[4]And in certain cases, the hierarchy intends to commit itself fully to an interpretation, pronouncing infallible and irreversible judgments. In other cases the hierarchy, though perceiving that some element of judgment is missing, desires to give the directive that is best at that moment, pronouncing itself in minor and attenuated form, which, even if it is not guaranteed infallibility, is always connected to practical safety for the faithful. Its judgments, even in this case, even if not one hundred percent infallible, solicit the religious respect, internal and external, of the faithful, so that, by accepting them, even though they are not irreformable, they are certain of having spiritual advantage.

The word also needs to be set forth in a form that is understandable and congenial to the times, to human beings, to tastes, to new civilizations. Here a great effort is required in our days; here the work of theologians, priests and lay people, who, having at their disposal time, culture and sometimes some divine help—if offered in the form of humble and prudent service—act almost as intermediaries between the hierarchy and the rest of the faithful. That is, as popularizers, they bring the teaching of the hierarchy to the faithful and future priests in a plain and developed form; as researchers, they prepare material developed on a technical level for the hierarchy.

5. *Our assent to the word must be an affectionate "yes"*. You are accustomed to recite the Act of Faith and then, separately, the Act of Love. And yet, the two acts should ideally be joined. You cannot trust in God unless you love Him; you cannot love Him

unless you trust Him, unless you say "yes" to what He tells you and asks you. So then you answer "yes", not only with your head, but with your heart, with all your being, with your works and a life lived in a holy way. "What good is it, my brothers," said St. James," if someone says he has faith but does not have works? . . . Faith of itself, if it does not have works, is dead" (James 2:14; 16-17).

It is, therefore, *a difficult "yes"*. We do not see the things that God has said of himself, but only glimpse them, like the sun behind the mountain; they are known "indistinctly, as though in a mirror" (1 Cor. 13:12); the other things that God has asked us to do, we must carry out on trust, as though with our eyes closed, with the abandonment of Abram, who, when called by God, "departed not knowing where he was going" (Heb 11:8). It is costly, then, to channel a whole life in the direction required and willed by God, when our laziness likes the opposite direction. Like each of us, St. Augustine experienced it. "I found myself," he says in the *Confessions*, "in the situation of someone who is in bed and knows that he must get up, but does not have the courage and groans: 'One moment more!'" And the movement is put off, put off again!

And it will be put off forever and nothing new will happen unless God intervenes by force to pull us out the bed of our laziness and our sin with his grace. It is the supernatural aspect of our "yes". St. Paul said: "No one can say 'Jesus is Lord' except by virtue of the Holy Spirit" (1 Cor. 12:3). We cannot come to accept the Gospel as we should, "without the inspiration and illumination of the Holy Spirit, who gives everyone the sweet joy of consenting to and adhering to the truth."5 Here is the mystery: If, on one hand, the "yes" of faith is a free response of man to God who speaks, on the other it is a gift of God to man, which man must implore and preserve with humble, trusting and repeated prayer.

2. Paralipomena⁶ [Supplement] to the Talk

Here my talk for Pentecost ended. If you don't mind, I will take it up again, returning to the four points.

1. John Kennedy spoke of a "new frontier." I used to dream that the "new frontier" of the diocese of St. Tiziano [Vittorio Veneto] would be down there in Burundi, where the word of God, proclaimed by our priests, is adding new members to the people of God. But: "Up here, there is a still newer frontier" some people have said to me. It's true. We must, unfortunately, contend with this "newer" frontier, within which, right here in the midst of us, there are people, though baptized, in three categories: practical atheists, skeptics, and atheists by conviction. The first—fundamentally not dishonest or wicked, but distracted and hostile, not so much to God as to the Church and some of its institutions—live as though God does not exist, centering their attention exclusively on values from which God is absent; the second doubt that God exists; the third repeat today what Heine said a hundred years ago: "Do you hear the bell ringing? They are carrying the last sacraments to God who is dying!" On the "dying God" there is—very recently—the strange theory, which has come from America and proposed by people who call themselves Christians and theologians—of the "death of God" or of "Christian atheism."

The theory says: we must present to people of today a Christianity that is suited for them, made for them. Now, the people of today no longer need God and religion. So let's offer them an areligious and atheistic Christianity. Let's offer Christ as a model for every man, one who loved other people completely, but let's drop the vertical Christian dimension of a God who creates us and descends to us to save us and of us rising to him through religion devotion! Let's keep only the horizontal dimension: love our neighbors, help each other, favor progress! This is the "kingdom of God!" Let's "desacralize" man, "secularize" religion" and empty Christianity of God!

67

It seems rather comical for there to be "theologians" who promote atheism. They are like the barber who put the following sign above the door of his shop: "Here we take the hair from the heads of bald men!" They also seem to mix together religion and secularization, Christianity and atheism. "Secularized religion" sounds like "areligious religion"; atheistic Christianity means "Christianity emptied of its Christianity!"

As for the "kingdom of God," its true growth, says the Pope in his magnificent profession of faith,[7] "cannot be confused with the progress of civilization, human science and technology, but consists of knowing ever more profoundly the inscrutable riches of Christ, in hoping ever more deeply for the eternal goods, in responding ever more ardently to the love of God." And is it really true that today human beings no longer have any need of God? Once, it has been said, science and technology were in their infancy, and religion grew gigantic. God was made to intervene as an explanation for the great many things that were not known and as a remedy for the many diseases for which there was no medicine. But now! Science and technology are arriving, or are about to arrive at the point where they can explain everything, find the remedy for everything; more and more space is being taken from God; better eliminate him from now on from the arc of human experience!

In other words: religion is only a pre-scientific human and cultural phenomenon; it will gradually disappear until it is dispelled with the advance of science.

By speaking in this way, they suppose that science and religion, technology and God are antagonistic to each other. On the contrary, the truth is that science and technology are as necessary a component of man as religion is. Has science grown, become gigantic, by purifying itself of a thousand false theories and forms of ingenuousness that hindered it? Religion grows and is purified too; and religious people purify their own ideas on the Most High God from some forms of ingenuousness or superstition of the past;[8] they no longer think, for example, that they can entrust to God alone the task of constantly intervening and repairing the little breakdowns of the machine of the world and humanity! The conclusion to be drawn, if any, is this: if science has grown from a baby to an adult, religion too should be allowed to become adult! A purified science that has made progress should correspond to a religion that has been purified and perfected.

We should not say: "man is either religious or technical-scientific," but "a well formed man is scientific and religious and even when he grows gigantic in science, God remains as necessary to him as bread and the sun."

Let's imagine him, this "giant," ascending the successive steps of a ladder:

First: he has become so "gigantic" that he knows *all* the laws of the universe. It is a great step forward, even from the present state, but I ask: doesn't it still happen even now that, in those laws that he knows, an exception arises that he has not foreseen? Don't the formulas used to express the law still have to be considered provisory, relative, something to be perfected through new and future investigations? If yes, man does not entirely dominate the laws, but is still dominated by them. And anyone who is a true scientist must admit it, saying with a scientist's modesty: there is something that escapes the control of my instruments and my calculations; I think that it belongs to another field of research, in which philosophers work; the results of the work of the philosophers —I am sure of it—will tell me that what should be suppressed is not God but that way of presenting God that may possibly contrast with the very certain data of science.

Second step. The "giant" has arrived at the point of really grasping in his fist all the forces of nature in a way that no exception escapes him and he can press all the "buttons" to direct the entire cosmos. Yes, but there is still a problem: who is the origin of the forces and the cosmos? Who has given him, the "giant," the power to dominate them? Who if not someone, who existed before the forces he has discovered, who is above him, of whom old Metastasio said:

> ... I admire you in your works,
> Do I recognize you in me?[9]

Third step. Man not only dominates human acts themselves, but dominates them through technology; through mechanical apparatus, the acts are foreseen, channeled toward certain fixed ends, put into regiments with the acts of other persons, and accurately registered. That's fine, but I ask again: are the human acts subjected to technology in this way subjected to it completely or only in part? If completely, it would be the ruin of man, the end of thought and freedom; it would be absurd. If in part, it will certainly happen that once he has escaped the intricate web of mechanization and technology that have partially imprisoned him, man will hasten as soon as possible outside, into the open air of thought and liberty to enjoy periods of respite for originality and authenticity; his mind will yearn to know new things; along with having freedom, he will hunger and thirst for choices and options. Now, among the things that can be known and chosen, there will always be mystery, the infinite and God. Always, then, it seems that there must be in man a religious sense and a certain need for God!

2. God has spoken and His Word is found in tradition and the Bible. Here, however, at times it is easy to detect it and at times difficult. At times, in fact, we must ask ourselves: is this, what is written, what God wants to tell me and wants me to believe, or is it only a means used by God to present the truth, taking into account the given cultural surroundings? The tree in the Garden of Eden, for example, the serpent, the dialogue between the serpent and Eve—are they historical facts, are they too the object of my belief, or are they a symbolic story, used to present the historical fact and the dogma of original sin?

Let's suppose that it is a question of a conventional manner of expression; however, it is mixed with the historical fact of the sin of Adam in such a way that only after long studies and accurate comparisons with the literatures of the ancient east will scholars be able to distinguish the symbol from historical reality. It will take time for the Magisterium of the Church to assess the data offered by the scholars. If finally authorized by the Magisterium, the faithful will be able to hold that—saving the dogma that all human beings have sinned in Adam—the dialogue between the serpent and Eve is a symbol, an expressive means used by God. This delicate and slow work, by which—not without a final review by the Magisterium—a distinction is made in the Bible between the object of faith and a presentation of this object, is reserved for specialists, who must proceed with great prudence and humility; it coincides with the method called "use of literary genres" by Vatican II. It should be distinguished from the "demythologization" in fashion today, which denies the reality of the interventions of God in history: the incarnation, death, resurrection and ascension of Jesus are not—for the "demythologizers"—events that really happened, but symbols and myths. In order to be Christians and to become virtuous we must accept the myths without worrying about knowing whether they are true. They are beautiful, radiant themes, they spur us to action; it is enough to know this; why concern yourself with anything else? But it is evident that this demythologization is a radical de-historicization; it completely empties Christianity of its content, and makes true faith impossible.

3. The principal guarantee that the word of God is preserved faithfully in the Church is the Magisterium of the Pope and bishops. The obedience of the faithful to the Magisterium is very urgently recommended by the Council: "Bishops, teaching in communion with the Roman Pontiff, are to be respected by all as witnesses to divine and Catholic truth. In matters of faith and morals, the bishops speak in the name of Christ and the faithful are to accept their

teaching and adhere to it with a religious assent. This religious submission . . . must be shown in a special way to the authentic Magisterium of the Roman Pontiff, even when he is not speaking *ex cathedra*."[10] If we have trust in Christ, who is the head and guide of the Church, how can we not give sincere and profound inner religious assent to the statements of those who Christ and the Holy Spirit have put in place to govern the Church of God? (cf. Acts 20:19).

And if we truly love this Church, how can we not feel like participants in her life, her extraordinary adventures and her destiny? She is the ship that ploughs the waters in the sea of history; we cannot look at her like simple spectators, criticizing from shore, we must feel that we belong to the crew, co-responsible for the crossing and helped by those who are her captains and pilots. They speak to us and give us directives: for the good and the success of the ship, we must agree to them and carry them out at the cost of some sacrifice, with humble and disciplined submission.

This humble and disciplined submission has been made a little more difficult by the ideas that are circulating in the air. Some people do not want an "institutional Church," that is, one furnished with organizational structures and with a hierarchy: they would like it to be "charismatic," in such a way that everyone, especially the "poor" and the obscure, can each individually live their own faith in in with spontaneous enthusiasm, without constrictions and directives.[11]

But the Church in which we live the faith must correspond not to our tastes, but to the design of Christ, who has put in place for her some untouchable structures, for example, the primacy of the Pope, the episcopate, the ministerial priesthood and the diaconate. Those who look suspiciously on these structures come to see in them an obstacle to spontaneity and vitality. On the other hand, those who look at them with sympathy and love for Christ and in the light of the Church, discover that they are necessary conditions for the vitality of the Church and for the expansion and preservation of the faith. In the Church, either hierarchy (although with powers duly exercised in a style of service) or anarchy.

Others accept the essential structures, but would like them to be expedited in function; other structures, then, that are not essential, they want to be removed or replaced immediately, without delays. The Council itself has proposed the reform of the Church in her human institutions that have been revealed to be outdated. Reform, however, requires time and prudence: the Catholic Church today has the proportions of a great transatlantic liner with half a billion people on board; it cannot turn itself around on a dime like a little fishing boat. Experience also says that souls must be well prepared for every reform. Do we make a change, for example, and introduce the living language in the liturgy? They cry that the tunic of the Christ has been torn. Do the bishops initiate a prudent, cautious and partial disengagement from politics? From the right they are scolded for the disengagement, from the left they protest, because the disengagement is too cautious, too prudent and too partial.

Confusion also derives from different attitudes: there are the aristocrats or purists in ecclesiology; and these will not accept that something must change, they do not admit that sometimes the Church has made mistakes; they always strike the *mea culpa* on the breasts of others. There are, on the other hand, others who seem to find everything beautiful outside of their own church: self-lacerating, triumphalists in reverse, they seem to enjoy pitilessly bringing out the true or presumed faults of the Church their mother. The first disturb one faction of Catholics, the second, another faction. A third faction, disoriented, does not know whom to believe. These attitudes induce a really delicate situation. We can never recommend enough prudence in speaking and writing and the constant commitment to instructing, explaining and educating the mass of the faithful. They will never trust the Magisterium unless they love the Church. But they will not be able to love the Church unless she is presented to them well and, above all, unless they can see her, outside of the pages of the conciliar texts, as a true communion of lived fraternity and charity!

4. Peter and Paul give us a noble example of how to respond to the word of God. At Capharnaum the listeners had found Jesus' discourse on the Eucharist disappointing, and they had gone away. A little sadly, a little ironically, Jesus had asked the Twelve: "Do you want to leave too?" Simon Peter answered him: "Lord, to whom shall we go? You have the words of eternal life, and we have come to know and believe that you are the Holy One of God" (Jn 6:67-6). Paul was exhorting the Philippians to a perfect life. Suddenly, he interrupts the exhortation, saying: "Not that I have . . . now reached perfection, but I continue to run" to reach it. And with what vision in front of him? Impelled by what power, O Paul? He answers: "One unforgettable day, on the way to Damascus, I was seized by Christ . . . from then on . . . "I have done one thing only. I forget what is behind and leaning forward to what lies ahead, I run toward the goal . . ." (Phil. 3:12-14).

Let's imitate the great apostles. Like Peter, let's profess courageously that Christ alone has the words of eternal life! Like Paul, let's allow ourselves to be seized by him and let our life be a race to seize him!

Pietralba, July 11, 1968

Notes

1 *Opera* 4:188-97.

2 LG, no. 17.

3 Augustine, *De Predestinatione sanctorum*, 4, 27; PL, col. 980.

4 DV no. 10.

5 Vatican I: DS, no. 3010.

6 *Paralipomena*: a Greek word meaning "things omitted" or passed over in another work. Catholics were once more familiar with this word than they are now, since the Old Testament in the Latin Vulgate called the Books of 1 and 2 Chronicles the *Paralipomenon.*—Trans.

7 The *Credo of the People of God*, which was introduced by Paul VI to close the Year of Faith.—Trans.

8 Already Rosmini had said: "Think highly of God." Now Paul VI (*L'Osservatore Romano*, June 1, 1968): "We must purify the banal and false concept that we often make for ourselves of divinity and try without rest to give the name of God the infinite riches of his endless transcendence and the ineffable sweetness, full of reverence and love, of his omnipresence, of his omnipotence."

9 *Metastasio* was the pen name of Pietro Trapassi, an eighteenth-century Italian poet who wrote the librettos for many operas of the period. —Trans.

10 LG, no. 25.

11 Cf. Ignazio Silone, *L'avventura di un povero cristiano* [Adventures of a poor Christian] (Vincenza, 1968).

The Basics of Belief

The Creed Today

Easter Homily[1]
1974

I wish everyone a happy Easter, that is, I wish that they may "walk in a new life" (Rom. 6:4).

But the new Christian life requires first of all clear, firm and stimulating ideas: the ones in the Catholic Creed.

I believe in one God: Don't come and tell me that you are not sure that God exists because you have never seen him. You haven't seen your great-grandfather either, and yet you are certain that he existed. Don't tell me that the world and you yourselves were the result of eternal matter that sprang into being by itself, at first unformed and confused, then with an ever clearer and more definite character as it moved, revolved, and advanced through the centuries. Not even a little white dot on a blackboard can make itself today; why should an immense world have spontaneously sprung forth from nothing billions of years ago? Can something that doesn't exist act "spontaneously"? Today's bees work hard, but they have not changed by one little bit the type of hives that they were constructing at the time of the Egyptian Pharaohs; why should the work of the monkeys, solely because it was work, have made them, as I read in a Marxist text, take a qualitative leap from monkey to man? And why should matter, just because it is eternal, explain everything? Any kind of film needs a director, and a few actors, technicians, etc., doesn't it? "Yes, but only if it lasts for two hours," some people will say. "If it lasts forever, it doesn't need anything: eternity alone is enough to explain the film." Really? Who would have the nerve to say anything so silly?

The Bible says: "Truly foolish are those who . . . considering the works (of this world), cannot recognize their maker" (Wisdom 13:1). Tolstoy said: "One fine day a savage ceases to believe in his god of wood; what does that mean? Not that God does not exist, but that he is not at all a god of wood." "But we are not savages, but scientists," I've heard people say to me. I answer: "For many scientists, the more progress they make, the more they believe." Fabre, a great expert in the study of insects, for example, said, "I do not believe in God, I see God." And then too: worthy scientists discover the laws and the forces of nature, they don't produce them! Eustachio Rudio and William Harvey, in the 1600's, at the University of Padua, discovered that our blood circulates. But who thought of that circulation and brought it into being? Do write in letters of gold in the book of great men the names of Rudio and Harvey, but please don't erase the name of God, the inventor, author, and preserver of the circulatory system, through an apparatus that is simply marvelous.

I believe in one God in three persons. One lady, in a parish on the mainland, once interrupted me: "One God in three equal and distinct persons! Just hearing these things I seem to be back in the school of the Sisters of Nevers. Incomprehensible things, from the Middle Ages: what we're interested in here is asphalt for our streets, and a playing field for our children!" That lady, clearly, wants a God made to the measure of man . . . or of woman! But God cannot be measured: God is infinitely above us; we are little, He is very great. "There is nothing about which we know everything," Pascal said, "not even ourselves." Imagine coming to know everything about God! Naturally, there must be mysteries for us in the divine life. After God has spoken to us about them, we have only a glimmering about them for now. God, who is perfect intelligence, knows himself; thus we have one who knows, the Father, one who is known, or the Son. Because the Father and the Son know each other as infinitely good and beautiful, an extraordinary love blazes between them: we call it the Holy Spirit. They are three, they are distinct, inseparable, absolutely perfect, and equal. When I know and love myself, we are also three: me, my knowledge of me, and the love that I have of myself; but the knowledge and love are inferior to me, born from me, yes, but after me: in God it is different.

Michelangelo said: "When the sun shines in all its brilliance, our eyes cannot bear it; and yet the sun is only the shadow of God." Dante said: "Mad are those that hope that our reason/ can look along the infinite way/ that holds a substance in three persons."2

I believe in Jesus Christ, God from God, light from light. These words have always expressed the faith that we have always had: Catholics, Orthodox and Protestants. They flow from other words: "You are the Christ, the Son of the living God," Peter said, and Jesus accepted, praised and rewarded these words (Mt. 16:17). "The Word was made flesh and dwelt among us," wrote John (Jn 1:14). And Paul: "Christ Jesus, though he was God, emptied himself, taking the form of a slave, and became man" (cf. Phil. 2:6-7).

A book is being sold in bookstores that holds the opposite view. True God? Why no, writes Hans Küng, the *true man*, Jesus of Nazareth, is (only) a powerful and effective revelation for the faith in a *true God*.3 In his book, Küng speaks well of Christ in a way, but he omits any mention of the miracles that he performed, his declarations about his own mission and identity, or the powers that he gave to the Apostles, whom he chose with care from among the people, kept with him, and prepared in view of special tasks.

Who then is the Christ of Küng? A good man, an intelligent man who made a gross blunder in believing that the end of the world was imminent, and a man who preached the word of God. But did he present his identity card, did he say who he was? No, not even to Caiaphas, who had even implored him in the name of the living God to say whether or not he was the Christ. Did he found the Church? He didn't even foresee it. Küng asserts this because he accepts in the Gospel only what interests him, rejecting everything that appears out of the ordinary and supernatural. The Christ that emerges from his book is a poor Christ, a paltry Christ. He is not the real Christ, the one who was seen on the roads of Palestine, who gave sight back to the blind man, who raised Lazarus, and who, after he rose, appeared in the upper room and in Galilee. It is this Christ, the real Christ, who we need to be able to say with Thomas: "My Lord and my God."

I believe in the Catholic Church. "Christ, yes," I hear people say, "The Church, no." But we must see whether Christ will allow himself be separated from his Church. He said to his apostles: "Those who reject you, reject me." (Lk. 10:16). About him, St. Paul said: "Christ loved the Church and gave himself up for her" (Eph. 5:25). Poor Church. Immaculate in her head, Christ, assisted by the Holy Spirit; stupendous because of the Bible and the sacraments and other means of sanctification; she also contains sick members that stain her with sins. We do well in the Church if we love her, and if we try to improve her, beginning with ourselves. Some people, on the other hand, are in the Church only as troublemakers. They are like that employee who first begs and moves heaven and earth to get into a firm, but who, once he has a job there, is forever restless, a pestiferous insect on the skin of his colleagues and superiors. Yes, some people look at the sun only to find spots in it; in the history of the Church, they nit-pick, looking only at faults; some Popes who were in error, the Inquisition, Galileo, the Crusades; they do not consider the different times, the great saints, the great institutions; they hold up religious habits that have been abandoned like a flag. "My Pope is Pope John." "My Pope is the POPE," whether he is called Pius, John or Paul." And then which Pope John? Has anyone taken the trouble to count Pope John's condemnations of Communism? There are 74.[4] Anyone who is a Catholic does not distinguish between one Pope and another, nor between the various documents of the same Pope; much less do they claim to teach the Pope how to be Pope.

I await the life of the world to come. Amen. These are the last words of the Creed. For this reason, perhaps, we do not stress them enough. And yet the Bible recalls to us often that we are only here in passing, on our way toward another life. "A voice said, 'Cry out!' and I answered, 'What should I cry out?' 'Every man is like the grass and all his glory is like the flower of the field'" (Is. 40:67). "Provide money bags for yourselves that do not wear out, an inexhaustible treasure in heaven that no thief can reach or moth destroy" (Lk. 12:33). St. Paul says to us: are you risen with Christ? Then "think of what is above, where Christ is seated at the right hand of God. Think of what is above, not of what is on earth" (Col. 3:12).

If I may be allowed to comment on St. Paul, let's keep our feet solidly planted on the ground. Christians, just because they are Christians, must give a greater contribution than the others to progress and the advancement of humankind.[5] Our eyes, however, must be turned above, where the greatest and best things await us: New heavens and a new earth.

Notes

[1] *Opera*, 7:319-22.

[2] *Purgatorio*, 3:36.

[3] Hans Küng, *Christ sein* (Munich 1974), p. 434, translation mine [That is, Luciani's. He read it in the original German. The English title is *On Being a Christian.*—Trans].

[4] Cf. *Il Gazzettino*, April 11, 1975.

[5] GS, nos. 34, 37, 39.

Faith and Conversion

Homily for the Feast of the Madonna della Salute[1]
November 21, 1975

A faithful copy of this painting of the Madonna della Salute, which we are venerating here, is being exhibited today, tomorrow and the day after tomorrow in the Cathedral of Santa Maria in the state of Rio Grande do Sul (Brazil). It was requested by the descendants of Venetian immigrants, who live down there in great numbers. They also requested that the Patriarch personally bring it onto Brazilian soil. At the urging of the Pope I had to consent! So I went to Brazil fifteen days ago, and returned just this morning. On Sunday, November 9, at the *romaria* (pilgrimage) for Our Lady; I concelebrated Mass with fifteen bishops before 200,000 people. On the way that led into the large square where the gathering was held, a banner told me: "When you return to Italy, tell the Venetians that we have remained faithful to our devotion to Our Lady!" But even louder than the banner spoke the monument to the Italian emigrants in Caxias do Sul. It rose majestically in bronze, halfway up a hill, at the end of a long *avenida* (avenue). An emigrant has a hoe on his shoulders and tied to the handle of the hoe, the bundle of the expatriate; on his right his wife, in the typical dress of our Venetian grandmothers, carries a baby in her arms, but with a rosary peeking out of her apron pocket.

With this monument still before my eyes, I think of Our Lady not so much as our mother as our sister. A sister who had the same problems that we do, who had to emigrate to Egypt, and who we must follow and imitate especially in her faith. "Blessed are you because you have believed," (cf. Lk 1:45) her cousin Elizabeth said to her. And she did believe. She said "yes" to God, who spoke to her

84

through the angel: "yes", like a humble serving woman to her master (cf. Lk 1:38). She kept in her heart the words of Jesus, even when she did not understand them perfectly (cf. Lk 2:50-51).

We should think of our faith in two different stages. 1. It may be the fundamental and decisive act by which a person becomes and remains a believer. 2. It may be the permanent attitude of the believer after he has accepted the faith. In the first case we make the choice for Christ, accepting him in our hearts. In the second, we take the following spiritual position: "Jesus, I have chosen you in earnest: I not only believe that everything that you have said and that the Church asks me to believe is true, but I want to orient my whole life according to your teachings."

The first choice is also called conversion. I will try to describe it. A person craves the good things of this world and especially human glory: he believes it is the very highest summit he can seek, and thinks he can achieve it by his own powers. He thinks he is a great person; he wants to be above everyone else. But then he experiences a complete change inside. He now feels that there is something above the glory that human beings promise: the glory to which Christ calls us. He now feels that human glory is not an absolute, but a relative thing; it is not the highest thing, but if anything, a rung on the ladder that mounts to the true summit. He feels that he is not great, but small, and that he needs the help of God to be able to do any good at all. This is conversion.

A classic example of this is Abraham. He had his own plans for his life and his future. God came, spoke to him, and changed all his plans: "Not in this country but in another one, far away; set out right away." And Abraham set out, blindly, without even knowing where the new country was, abandoning himself completely to God's plans.

St. Augustine is another example. The son of a pagan father and a Christian mother, he was not baptized. As a very learned professor, he read the Bible, but found it dull and badly written compared to the classics that he was familiar with. What was his life as a youth like? "I loved to love," he wrote—he loved the carnal mystery of women, fame and friendships with famous people. For the sake of glory he moved from Carthage to Rome, from Rome to Milan, from literature to philosophy, from philosophy to the Manichean sect. His worried mother followed him: in Milan she persuaded him to leave his concubine. But Augustine's soul was so engulfed by habit that he took another lover. He was incapable of freeing himself from sin, yet he was constantly troubled by an insistent inner voice. He wrote: "There were two men in me, who were fighting each other." And again: "I was like a person in bed, in the morning. They knocked at the door and said: 'Augustine, get up.' And I said: 'Later, later on!' But outside, they continued to knock. One day they said to me, 'Victorinus, the great professor who translated Plato and Plotinus, has become a Christian.' It was a blow. Another day they said to me: 'Two court officials have left everything and become monks.' Another blow for me, who was incapable of leaving anything. Another day there fell under my eyes the words of St. Paul: 'Now is the time to awake from your sleep' (Rom 13:11). It was the coup de grace, it was the Lord pulling me out of the bed of my miseries, once and for all."

This is more or less what happens in every conversion: a merciful God, who never tires of calling, who does not become discouraged by our rejections. On one hand our free "yes" after so many "no's" on the other. There must be a break with the past: the motive for our life must be changed from within; we must broaden our area and views. "A New Frontier" said John Kennedy. And we should say: new frontiers, frontiers of heaven. Let's decide to be citizens not only of this little transitory world, but of the great world that never ends! Like Our Lady, we must say "yes" to God, but with our whole heart, clinging to him with our whole being without fear of risk. With God the risk is not risk, but security: we abandon palpable human certainties that are in reality fragile uncertainties, we rest in a security that has only one fault: it cannot be seen and touched.

There can be a misunderstanding on the subject of faith. We think someone has his life in perfect order when he possesses the whole package of truths contained in the Creed. Alas! It is not a matter of possessing the truths, but of allowing yourself to be possessed by them. The truths of faith are not cold, inert things, but incandescent fire, one that urges us on, makes us restless, a fire bursting with energy that compels us to take eager and passionate action. How can I say: "I believe in the Son of God . . . who for us men and for our salvation came down from heaven . . . was made man . . . suffered under Pontius Pilate," without saying to myself "What am I doing to respond to so much love? What response do I give to the extraordinary offer made by Jesus? He loved his brothers and sisters to the point of dying for them. What do I give to my poor brothers and sisters?"

I say: "I believe in one, holy, Catholic and apostolic Church." If she is *one*, I must not divide her by my disobedience, my constant and systematic protest against legitimate authority in the name of an excessive pluralism. She is *holy*, therefore rich in saints and many merits; I must come to know and recognize these merits, and make them known in preference to her few historical weaknesses and faults, and not the other way around. Is she *holy*? Then she should be made more and more pure and resplendent by putting into practice what the Council has said – precisely in view of a greater sanctity in the Church. Provided, of course, that the Council really said it. Many people today, in fact, attribute to the Council what it has not said or actually the contrary of what it said, with the fine result that they bring to the Church not sanctity but confusion. *Catholic.* Let's honor, by all means, the particular churches and their own traditions, but let's take care that we do not slip into a federation of churches: the existence of these churches "does not lessen in any way the primacy of the chair of Peter, which presides over the universal assembly of charity."[2] *Apostolic.* This means not only that the Church preserves the teaching of the Apostles, but that the tasks and the powers assigned by Christ to the Apostles continue in their legitimate successors, the bishops.

There is still one step to take. If someone is possessed in earnest by a great idea, he does everything to transmit it to others. Faith is a treasure, a fortune, the Pope says, and I want my children to have it too. The apostle, the catechist, and the missionary repeat the same reasoning with still greater fervor. But how do we go about transmitting faith? In Brazil, the other day, I heard the following proverb: "*Miguel, Miguel, nao tens abelhas e vendes miel!*" "Michael, how can you claim to be selling honey, when you don't even have any bees?" I have been told that as a bishop I must sell the honey of the faith, of the love of God. How can I do it, if I do not have it first? What kind of faith will the sons, the pupils, the Christians have, if their fathers, teachers and priests have no faith or it is only a smoldering wick instead of a shining beacon?

My brothers and sisters! I think that among the many problems of the Church, the most serious today is evangelization, that is, preserving, defending and spreading the faith. The Council stresses the "free faith and obedience of Our Lady,"[3] it stresses that she too "made progress in her journey of faith."[4] Let's ask her today for the health of our faith! And that is the grace that the Church in Venice may preserve pure and without spot, whole and not lame, her faith of centuries past, always accepting humbly what God has revealed and what the Magisterium has set forth. May she also have before her eyes a luminous example of faith in the life of her bishop, her priests, and the heads of her families![1]

Notes

[1] *Opera* 7:198-201.

[2] LG no. 13.

[3] LG no. 58.

[4] LG no. 58.

Light in Our Darkness

Homily for the Feast of St. Lucy[1]
December 13, 1977

For the Christian people, St. Lucy, virgin and martyr, is the saint who helps those who need light: light of the body and light of the soul.

But the light of the soul is God; of this light it has been written: "He is the true light that gives light to every man" (Jn 1:9); "the light shines in the darkness, but the darkness has not welcomed it" (Jn 1:5).

1. The phenomenon of this refusal to welcome belongs to all centuries; in a certain measure, it is taking place even today; in the middle of Christian civilization we observe tremendous darkness in two principal forms. The first form is religious indifference: today rather than atheism true and proper, what is widespread is abandonment of the faith as something that is no longer of interest, that is, something useless, that does not make sense. Another form is dissent: that is, a number of people declare that they adhere, at least in part, to the truths and values of Christianity, but refuse either the Church or this church here: sometimes they even engage in violent demonstrations against her.

2. I will try to explain what seems to me to be the causes of this painful phenomenon, which also touches our church in Venice. The first cause is perhaps our inadequate catechesis for children and young people: we instruct them, but not in such a way as to help them live a intense Christian life; at times, the parents, behaving in a way contrary to the catechesis, cancel out the work of the catechist:

at times the parents are truly Christian, but their educative work is supported neither by the Catholic associations, which, unfortunately, have partly collapsed, nor by the schools. The old school was, perhaps, too rigid, it sinned by excessive reliance on the theoretical. But today we have gone to the opposite extreme: now that students are promoted with the greatest ease, seriously committed students are disqualified and discouraged; by the introduction of politics, minds are also divided and their serenity is at an end; by subjecting everything to discussion, much time is wasted, and people are set off on their way to superficiality, to doubting everything or to presumptuous self-importance.

Second cause: once young people lived dispersed among adults; today—by reason of the increased emphasis on education and by the delayed entrance of young people into the work force—they spend a great deal of time together in school, sports and various groups; in this way they form a new social class, which undeniably has enormous unresolved problems; it is much easier for them to be strongly influenced by ideologies, publicity and the fashions of the day; they are more exposed to galloping secularization.

Third cause: individualism. People talk a great deal about duties, but they are always the duties of others, who are considered exploiters and parasites. They constantly demand this or that right in a climate of bitter conflict. Scapegoats, usually, are the state and institutions, who they demand must foresee and provide for everything without being able to ask for the sacrifices that are also necessary.

Fourth cause, pleasure and ease assumed as the supreme norm. Effort, sacrifice or deep and constant commitment create fear in many, who, instead throw themselves headfirst into "consuming" the goods constantly suggested by a commercial advertising that has now became the master, advisor and prompter most frequently listened to. A parallel publicity campaign has toppled moral laws, which are called taboos, so that young people will throw themselves very early into precocious sexual experiences that banalize love, cause them to neglect serious work, make them insensible to religious values and hostile to the Church, which, as is her duty, preaches a premarital chastity that they call repression.

Fifth cause: equality understood in an exaggerated way. Everyone is equal, they say: and therefore they struggle against the meritocracy; jobs should be given not to those who, through natural or acquired gifts are more capable, but to those who have greater seniority at work. Equal and therefore the way is open to extreme feminism. We are in agreement that we have to make amends for the injustices committed against women in the past; that women are equal in dignity and worth; but that does not mean that women are identical with men and that they have the same tasks to carry out, at the expense of the complementarity that makes men and women complete as human beings. Equal, and therefore they struggle against authority. They talk a great deal about authoritarianism. But "authoritarianism" means the exaggerated exercise of authority, and it is right to reject it. Authority, on the other hand, exercised in a correct way and at the service of others, is necessary whether in the family, society or the Church.

3. How should we act before the widespread lack of religiosity from the said causes? There is one thing we should not do: become discouraged, remaining with hands folded and closing ourselves up in the "besieged citadel." Instead, we must get down to work and gather our strength to make a Christian "model of life" lived by many people into a reality. A mother of a family, who had to leave her children alone in the house for a few hours, instructed them this way: "If something dire happens, don't shout 'Thief, thief!' That would not be of much interest to the neighbors. Shout 'Fire!' That would be of great interest to the neighbors, who will be afraid that the blaze will spread." This is the case with us: something very dire is happening; without dramatizing too much by crying 'fire,' we must nevertheless try to have many people with us, to involve the apathetic, those who would like to only stand and watch;

and thus, united and organized, we must not isolate ourselves, but insert ourselves as a leaven in the mass in order to improve society and remove at least the most serious injustices.

I said something dire is happening. I will try to explain myself better with an example taken from the Dolomite mountains, where I come from. Up there you often see, high up, some villages halfway up the slope. Some people ask themselves: how do people manage to live securely in those places when in winter and spring avalanches and landslides could sweep away houses, stables, church, everything? But they have thought of that: above the village, as a protection, there are forests of spruce and larch trees so dense and clinging so fast to the soil with their vast and deep roots that neither avalanches nor landslides can pass: everything lies in preserving the density of the woods and not removing any plant unless they have foreseen replacing it with another. The village is a symbol of our society; the trees planted in the woods are the principles of religion and morals. As long as these are firm and rooted in souls, society is protected and secure; the day you make them disappear, the avalanche falls and creates ruin; the landslide of the passions becomes unstoppable. We are seeing it: the police, the guards, the police dogs, the burglar alarms, the safe deposit boxes are increasing, but they are little use; when the woods of the great religious principles and the fear of God are thinned out, the avalanche of violence can pass; the earth moves, and violence, shooting, Molotov cocktails and kidnappings run rampant in an atmosphere that is now made up of disorders, insecurity and fear.

4. Work, then, for the defense of the great principles. But above all, we must pray; the light of faith is something that does not depend only on us: it will not shine in souls again unless God intervenes. It has been proved by the experience of an arc of more than a thousand years, an arc that goes from the ancient Augustine to that recent Augustine named Giovanni Papini.[2]

St. Augustine, educated by a Christian mother, had never lost his attraction to Christ; but he protested, and bitterly, against the church, and for many years led a life that was not morally good, in an irregular union with a woman. He needed a long road to return, and in the last few months he seemed to wriggle like an eel. "I sighed," he wrote, "feeling bound, not by iron fetters but by my iron will [that is, by the tenacious love for his concubine]. The corrupt will had been converted into passion, and from serving passion, it had become a habit, and because I had not resisted the habit, a need had been created . . . I was convinced, I had nothing to oppose [to the Lord], except for these words full of laziness and sleep, "soon, soon; wait a little while longer." But the 'soon' never came to an end and the 'a little while longer' dragged on for a long time."[3] The Lord helped him: good reading, examples of generous and resolute Christians, imitation, remorse and shame gave him no respite: he ended up surrendering to grace. "Too late have I loved you, Lord," he would write later. For others, the road was different, but always guided by God. Silvio Pellico wrote: "That unworthy mixture of faith and wavering (of mine), how long would it have lasted? Perhaps my whole life. God kindly provided for this by means of misfortune"meaning his imprisonment.[4]

Theodore Ratisbonne, a Jew, brother of the more famous Alphonse Marie, wrote: "The whispered words of Abbè Bautain, warm and luminous . . . dissipated without resistance the accumulated clouds in my mind." Gilbert Keith Chesterton, after the doubts and uncertainties of his youth, became first a fervent Anglican, then, by meditating and conversing with faithful Anglicans and studying, crossed over to the Catholic Church. He declared: "A church that wants to have authority must possess absolutely clear ideas when it comes to the great moral questions . . . it must say a yes or a no: but the Protestant churches are completely lost in the face of such moral questions . . . clarity and resolve before the powerful questions of modern life—I find them only in the Catholic Church; therefore I became Catholic."[5]

And we come to Papini. Domenico Giuliotti wrote to him on January 10, 1920: "You are still, although it does not seem so to you, and to the disgrace of your baptism, a Protestant, rationalist, modernist, in short, compositionally a heretic. Your eyes do not see, your ears, stopped up by the wax of ignorance, do not hear. You have traveled almost all the roads of knowledge; you have been lost and found again in almost all the labyrinths of thought . . . you are a meditative person and an artist, but when you talk about Catholicism you are mediocre. And you are mediocre because you are ignorant of it . . . I tell you that it is easier to doubt your own existence than that of the foundation of the church through the work of Christ . . . When Christ said: 'You are Peter . . .' he wasn't joking. Either our soul builds with Christ on that rock or everything, as you can see, collapses on it . . . For twenty years your pen has written at the dictation of the devil . . . You need to erase and write again. Your books—some infamous, others empty, others beautiful but profane—throw them resolutely and joyfully into the bonfire of the vanities. And begin again from the beginning. After the 'black half' the "white half" must shine on your new life. Turn yourself around, renew yourself, purify yourself again internally . . . if you hope, you will obtain; if you desire the light, you will see; if you knock, it will be opened to you. It is impossible for God, who certainly loves you, not to help you."

Papini answered the letter, but did not surrender and continued as before. A short time afterwards, however, he wrote to Giuliotti from our Venice: "I go every morning to San Marco. Tonight the bell of the basilica woke me and suddenly there came to my lips, I don't know why, the Hail Mary that for so many years I have no longer said and that it seemed to me I wasn't able to recall very well."

Jubilantly, Giuliotto wrote down a note: "It is the first action of grace, it is the irresistible maternal call of the *Mater Salvatoris* [Mother of the Savior], and of the *Virgo potens* [powerful virgin]. Tomorrow Giovanni Papini will say: 'I believe.'"[6]

And so it was. Let's hope that, helped by grace, many of our brothers and sisters, who are good and generous from one point of view but who today declare themselves either atheists or indifferent or dissenting, who are floundering in the darkness of unbelief, that is, in the poorest of all forms of poverty, will say "I believe." Let's pray that, like Augustine, they may receive from God the strength to answer the voice that is calling: "Awake, O sleeper, arise from the dead, and Christ will give you light" (Eph 5:14).

Notes

1 *Opera* 8: 334-38.

2 For Papini, see "Something Less than a Syllabus," note 20.—Trans.

3 *Confessions* 8:5.

4 Letter to Abbot Beccari, December 15, 1832. [Silvio Pellico (1789-1854) was an Italian poet, dramatist and patriot. The best known of his works is *Le mie prigioni*, his account of his imprisonment for his work to liberate Italy from Austrian control.—Trans].

5 G. K. Chesterton to the Washington News Service, [1923. Unfortunately, I couldn't find the original English text.—Trans].

6 *L'ora di Barabba* (Vallecchi, 1946).

Mysteries of Our Faith

How Jesus Returns at Christmas

Homilies in the Cathedral in Vittorio Veneto
December 24-25, 1961[1]

I

Tonight everyone, everywhere, is saying: "Christmas has come again!"

It *has* come again, but in what way?

After being born of the Blessed Virgin once, Jesus will not be born again in the same way; so Christmas is not coming again in this sense. He has already returned to heaven, and he will continue to remain there, even as a man. The immortal king of the ages: *"Christus heri, et hodie: ipse et in saecula"* (Heb. 13:8).[2]

Though radiant with glory, in a very different situation from the one in Bethlehem, he is still the same as in Bethlehem. In Bethlehem, he had a heart full of love for us; that love still swells his heart even now.

We are remembering Bethlehem this evening; he remembers it better than we do, and with longing. And he says: "I am not being born again, but if necessary, I would be ready to start over and do everything again from the beginning." And he draws near us; and in a way only he can, he tries to touch our hearts. And he speaks: "Let yourselves be captured, don't run away from me, as you always do!" This is the way he returns at Christmas.

So "celebrating Christmas" does not mean just being with our own relatives, in the intimacy of our own homes, savoring sweet memories. No. It means above all hearing in our souls the voice of Christ, who is drawing near, and letting ourselves be seized by his love.

It is, in fact, about the love of Jesus that we must speak this evening. It is the love that moved Him to come down from heaven.

"Father," he said, "What miserable adoration men give you down there! I will go down myself; I will put myself at their head, I will be one of them, and they will worship God with me; it will be a worthy and resounding worship, and I will bring them after me, saved, to you in heaven!"

"All right, I accept, go ahead and go down," God the Father answered "and I will leave you free in regard to the way to choose. There is a comfortable way: birth as a rich man, an easy life, full success, a triumphant return. There is also the hard way: birth in poverty, a life of toil, apparent failure, death on the cross: choose, you are free."

"I choose the hard way," answered the Son (cf. Heb. 12:2). "If I chose the other one, it would be more difficult for them to recognize me as a brother. I choose the hard way: I want them to be able to say: 'Our priest is able to sympathize with our weaknesses . . . He has experienced them all, except for sin'" (cf. Heb. 4:15).

Now that the choice has been made, look at him in action. "Rich though he was," says St. Paul, "he made himself poor for love of us" (2 Cor. 8:9). Poor in earthly goods, so that we might become rich in virtue and holiness.

He was in the condition of God, Paul says again, really equal to God, but he did not consider staying to enjoy the honors given to God a kind of prey to be held on to with the teeth at any cost; he emptied himself of those external honors and took on the livery of a slave, made like one of us (cf. Phil. 2:5).

And he did not let himself be moved from that way. What, in substance, were the three temptations in the desert? This: an attempt to make him change his program and his way. "What do you mean, personal sacrifices! Spectacular exhibitions, and a glorious and worldly reign, that is the way to go!" said the devil. And Jesus: "Away from me, Satan. The plan is already traced out, I even had it written by the prophets, and that is the way it will stay" (cf. Mt. 4:111).

St. Peter also had experience of how firm Jesus was in his proposal of sacrificing himself. Our Lord was foretelling that in Jerusalem he would suffer greatly and die. "For the love of God, Lord! This will never happen!" St. Peter burst out. And Christ, immediately: "Go away from here you tempter. You are a scandal to me. You have no sense of the things of God" (cf. Mt. 16:21-23).

"I have not come to be served, but to serve," he kept repeating. (cf. Mt. 20:28). "I have come to seek out, and to save" (Lk. 19:10). Yes, he is the great seeker of souls and rejoices when he can bring just one of them to salvation (Lk. 15:7, 10). Go through the whole Gospel: you will find so many things, but this above all: he loved us, he loved us so much, he loved us through sacrifice. Paul sums up the whole Gospel well when he says, *"dilexit me et tradidit semetipsum pro me"* (Gal. 2:20): "He loved me and gave himself for me."

But St. Paul was not content with summing up; he drew some practical conclusions.

That love, he said, is only the first love; now must come the second, mine. Christ has written the first page of the book; now I must write the second. The immense love that Christ has for me leaves me no peace, it compels me, it cries out to me: "Get moving, Paul, and do something for him in return" (cf. 2 Cor. 5:14).

And he really got moving: he set out to follow Christ as though on an impassioned and passion-inspiring adventure. That time when I was on horseback on the way to Damascus, he says, Christ seized me and made me his. I was happy to become his prey; so happy that, from that time on, I have tried to run after him in an extraordinary chase in which one is at once hunter and prey (cf. Phil. 3:12).

Here is a program worthy of a true Christian. You will say: but who puts it into practice? Cardinal dalla Costa,[3] who they buried yesterday evening, he put it into practice. I was close to him, as a student, for about two weeks. That meeting made a very deep impression on me. Words that were sword and fire in church; outside church, a kindness to the poor, the sick, and the children that captivated people. And such faith that it seemed that he saw the Lord with his own eyes and that outside of the Lord nothing mattered to him. I never saw him again after that, but I read his books and heard about his virtues. He belonged to the breed of bishops who, hard as rock, turn to their persecutor and say to him "Go ahead, do your job and strike. But remember that if you are the hammer, I am the anvil. The hammer will break but the anvil will not break and the Church will remain!" At difficult moments, when it was dangerous to speak certain truths, he went into the pulpit at Padua and spoke those truths, to a full cathedral. And he topped them off with the following words:

"On the great day of my consecration I was told: You will not call evil good and good evil, truth error and error truth, virtue vice and vice virtue. Faithful to this terrible summons, my words must be those of truth and justice, always and in everything, and before God, I trust that they will be. What indeed could induce me to lie? Fear of offending the great? I have never known it. Hankering after money? It has never tormented my poor heart. The desire to climb higher? I would have been happy to go lower."

There are then, still some people, and even some who are close to us, who love the Lord and who follow him at the cost of any sacrifice, and who encourage us by their example to do the same.

Let us follow him too. It will be a "Merry Christmas" for us if tonight we leave this cathedral with an ardent love for Jesus Christ in our hearts and this decision in our wills, "Lord, this time I will really let myself be captured, I will be your prey, and at the same time the hunter who pursues You."

II

There he is, a rosy little morsel of flesh. He seems like a mere nothing, truly nothing as a power, as a presence, as a voice.

There he is, in a manger prepared for the animals. And the manger is in a drafty, dimly lit, bad-smelling cave. And the cave is near a poor village, unknown to the world.

Why then is he the master of the world? What system is he using now? That is the word, it is really a new system. Jesus wants to introduce a new mentality from his first appearance. There are enough of those who become great by posing and strutting. It is now that we are going against the current.

Bethlehem is the real "new style" and the "style" will be continued in the thirty-three years that follow. He flees to Egypt; he is one of the conquered and the persecuted. He works in a shop; he is an apprentice and a worker under a foreman. He preaches and throws himself into his work, even performs miracles, but he is a fiasco. He hungers and thirsts, he has nowhere to lay his head. He has friends and disciples, but they abandon him. He has one garment left, they strip him even of that. He still has his mother; he gives her away too, before dying!

Have you ever seen a root in a parched and desert land? It is he, it is he, "spurned and avoided by men, a man of suffering, accustomed to infirmity" (Isaiah 53:3). I repeat: he wanted to introduce a new style, a new climate.

Once the climate has been introduced, the teachings come.

"Do not lay up for yourselves an earthly treasure where moths and rust corrode and thieves break in and steal" (Mt. 6:19). "Blest are you poor" (Lk. 6:20). "Woe to you rich, for your consolation is now" (Lk. 6:24). "It is easier for a camel to pass through a needle's eye than for a rich man to enter the kingdom of God" (Mt. 19:24).

Our Lady had already sensed the new climate, when she said, "He has deposed the mighty from their thrones and raised the lowly to high places" (Lk. 1:52).

Later, the Apostles will also understand, and St. James and St. Peter will say: "God resists the proud and bestows his favor on the lowly" (James 4:6 and I Peter 5:5).

My dear faithful! In the light of these great teachings, matters appear differently: what seemed great and very important becomes small; what seemed very close and vivid becomes distant and grows pale. The soul, on the other hand, with its problems, comes into the foreground, becomes more vivid, and appears in its true importance.

There is so much talk about the "Italian economic miracle."[4]

From the "soul" point of view there are some reservations to be made in regard to this miracle. It will be a miracle in reverse if the goods produced become, instead of our servants, our masters, our tormentors, and our evil demons. It will be an illusory "miracle" if many, too many, are not allowed to enjoy it. It will be a deficient and false "miracle," if in spite of our abundance, hunger, malnutrition and disease continue to gallop undisturbed over very vast zones of Asia, Africa and even Latin America.

There is talk of "broadening the democratic area." Democracy, it is clear, hungers and thirsts for space. And doesn't God hunger and thirst for souls? When I pray, "Your kingdom come," I think of the divine area to be broadened. Out of three billion or so human beings, two billion are not Christians. Out of a billion Christians, not even half a billion is Catholic. Out of not even half a billion Catholics, many do not profess their faith or behave badly. May your kingdom come, Lord, may your area increase!

There is talk of an "opening."[5] Let's throw open, really wide open the doors and windows of our souls. Let charity in, let resentment, rancor, and envy out; let humility in, let pride out. More air, more oxygen for the lungs of our souls! As St Paul said: "Your thoughts should be wholly devoted to all that is true, all that deserves respect, all that is honest, pure, admirable, decent, virtuous or worthy of praise" (Phil. 4:8).

There is talk of "choices" to be made, and, it is added, "responsible choices." But the first "choice," the choice of choices, must be Christ. We choose him the first time by a free and spontaneous, mature and fully conscious act; afterwards we repeat the choice every day. Because every day, we must say: "O Lord, I prefer you to everything that is sin."

There is talk of "structures and infrastructures." The "infrastructures" are the streets, the telephone connections, the aqueducts and similar things; the "structures" are the new foundations of the state and business enterprises.

But there are also the "infrastructures and the structures" prepared by God for our souls. A marvelous and invisible "structure," but a true and very certain one, is grace, or the divine life placed inside of us. God living in me, me becoming a brother of Christ, traveling through the world like an authentic sun, admired by the angels, on the way to an immortal destiny, is there anything more important than this? Or than that which guarantees, nourishes, repairs, and restores (in case of loss) this life and this journey? Here is where the "infrastructures" come in: prayer, which connects me to God, confession, Holy Communion, and the Mass.

There is talk of the "availability" of this or that political party. Let us also talk about religious availability! Are we, or are we not people that Christ has at his disposal?

Ignatius, the bishop of Antioch, was traveling towards Rome, chained and destined for the wild beasts in the amphitheater, when he heard that in Rome they were working to free him. He took up his pen and immediately wrote to the Romans: "I beg you, do not show me a misplaced benevolence! Let me be given as food to the beasts. I am the grain of God, and under the millstone of the teeth of the beasts, I want to become the immaculate bread of Christ."[6]

There is no wild beast waiting for us. But we must put a sign outside the door of our souls this Christmas. And on it, we must write: "This soul is available for Christ." Yes, every time Christ presents himself, we must be happy to "take him on board." With him at the head, as guide and pilot, with him as the captain of our boat, life is more secure and more beautiful!

Notes

1 *Opera* 2:370-75.

2 "Jesus Christ is the same, yesterday, today and forever."—Trans.

3 Cardinal Elia dalla Costa was the Archbishop of Padua and later of Florence. He was known for his courage in speaking out against the Nazis and helping to save Italian Jews from deportation during WWII.—Trans.

4 Luciani is referring to the seemingly miraculous recovery of the Italian economy after World War II.—Trans.

5 This refers to the "opening to the left," that is, the proposal being made at that time, and supported by some Catholics, for a coalition of socialists and the Christian Democrats in the Italian government. The other slogans he discusses are political as well.—Trans.

6 St. Ignatius of Antioch, *Epistle to the Romans* in PG 5, col. 689. —Trans.

The Proof of Christ's Love

Homily for the Feast of the Holy Redeemer[1]
July 16, 1978

The three readings we have listened to help us to understand a little the mystery of the redemption, which Venice has honored every year since the vow of 1577.[2]

I

1. The third reading (Jn 3:14ff) tells us the profound *why* of the redemption. "God so loved the world that he gave his only Son." Here is the why: "God so loved the world." God experiences a strong will to save us, you might say, great pleasure in saving us. The redemption, however, is not only an event in the past, recorded by history and filed away once and for all. It is a continuing event: we are still being saved, we are still so greatly loved. All of us, even if we are sinners. In fact, in a certain sense, the more sinful we are, the more we are loved. "In a certain sense": God actually sees in us sinners two things: the ugliness of sin, and us who are sick with this ugliness. The sin disgusts him; we sick people arouse his compassion. The prodigal son was given a great feast. That great favorite of God who was David was reproved and had punishment inflicted on him, when he fell into serious sin. Once he had repented, however, all the old benevolence and friendship were restored to him. I repeat: we are so greatly loved by God.

2. The first reading (Isa 49:17, 53:25) indicates what was pleasing to God the Father in the Redeemer and, indirectly, how the redemption took place. For centuries, theologians, with St. Anselm

107

at their head, have attempted to present the redemption as a payment. Because they offended an infinite God, our sins were thought to have an infinite weight: it was only possible to make amends for them, therefore, by the death of the Son of God on the cross. Here, obviously, the stress was put on justice: we find ourselves facing a God who wants to be paid to the last penny.

I bow to the great St. Anselm, however, it seems to me that the stress should be placed instead on love, on tenderness. God is love and tenderness, and great tenderness was aroused in God the Father by the fact that his Son, also out of love for mankind, should be made small and poor, allowing himself to be scorned and put to death. We have heard: "He was spurned and avoided by men; a man of suffering, accustomed to infirmity, one of those from whom men hide their faces" (Isa 53:3). The consequence? "Therefore," says God, "I will give him his portion among the great, and he shall divide the spoils with the mighty, because he gave himself up to death" (Ibid., v. 12). This passage almost perfectly matches a hymn quoted by St. Paul: Christ Jesus, "though he was in the form of God, did not deem his equality with God something to be held on to at any cost. Rather, he emptied himself and took the form of a slave, being born in the likeness of men. He was known to be of human estate, and it was thus that he humbled himself, obediently accepting even death, death on a cross! Because of this, God highly exalted him, and bestowed on him the name above every other name, so that at Jesus' name every knee must bend, in the heavens, on the earth, and under the earth, and every tongue proclaim: Jesus Christ is Lord!" (Phil. 2:611). "Therefore," it is written in Deutero-Isaiah, "because of this," it is written in St. Paul. God has therefore rewarded Christ's *escalation* in reverse: with the well-known "policy" of God, even in his Son, God the Father has given grace to one who humbles himself (cf. Prov 3:35, James 4:6, 1 Peter 5:5).

The road of the redemption is the road of the humiliations chosen by Christ for love of us and pleasing to God the Father. Palestine was a nothing in the cosmos; Bethlehem and Nazareth were nothing in Palestine; dying on the cross was less than nothing, something absolutely shameful for everyone. That Christ accepted this way and these stages, offering them for us to God his Father, who admired them as proofs of love and crowned them with his resurrection and ascension into heaven—this is what the redemption is.

3. But this redemption, as I said above, was to continue in the Church, which is the extension of Christ. How? We are told in the second reading (Eph. 5:25-27), which describes the Redeemer's solicitude for the Church. It was the custom in the East that on the day of her wedding a bride would first take the "nuptial bath"; after which she would be dressed and solemnly conducted by a paranymph to her bridegroom. Christ, says St. Paul, prepared the Church, his bride, by himself, personally, without need of any paranymph. For this reason she is "glorious, without spot or blemish." The "nuptial bath" in which he has purified her is Holy Baptism, "accompanied by the word." At the Council too, we said that the Church can be called the bride of Christ, inseparable from him.

Today Christ does not exist without the Church, nor does the Church exist without Christ. It was the first intuition that Paul had, when he was stopped on the road to Damascus. "Saul, why are you persecuting me?" the voice scolded. And he: "Who are you, O Lord?" And the voice: "I am that Jesus whom you are persecuting" (cf. Acts 9:45). Saul did not yet know Christ, and was persecuting only some Christians, whom he considered dissenting Jews. He understood then, and forever afterward, that Christ and Christians, Christ and the Church, make one body, are one thing.

II

These few thoughts are very well known. The important thing, however, is not to know them, but to bring them down into our lives.

1. We are loved immensely by God, we have said. But how do we return this love? "If you love me," Jesus has said, "you will keep my commandments" (John 14:15). Commandments which, in essence, can be reduced to two: to love God with all our hearts and our neighbor as ourselves.

Those who love God are those who try to do the will of God. The gondolier is one with his gondola; he does not move himself by his own motion, instead, he lets himself be moved by the movement of the gondola in which he is standing. But are our hearts really on board God's boat, and are they going in the direction he wants them to? I don't know about you. I know about myself; I know that sometimes I am afraid when I say in my prayers, "Oh my God, I love you with all my heart, above everything else."

While rereading during the past few days the life of St. Lorenzo Giustiniani,[3] I ran across his famous constitution on women's fashions. There was a bishop! No longer, he prescribed to the women of Venice, shall you *"Portare manichetos breviores duobus digitis supra nodum majus"* . . . etc. [Wear sleeves that are shorter than two fingers' length above the elbow]. And the women who do not obey are excommunicated; nothing less. What will the saint think of me, his unworthy successor? Down there in Venice in 1978, he will say from heaven, there is the most audacious nudity, there are abortions being advertised, contemptible, ugly deeds, reported by newspapers throughout the world; there is a patriarch, my successor, and he remains silent and continues to pray tranquilly: "Oh my God, I love you with all my heart, above everything else!" My brothers and sisters, how gladly I would speak, if I had any hope that people would listen to me![4] At least have the good grace to recognize that it is not easy today for your pastor to carry out his duties, and pray for him.

St. Francis de Sales spoke of the two loves as twins.[5] Jesus, in fact, did not want them to be separated, but united. "If you bring your gift to the altar and there recall that your brother has anything against you, leave your gift at the altar, go first to be reconciled with your brother, and then come and offer your gift" (Mt. 5:2324). Love of neighbor, in turn, must very often be accompanied by justice. How can I love my neighbor if I act unjustly toward him? On the other hand, it is love that puts a bit of warmth into the usually cold relationship of justice. In *Les Miserables* by Victor Hugo, Jean Valjean, who is fleeing, is welcomed by Bishop Myriel in his home. "But do you know who I am?" the fugitive asks. "Yes, you are my brother," the bishop answers. Recently, the Communist Garaudy commented, "Myriel entered into the sphere of love and into its risks, because love is always a risk and goes beyond any kind of justice."[6] I have quoted this because today people talk only of justice. But just as charity without justice is not enough, so too without charity justice is not enough. In 1974 the French minister for social action, René Lenoir, declared on television: "The law cannot solve everything," and cited the case of a sick old woman who was literally overwhelmed by the visit of a young lady; it was the first visit she had received in forty years.[7]

2. I spoke above about an *escalation* of Christ in reverse. This means humility, meekness and obedience. Virtues that people today fail to recognize as virtues; without them we could not be Christians, nor could we hope for an end to the violence that plagues today's world. St. Francis de Sales used to tell, smiling, the story of the old gentleman who had lived a good eighty years in Paris, happy and contented, without ever feeling the desire or the need to be away from the city for a single day. It was enough for the king to send him an order to end his days in Paris; he was seized by an irresistible desire to go to the country.[8] That is how we are made today:

whatever the others are doing or want to do, don't do it; whatever the others are not doing or prohibit, do it. It is the spirit of protest, and they call it greatness and maturity!

3. In the Church too, we are sometimes "perverse." "Christ yes, the Church no," we say. Even if Christ said to Peter: on you I will build *my* Church. Even if the ancient Fathers taught "No one can have God for his Father unless he has the Church for his mother." Today they also say: "Church yes, hierarchy no." Hierarchy no, because the Church is only a *koinonia*, a communion; because today every society must be democratic, with powers that rise from the base to the top. The Church, however, is an atypical society. Yes, in the state, the powers come from the people. In the Church, on the other hand, they come from on high, from priestly and episcopal ordination. This is by the will of Christ, who said to Peter: "Feed my sheep" (John 21:17), and to the apostles, "Whatever you declare loosed on earth shall be held loosed in heaven" (Mt. 18:18). It is true that Christ has also explained precisely in what way the powers are to be used. Government, he said, must be service, and carried out in the style of service. It is also true that Pope, bishops, and priests do not cease to be human beings subject to error and that often they make mistakes. These mistakes, however, if they do authorize the faithful to make respectful observations, do not authorize them to leave the Church, or say bad things about it, or oppose to the true Church ephemeral little dissenting churches.

Bernanos, it seems to me, used to say, referring precisely to the Church: "Rather than stay in a luxurious house belonging to strangers, I would prefer to live in my own family's house, even if there are a few broken down chairs and a few rickety tables." I feel the same way, and I add: remain there, and do everything possible to fix those chairs and those tables.

Notes

1 *Opera* 8:555-59.

2 In 1575, Venice was ravaged by a plague which lasted two years. After the prayers of the people for deliverance were heard, the city instituted in thanksgiving the annual Feast of the Holy Redeemer, celebrated on the third Sunday in July, and built a basilica of the same name, in which this yearly Mass was celebrated.—Trans.

3 St. Lorenzo Giustiniani (1380-1455), Luciani's predecessor in his see, was the first bishop of Venice to be given the title of patriarch by the Pope. He was known for the great austerity of his life and his stern moral preaching in the corrupt Venice of the fifteenth century.—Trans.

4 Luciani actually spoke out on abortion and other moral matters many times. The examples included in this collection are only a few of these.—Trans.

5 *Oeuvres* X, 270.

6 Cited by J. M. Belloso, *La dimension critica y configuradora de la caridad in I Cor. XIII*, 1977, 1, 50.

7 cf. *Nouvelle revue theologique* 110 (1978), p. 33.

8 St. Francis de Sales, *Theotime*, 1.58, c. 5 and *Pleiade*, pp. 724-2.

The Mystery of the Eucharist

Homily at the Holy Thursday Mass "In Coena Domini"[1]
April 19, 1973

At the high point of every Mass the priest announces "the Mystery of Faith," but during this evening's Mass, those words produce a special impression on us. The way in which Christ can be living and real, in body, blood, soul and divinity, under the appearance of bread and wine remains obscure to us; what is very clear is the incredible love that moved our adorable Savior to invent for our benefit something so completely unexpected and unimaginable. He was on the eve of his death; he was about to offer himself in sacrifice for us to the Father. And he reasoned like this: "Even after my death and ascension to heaven, I want to remain with my human brothers and sisters! I want my sacrifice to be prolonged on the earth; I want every Mass to be a mysterious representation-reproduction of the Cross in order to apply to humanity the benefits of the redemption. In communion, then, they will eat My flesh, they will drink My blood, uniting themselves to Me as the weak person unites with the strong, as friend unites with friend, to have the resurrection and the life."

It is an invention that makes people dizzy when they hear it announced. In fact, when they heard Christ speak of his body made food at Capernaum, several listeners said, "This language is too strong; who can listen to it?" And they went away. The story is being repeated now. Some theologians assert: "It is too strong to admit the Eucharist as it is proposed by the Church, we will go away unless some of our explanations are accepted there." And they propose them to us under the form of conditions and reservations.

I. BELIEVING HUMBLY IN THE EUCHARIST

Some people say: I receive the Eucharist in me; if I have faith, at the time I eat the bread, Christ's presence blossoms in me and in some way created by me myself. When Communion is over, however, the presence also ends, and nothing remains but mere bread. Others say: with the consecration, the bread and wine do not change, but remain bread and wine. What changes is only the meaning and purpose of the bread and wine. In themselves and usually, in fact, bread and wine mean ordinary food; they have the purpose of nourishing. Thanks to the consecration, on the other hand, they are subtracted from the profane field; they acquire a new meaning and purpose, a religious one: they signify Christ and have the purpose of producing eternal life. We should not speak, then, of changing of substance (transubstantiation), but of transignification and trans-finalization. What can we say?

Though he was distressed when faced with abandonment by the crowd, Christ held firm, repeating his statements: "My flesh is true food, my blood is true drink." The Magisterium of the Church, imitating Christ, also holds firm, and states, as always: after the consecration, under the appearance of bread and wine, there is no longer bread and wine, but there is the body and blood of Christ." A Catholic, then, cannot admit that, when the Mass is ended, Christ is no longer in the consecrated particles remaining in the tabernacle. And as for the words "transignification, and "transfinalization," they can be accepted, not in place of transubstantiation, but added to it. It is true, in fact, to say that bread and wine have a new purpose and new meaning, if they have really become the body and blood of Christ. But it is heresy to say that the bread remains bread, only acquiring a new meaning and a new purpose.

Please understand me: we are talking here about mysterious things; it is right and proper to accept them out of faith; it is something else to give them a satisfactory explanation. We can attempt to explain, but any explanation will be acceptable only insofar as it does not destroy the thing to be believed that we are trying to explain. It has been written, for example: Christ is present in the Eucharist, but "without him being localized in the bread and wine." This explanation preserves the faith, if it means that the body of Christ, in a new and miraculous way, incomprehensible to us, stands in the same place where the bread and wine stood and where only the appearances of bread remain. It does not preserve the faith if it means that the body of Christ has no relationship of place with the appearances remaining in the bread.

It has also been written: "There is no physical-chemical change in the bread and wine." This explanation is in accordance with the faith if it states that the change is not verifiable by physicists and by scientists; it is against the faith if it denies -that some change beyond the reach of the senses takes place. For centuries, in fact, the Church has been singing *"visus, tactus, gustus in te fallitur"*: sight, taste and touch in the Eucharist cannot discover the truth; nor can the microscope, the scalpel or electrolysis discover it. It is a matter of metaphysical realities within the reach of faith and not of science.

It has been written: the word transubstantiation is now old, difficult and unpopular; in its place we should use "mysterious conversion," "essential transformation"; we should no longer say "substance" of the bread, but "reality or objective reality of the bread"; we should no longer say "accidents" of the bread, but 'property of the bread, perceived by the senses." All this can be accepted very well; it is enough only that we do not deny what the Council of Trent called the "singular and wondrous conversion." Singular or unique, wondrous or mysterious conversion of the bread into the body of Christ.

II. LIVING THE EUCHARIST

But the Eucharist is not a truth only to be believed, but to be lived. Here too something is happening today that we need to pay attention to.

This opinion is going around: the Mass is a ceremony that gathers the faithful together so that they might feel solidarity and a sense of community among themselves.

Some people add: this sense of community will be still more authentic if, instead of being produced by the Eucharist, it exists before it. So then the Mass celebrated by a small heterogeneous group that gathers around a small table, in an ordinary dining room is good; it is still better if the usual sacred ecclesiastical formulas, inauthentic and cold, are replaced by ordinary and spontaneous words, created and invented there on the spur of the moment, in the warmth of friendship and the breath of the Spirit.

My brothers and sisters! It is not a matter of communicating only with our friends as if we are at a club or a wedding dinner, but also, and first, with Jesus Christ, something that is not testable and that cannot be measured with the yardstick of feeling. Nor is it a private affair, left to the individual judgment, but rather a public, official action, which affects the whole Church and therefore requires an application of norms issued from on high, though after the opinions of the base have also been heard. The Eucharist is, on top of everything else, a means of producing union and love between Christians. Of course, those who participate in it must try to have feelings of charity for their brothers and sisters, but it would be a mistake to say: I don't feel like communicating together with this or that person, as long as they don't share my ideas or as long as they have not fixed this or that! In addition, the Mass is essentially, is the sacrifice of the Cross, represented in a mysterious way, the application for every Christian of the merits of Christ, an anticipation of the liturgy of heaven. Living the Mass, then, is to unite our sufferings, our voluntary sacrifices with the immolated Christ, and to transfigure our lives through hope in the glory of the Lord, while awaiting his return. Eating the immolated Lamb is to share his desires and his will, to espouse his sorrows and interests, to desire to make his feelings ours, to be endowed with his goodness and mercy. "Blood of the covenant," says the celebrant: yes, covenant, pact between the Man-God and a poor sinner; a reciprocal gift of one to the other, the fusion of two hearts, all the closer the more it has been desired and prepared for.

This year marks the centenary of the death of Alessandro Manzoni. The thoughts set forth above had been deeply engraved in his heart and lived experienced personally in his life, at the time he wrote the two following verses:

> Come, O Lord, take your rest,
> Reign in our breasts;
> Clear away from our feelings
> All that is not immortal.
> Descend: every visit of yours,
> Prepares for a return of yours,
> Until that golden day
> That enraptures us in You.[2]

May the feelings of this great man also be ours on so great an evening!

Notes

[1] *Opera* 6:70-73.

[2] "Per la prima Comunione," from *Tutte le poesie*.

Crosses

Homily at the Good Friday Liturgy[1]
April 12, 1974

During the reading of John's deeply compassionate account, I have contemplated him together with you: full of sorrows, nailed in his hands and suspended; nailed in his feet and immobilized. There I was, facing him: I who cannot bear obstacles, I who shrug off every annoyance, I who am drowning in ease. And yet I profess to be his disciple. I have a beautiful crucifix hanging on the wall of my study; another crucifix at the end of the rosary that I carry in my pocket; I make the sign of the Cross I don't know how many times a day; every day I celebrate the Mass, the sacrifice of the Cross represented on the altar. In spite of all this, I am so afraid of crosses.

Reflecting on crosses, I have made a distinction. There are some that do not make us tremble. For example: the pain that is heavy, but that you have the strength to bear. Competition, which exhausts you and leaves you breathless, which makes you thirsty and wears you out, but at the same time, stimulates you to overcome your opponent and reach the finish line in glory. These are very small crosses.

The cross is a beam fastened to a crossbeam. It is, therefore, the road blocked in front of me. I thought I would be able to go on and someone stops me, unjustly blocking all of my hopes. I cherished legitimate desires and I see them destroyed from beginning to end. I wanted to keep my feet on the ground and I find myself separated from the earth, lifted up and nailed where I really didn't want to be. And without any glory; the same people who sympathize with me outwardly for propriety's sake, deep down are laughing at me. This really is a cross, this wounds the depths of the heart, it twists the soul, and makes this cry rise spontaneously to the lips: This I really didn't want, Lord! Let this cup pass from me, Lord! *Transeat*, Lord!

Jesus too experienced this; in the garden he felt prostrated, annihilated, sorrowful unto death. He too, said: "Father, if it is possible let this cup pass from me." Afterwards, however, he accepted it heroically. Afterward, he said: "let not my will, but yours be done." (Luke 22:42)

My brothers and sisters! Let us also try to say our *Fiat* and carry our daily cross. To us too, as to Christ, a little bit of strength will come from the Father. On our painful journey, there will also be some Simon of Cyrene to help us; a mother to suffer along with us and console us.

In any case, every cross is a passing thing; it is the road, not the goal. And no crosses without heaven in view. St. Peter wrote: "Rejoice in the measure that you share Christ's sufferings. When his glory is revealed, you will rejoice exultantly" (1 Peter 4:13).

Notes

1 *Opera* 6:310-11.

A New Creation in Christ

Mass at the Easter Vigil[1]
1974

1. We are Christians, we can all recall the memorable events that filled Easter day. Early in the morning, the three holy women hurried to the sepulcher. On Friday evening they had been forced to interrupt the embalming. "Poor Jesus! He is dead, alas!" they say. "May we at least be allowed to give him all the honors he deserves! But how?" For them it is a great problem. You know what happened next. The enormous stone is found rolled to one side. The tomb is empty; there remain only the shroud and the face napkin; the seals have been broken; the guards have disappeared. Instead there is an angel, a messenger of joy and peace: "Are you looking for Jesus Christ the crucified? He is risen, he is no longer here."

The amazement of the women, the incredulity of the apostles, the sorrow of Mary Magdalen, the running and feverish searching of Peter and John. In the evening, on the other hand, we find all these people convinced: they had to yield to the evidence. The Master is really alive and alive in an extraordinary way. Lazarus, after his resurrection, had returned to the kind of life he had before. The Master, on the other hand, enters the room with the doors closed, he experiences no difficulties of distance or time. Within a few hours, he has appeared to Magdalen, to the two at Emmaus, to a group gathered in the upper room. Eight days later, even Thomas, who had at first been skeptical and unbelieving, lets all of his doubts fall before the wounds of Christ, which he has seen and touched. All of the people become witnesses. Placed in prison and given warnings, they answer through the mouth of Peter: "We cannot be silent about what we have seen and heard" (Acts 4:20). St. Paul, a witness too, in an extraordinary way, on the road to Damascus, will write: "Neither death nor life, nor angels nor principalities, nor present things, nor the future things . . . nor any other creature, will be able to separate us from the love of God, in Jesus Christ our Lord" (Rom 8:39).

At the time of the apostles and after them, the Church is established, it is extended and it continues to work, relying on faith in the resurrection of Christ. "If Christ has not been raised," writes St. Paul, "then empty is your faith, then empty is our preaching . . . Then we are also false witnesses to God . . . we are to be pitied more than any other men" (1 Cor 15:14,15f). And he continued, have no fear! "Christ has been raised from the dead, the first fruits of all those who have fallen asleep" (1 Cor 15:20). The "first fruits," that is, the first of a long series of people, who, just as they have followed him in death, will follow him in rising again.

2. Christ is therefore the head of a long line. Though he has done all he can for our benefit, that doesn't mean that he must do everything himself, and that we must remain idle. He did not need us to create us, said Augustine, but he does need us to save us. We must make a personal contribution of effort and work to our salvation: St. Paul has recorded it for us in the second reading (1 Cor 5:68). We are close to Easter, he said, let us not celebrate it with the old dough leavened with wickedness, but with the new unleavened bread of sincerity and truth.

This ringing call to newness is exquisitely Paschal and typical of Paul. For Paul, "whoever is in Christ, is a new creation. The old order has passed away" (2 Cor. 5:17). The phrase "old order" means sin, passions, and shame. "New creation" means: Christ resurrected in us. "All of you who have been baptized into Christ have clothed yourself with him" (Gal 3:27). And St. Paul does not limit himself to writing these things: he lived them. Very often he said: "Imitate me, as I imitate Christ" (1 Cor. 11:1; cf. 1 Cor. 4:16; Phil. 3:17; 1 Thess 1:6). He must have excelled in this imitation, if he could write: "The life I live now is not my own; Christ is living in me" (Gal. 2:20); in Paul heartbeat, breath and life were Jesus!

People will say: beautiful things, but for ascetics and mystics! No, to imitate or not to imitate Christ, at least with a sincere and continual effort, simply means to be or not to be a Christian. And this is the disgrace of us Christians, if we bear the name of Christ and not the virtues: not the gentleness, not the generous devotion to our brothers and sisters, not the effort to please the Heavenly Father by a holy life.

Another disgrace of ours: neglecting the means that God has given us for us to imitate him and making empty the courtesies that he has used toward us. The Bible speaks of the Most High who cares for Israel, guarding it like the apple of his eye, and like the eagle bears it up on his own wings to lofty flights (Deut. 32:11). In the Gospel Jesus has portrayed himself as the shepherd who carries the lamb lovingly around his neck. We are those guarded ones, those protected ones, those lifted on his wings, the sheep around Christ's neck. By Baptism, in fact, the Lord has made us his brothers and sisters; by Confirmation he has strengthened us and made us better prepared for the blows of life, by Communion he enters into us as food, medicine and energy; by Reconciliation he lifts us up again from our falls and puts us back in shape. We could have become giants; instead perhaps we remain the pygmies or stunted people of Christianity. We could have become shining beacons; instead, we may have given off light for a time, then we have allowed ourselves to turn into nothing but smoldering wicks.

An English poet (Young) complained, weeping, that man is born an original and dies a copy. I am only sorry that Christians in their lives make themselves into bad copies of bad human models. It is very pleasing, on the other hand, if they strive to become a copies or portraits of that very beautiful model that is Christ. He has constantly said: Follow me, learn from me. St. Paul writes of God the Father: "Those whom he knew, he predestined to share the image of his Son, that the Son might be the firstborn of many brothers" (Rom 8:29).

And here is the criterion by which we will one day be judged. We will appear before the Lord. There will no longer be any distinctions, degrees, medals or decorations on us. We will no longer be presidents, or patriarchs, or titled people, or cabinet ministers, or generals. On that day, Schiller has said, men will be nothing but men; my soul and your soul will be naked in the sight of God, who will check: "Does it or does it not resemble my Son?" The only thing that will save our souls will be the image of Christ, transparent and shining in them. Let's try from now on, therefore, to have them bear, living and resplendent, the image of Christ.

On the day of Christ's resurrection, may a resurrection take place in us, from the old to the new, from sleep to action. The Lord orders us: "Awake, O sleepers, rise from the dead, and Christ will give you light" (Eph. 5:14). May this be a cry of liberation and may it signal the beginning of a new Easter for us!

Notes

1 *Opera*, 6:317-19.

Death and Eternal Life

Homily for All Souls Day, 1976[1]

Today we are commemorating all the faithful departed. It is not a bad idea to give a thought to our own deaths, which constitutes, perhaps, the problem that anguishes us most of all. When? Why? And what will become of us afterward? These are questions that all of us ask ourselves at one time or another. It is true that fashions change: the big question about the numerous dead people in books and TV detective shows is not "Where might his soul have gone?" but "Who killed him?"

1. What will become of us afterward? Science and philosophy try to give answers. But science can only observe that, at a given moment, for everyone, the thread of life is broken.

Philosophy takes me one step further. With Horace, I take note of my thirst for immortality: *"non omnis moriar,"* I will die, but I would like to not die completely; the better part of me, I hope, will survive. I look around me: I see that the duck has an instinct to swim, and that outside of the duck, water exists. I see that man has eyes, and outside of man, there are beautiful things to see. In me, there is a hunger and thirst to survive. I conclude: outside of me, therefore, there exists, there must exist, a life without end; otherwise, we would be the only beings who are mistaken, who are filled with unattainable desires.

2. Beyond this philosophy, which alas! is uncertain, the most certain and consoling words are spoken by Christ: death is not *the* end, but *an* end: the end, that is, of an initial and temporary period of an age that has no end. Jesus has said: "My kingdom is not of this world." Not only his disciples, but his adversaries believed in this

other world. The lawyer asks him what he must do "to inherit everlasting life" (Lk 10:25). The rich young man asks him the same question and Jesus answers: "Sell everything you have, distribute it to the poor and you will have a treasure in heaven." The young man becomes sad and he does not accept, but Peter intervenes: "And what about us?" he says, "We apostles have abandoned everything for you." Jesus answers: there is "life everlasting in the age to come" (cf. Lk 18:18ff). Precisely because it is eternal, this life is so precious that the fortunes of the present world pale before it. This is demonstrated forcefully by the parable of the rich man, whose crops had done extraordinarily well that year. He was planning how to gather together all the bounty of God that his fields and stalls had produced for him, when the words of the Lord sounded in his ears: "You fool! This very night your life shall be required of you: to whom will all this piled-up wealth of yours go?" (cf. Lk 12:16ff).

3. The certainty of another life does not destroy the bitterness of death. To help us understand it and to give us courage, Jesus willed to experience this bitterness in himself. For this reason, he wept before the tomb of his friend Lazarus. For this reason, when his moment comes, in the garden, he begins to tremble, and is seized with anguish (cf. Mk 14:34) and passes through a very painful agony. So that he might regain his courage, the Father sends him an angel to console him, but on the cross Jesus once again calls on the Father saying, "My God, why have you forsaken me?" (Mt 27:47).

4. If he is subject to death for us and like us, Jesus is, nevertheless, the stupendous conqueror of death. He defeated it in others, by raising to life the daughter of Jairus, the son of the widow of Naim, and Lazarus. After his own crucifixion, he defeated it by raising himself as the first of a never-ending series of others who will be brought back to life. "I solemnly assure you," he had promised, "an hour is coming, in which all those in their tombs will hear the voice of the Son of God and come forth. Those who have

done right will rise to live; the evildoers will rise to be damned" (Jn 5: 28-29).

Like Jesus, for the Christian, physical death remains, but not the terror of death. Those who hold on to the certainty that there is another life, and that their bodies will one day rise again, are not to fear. They can cry with St. Paul: "O death, where is your sting?" (1 Cor 15:55).

The summary response to the question "What will become of us?" is found in the "Credo" of Paul VI: "We believe in eternal life. We believe that the souls of all those who die in the grace of Christ, whether they must still be purified in purgatory, or whether at the moment they leave their bodies Christ welcomes them into heaven, as he did with the good thief, constitute the people of God in the world beyond death, a death that will be once and for all defeated on the day of the resurrection, when those souls will be reunited to their bodies [. . .] And with faith and in hope we await the resurrection of the dead and the life of the world to come."

Another question: Why death? The Bible answers: "Through one man [Adam] sin entered the world and with sin death, death thus coming to all men inasmuch as all sinned" (Rom 5:12). Death is bound up with sin, sin committed by one man alone, but which has repercussions for everyone.

Some people do not want to hear talk of original sin. At most, they say, there exists the so-called "sin of the world." That is, there exists around us a bad environment, not at all favorable to goodness: our personal sins are a by-product of this environment. Alas! This by-product, in the form of a tendency to evil, exists in everyone, even in those who live in the best environments. It is absurd, they retort, to make us suffer the consequences of what another has committed. It is mysterious, it is difficult to understand, but it is not absurd, if this other person is a leader who represents us, and, in some way, contains us; if because of this other person, we are deprived only of gifts that we were not entitled to in justice; if human nature, although wounded, remains good and open to the supernatural; if, as soon as the affliction has been caused by man, God has prepared for man the medicine, that is, salvation.

Here we are at a central point, to which those with different conceptions of life have applied their heads.

Rousseau has said: children are born good; it is society that ruins them. Certain experts in education repeat: children are born good; avoid giving them complexes, give them a culture; and they will be happy. If only it were that way, but we can see people going around with little culture who are good and happy. Without culture there used to be stupid wicked people; with culture and technology we now have wicked people who are shrewd and clever.

Luther has said: human nature is corrupt, it can produce only sin. Goodness consists of the fact that God covers these sins with a mantle of mercy. The Marxists say: man, taken individually, is egotistical and wicked. He will become good and happy if he is placed in a collective regime that achieves economic prosperity for everyone. It has been noted, however, that in a period of great prosperity, juvenile delinquency increases, while religious life prospers when the vow and the spirit of poverty are practiced in earnest.

The truth lies in between the two hypotheses: we all experience in ourselves moments of goodness and moments of wickedness; we are like a watch that has all of its wheels, but needs a mainspring that will make it move. The mainspring is the grace of God: if we do not resist it, our spiritual wheels will work and produce good. Naturally, these are mysterious things: we hold them through faith, we do not know exactly how they work, they do not lend themselves to verification. Should we be surprised? "There is nothing," Pascal wrote, "about which we know everything." And Chesterton: "How could physical science prove that man is not depraved? You do not cut a man open to find his sins. You do not boil him until he gives forth the unmistakable green fumes of depravity. How could physical science find any traces of a moral fall? . . . Did [the scientist] expect to find a fossil Eve with a fossil apple inside her? Did he suppose that the ages would have spared for him a complete skeleton of Adam . . . attached to a slightly faded fig leaf?"[2]

A third question: When? Here, everyone knows enough to answer that we do not know when. The consequence is: let's try to be prepared. The warnings given by Jesus still hold good: "Look" around you! You do not know when the master of the house is coming, whether at dusk, at midnight, when the cock crows, or at early dawn. Do not let him come suddenly and catch you asleep" (Mk 13:35-36). What the Lord said to the bishop of Sardis in the book of Revelation still holds good for the bishop and the people of Venice: "Wake up . . . if you do not rouse yourselves I will come upon you like a thief, at a time when you cannot know" (Rev 3:23).

Christ is only a thief in the sense that he comes to take us without warning. His coming does not cause fear if we are prepared. On the contrary! He says it himself: "It will go well with those servants whom the master finds wide awake on his return. I tell you, he will put on an apron, seat them at table and proceed to wait on them" (cf. Lk 12:37ff).

This vision of a heavenly banquet, in which Christ in person serves his friends, revives our hope and is a force that sustains us on the road of the world. It is a moral road, but it resembles the ordinary road on which people travel in the most varied ways: some on motorcycles, some in Alfa Romeos, some in Fiat 128s; some in Mini Minors; but the police, when they stop them, do not ask: "What kind of car do you have?" but rather "Have you observed the traffic laws?" Christ is anything but a policeman; if we are repentant, he is our friend, to the point of taking our defense, even in the event that we were opposed to him in the past. He will not ask whether we were rich or poor, Italian or German, ignorant or learned. He will ask only: "Have you traveled in a Christian way, according to the laws: the Commandments?" An exam that is not very difficult to pass. It will undoubtedly be passed by those who have prepared themselves by trying to die to their own passions day by day.

On the tomb of John Duns Scotus, the seventh centenary of whose death is being celebrated this year, is written: *semel sepultus, bis mortuus*. He was buried only once, but he died twice: the first time, through his good life he died to sin; the second time, he died physically. The second death is no longer frightening, if it has been preceded by the first.

Notes

1 *Opera* 7:486-90. Title from republication of the piece in *Il Magistero di Albino Luciani*, a cura di Alfredo Cattabiani (Padua: Edizioni Messaggero, 1979).

2 G. K. Chesterton, "Science and Religion," in *All Things Considered* [1908; reprint Philadelphia: Dufour Editions, 1969, pp. 124-25.—Trans.]

The Church

The House on a Rock

Homily for the Feast of Saints Peter and Paul[1]
June 29, 1976

When a house is built on a rock, what happens? It is the rock that keeps the house steady, united and compact.

Peter is the rock; the Church is the house. The Church, by the provision of Christ, will be steady, united and compact, as long as Catholics remain attached to Peter. This is the principal teaching of the Gospel that has just been read, and it should be emphasized on the feast of the Pope, which we are celebrating today.

Twelve years ago, Pope Paul wrote *Ecclesiam Suam*, the first encyclical of his pontificate. "The church is on a journey in the world; what roads should she travel?" he asked himself. And he answered: 1) Gain awareness of herself; 2) Renew herself; 3) Engage in dialogue.

AWARENESS OF HERSELF

Who and what are we? What do we Catholics possess? The Gospel stands in front of us like a mirror. Let's look at it and ask Christ: "How did you see us and delineate us, Lord? What did you want your Church to be?" The answer of Christ: "I am the vine, you are the branches; remain in me" (cf. Jn 15). Here is what we are: living branches inserted in a living trunk, who absorb its sap, who prolong it. With Christ we make a complete whole, a body, of which he is the head and we are the members. "You are all one in Christ (Gal 3:28). "Marvel and rejoice: we have become Christ."[2]

Do we think of this? Since by baptism we have become children of God, brothers and sisters of Christ, we have in our hands the greatest of all fortunes. What account will we make of it? Is it possible that we think only of money, career and health and not at all of these great realities? "Recognize your dignity, O Christians," St. Leo the Great says to us. "Seek the things of above, not those of below," says St. Paul. "Seek first the Kingdom of God."

RENEWING HERSELF

What happens when someone stands at the mirror? He discovers spots and defects in his hair, his face and his clothes, and does something about them. The Church too, looking at herself in the mirror of the Gospel, Paul VI says, discovers some defects in herself and must remedy them. And he explains:

The essential conception and the fundamental structures of the Church are settled. The Lord himself has kept watch over them. Here reforms are not necessary and are not possible.

In people, however, even those most representative of the Church, there can be defects and failings, which should be removed. Just as certain superstructures the Church has been saddled with in the past should be taken away. At that time, they were perhaps useful. Today they turn out to be cumbersome. David found himself uncomfortable and almost paralyzed when they clothed him in the heavy armor of Saul; if he wanted to recover his agility and freedom of movement, he had to put aside that armor.

Renewing herself, however, does not mean that the Church must adapt herself to the ways of the world, and the pagan conception of life. Nor is it enough for the Church to remove or change a few laws. It is above all the inside of Catholics that must change. Paul VI uses the evangelical word *metanoia*, which means completely changing our outlook. And he insists on two points: the spirit of poverty and charity. Poverty means being less attached to the goods of this world, having more trust in Providence, privileging spiritual goods over economic ones and being just and moderate in seeking one's own advancement. Charity means loving God with a supreme love: that is, loving no one and nothing as much as him, more than him, or against him; loving our neighbor as ourselves;

something that is easy to say but difficult to do with human effort alone.

DIALOGUE

Why engage in dialogue? Because being a Christian is a great good fortune, we must try to share this good fortune with others by talking and dialoguing.

How to engage in dialogue? By looking to the advantage of others, respecting their freedom and trying to have a sincere and humble spirit of service.

Who to dialogue with? There are three circles of people. The first circle embraces people as people even if they do not profess any religion or declare themselves atheists. We must state frankly, before everyone, that God exists. This is in order to render homage to the truth, out of love for our fellow human beings and out of fidelity to the Gospel. For us, to deplore atheism "is the lament of a victim rather than the sentence of a judge." Believers, in fact, are persecuted and beaten in many places. Will they be able to say it? Will they be able to say that the beatings hurt? Or will they have to say that the beatings are caramels and caresses?

The second circle is that of believers in God. Paul VI names the Jews, the Muslims, and the great Afro-Asiatic religions. Dialoging with them does not mean saying that all religions are equally good. One is the true religion by which God wants to be adored by us; many people, however, through no fault of their own, do not know of it. They are doing what they can; they should be honored and respected. Just as many values, both moral and religious, contained in non-Christian religions deserve respectful recognition.

The third circle contains our separated Christian brothers, Protestant and Orthodox. A rock that breaks off from a gold-bearing mountain, remains gold-bearing, said Pius XI.

We have a number of points in common with these separated brothers. Let's bring them out. The Protestants, for example, value the Bible a great deal; the Orthodox greatly venerate Our Lady. There are differences between us and them on points that Christ has left open; Catholics should understand and adapt themselves, and if necessary, yield. If, on the other hand, the difference is over doctrines established by Christ, the matter becomes delicate; the dialogue should be conducted with respect and love for persons as well as for truth.

To the dialogue "of the three circles," Paul VI has added "domestic dialogue" inside the Catholic Church. "Often," he says, "some people, instead of cultivating a calm and respectful dialogue, cultivate "arguments, dissension or disputes." Let's try to avoid these phenomena, let's listen to the Apostle, who wrote: "let there may be no divisions among you." (1 Cor 1:10). Still more, let's unite our humble prayer to that of Christ, who prayed: "Father, keep them in your name, those that you have given me, so that they may be one" (Jn 17:11).

Notes

[1] *Opera* 7: 376-78.

[2] Augustine, *Tract. in Ioh.* 21:8.

On the Way to the Priesthood

Letter From The Council To Seminarians[1]
September 28, 1964

My dear seminarians:

Once again this year, my commitments at the Council keep me from being with you at the beginning of the school year. May the following lines take the place of my presence.

I will begin by telling you that the recommencement of the work of the Council also gives me the impression that I am beginning a new school year. You change your class and your seat, I do too: at the first session in 1962 I was on the right, at the bottom. At the second session in 1963 I was on the left and at the top; this year I have moved to the right again, to seat number 779.

The vice-rector decides your seating; the Secretary of the Council does it for me. But I can't tell you what a line there was on Tuesday September 15, to get the number of our *sedes* or *locus* (that's what they call the seats). You would never imagine it, but archbishops and bishops have to wait patiently for their turn, crowding around and squeezing together every so often to make room for someone who must pass through. But there is nothing surprising about that; we are an assembly of twenty-five hundred men! I will say, in fact, that some of the old ones like it; they feel as if they were back in the seminary, and young again. One old Italian bishop, who, after taking his number in the entrance of St. Peter's, was scarcely able to open a passage for himself in the crowd, said laughing, "We are boys again!" And seeing that his neighbors, who were from other countries, did not understand, he translated, still laughing, "*Sumus adhuc pueri!*"

You receive announcements, advice, and disciplinary directives from the vice-rector. Here it is the secretary of the Council[2] who acts as the vice-rector. A deluxe vice-rector, of course, who speaks to us in very elegant Latin, with great vivacity and good humor. He warns us, for example, that this year there is a greater amount of work to be done, that we cannot waste time, and therefore even the two bars will not be open before ten o'clock! He took care to add: "It is useless to knock at the door before that time. The door will not be opened for you!"

Another warning: "Any Fathers who are not sitting in their assigned seats in the hall will be hunted down." That was only right, but he went on, "Understand us, venerable Fathers! Some Fathers wrote that they will be coming to the Council and they did not come; some wrote that they were not coming and came anyway; some, finally, send word that they are coming any day now. . ." The whole assembly burst out laughing, and by their laughter they made it clear that they understood, that they sympathized, that they would have all the necessary patience.

Again: "No fathers are to gather at the *tabernam mechanographicam* (the automated registration center), at least not simply to admire it." Fine, we are pleased by it, the Secretary said, "this gives great honor to us." But, he went on, do it with discretion, and when the employees are not busy, because even among the technicians of the center "no one can serve two masters"; he then recalled that in a sense, the Holy Spirit "must also assist the *machinas mechanographicas*, so that they may not make errors in tallying the Fathers' votes!" One of his quite frequent reminders is this: "Will the Fathers please return to their seats, because the voting is about to begin!" (*jam jam imminet*). Or: "Will the Fathers please listen, both those who are in their seats and those who have gone into the Diaspora!" (that is those in the side naves). The requests are often (with wise psychology!) softened by an epithet: to the Secretary, we are usually the "Venerable Fathers", but every so often we become the "Dear" or "Dearest" or "Most Honored" or "Most Eminent" Fathers!

During the first few days, you look around you to see what's new in the seminary, and to greet your old acquaintances. I do too. Here is the statue of St. Teresa; in 1962 she was directly opposite me, now she looks at me from the right. The book in her hand is still open, her eyes are still intent on waiting for God to finish his revelation, and you know that the goose quill pen that she holds in her right hand will very soon be racing quickly to transcribe the vision she has had . . . My neighbor from last year has ended up down there, opposite; now he has seen me and from a distance he waves to me in greeting. Bishop Msakila is in the open stall below me; his purple skullcap stands out against his deep black hair, which looks like an ink blot against his skin which is black, but not as back as his hair; every so often he turns his face toward me, with the most beautiful African smile, to communicate some impression to me.

On my right side, on the other hand, there is a Mexican I do not know, Bishop Garcia Franco Miguel. He came very young to study philosophy and theology at the Gregorian University, so he speaks Italian well. On Tuesday, September 15, after mutual introductions had been made, he suddenly pointed out to me a pair of Eastern bishops who were passing by wearing the *kalimavkion* (a kind of cylindrical hat with a black veil falling to the shoulders). "Do you know what those bishops are called?" he asked me. "No, actually I don't." I answered. "I'll tell you: they are called *viudas tristes* (sorrowful widows). And now look at that other one, in the red *kalimavkion* and red veil; he is a representative of the *viudas alegres* (merry widows). On the other hand, that bishop of the Armenian rite with that sort of little black basket on his head is a *sombrero femenino!*" (a ladies' hat). I couldn't help smiling, and I said: "Excellency, however can you allow yourself to slap nicknames on people?" "Oh, it's not on the people, it's on their clothes! And it wasn't me who made them up, but a very distinguished Mexican, the moving spirit behind the resistance to

President Calles, an organizer of the *Cristeros*, who used to play innocent tricks along with Padre Pro, even at the moments of greatest danger![3] Why not enjoy a few jokes even during the intermissions at the Council?"

They are, in fact, intermissions; I would not want you to think that the Council is made up and woven of little pleasantries: they are actually rare times of relaxation that take place during the breaks. The Council is quite different and leads to quite other subjects and concerns.

Among our other concerns, not the least is about you and your pastoral formation. The Council of Trent was famous especially for thinking of you seminarians. Vatican II will be concerned with you as well.

I said "pastoral" formation. In fact, everything you receive from the seminary, the quality and method of your prayer, the direction of your studies, the subjects you study in class, your method of studying, your spiritual direction, the type of recreation you have, your way of spending your vacations, everything must aim at this end alone: to make you into true shepherds of souls, modeled on the example of Jesus, the Good Shepherd par excellence. If, while you are in the seminary, you see a large circle of people all lovingly gathered around you to help you and encourage you, from the bishop, your parents, and the rector to your spiritual father, your teachers, the many people who are praying for your vocation, and the sisters who prepare your meals and iron your clothes, know that it is for this: to have tomorrow priests who are passionately devoted above all to saving souls, and who are able to get to know them and help them with the necessary sensitivity, and by the most suitable methods and means. Tomorrow it will not be enough for you to teach catechism and preach; people will want from you the lessons and sermons of shepherds of souls. It will not be enough for you to administer the sacraments, you will be required to administer them fervently, zealously, and disinterestedly. It will not be enough for you to "govern" a parish well or badly; your parishioners must feel that they have in you an authentic father of souls, who is deeply concerned about the spiritual good of his children and who cares little for those things called money, honors, and career.

In order to be like this, you will have to live with the Lord in a relationship of true and constant friendship. It is true that Jesus is invisible, but he is absolutely concrete, living and very close to you, and you can love him. He strives himself, if we allow him to do it, by anticipating us, helping us, and caring for us, to produce and increase his friendship in us. A priest who is rich in everything but lacks this real friendship is very poor and in great danger.

My dear seminarians, yours are the best years for establishing a firm and decided friendship that attaches you solidly to the Lord and detaches you from the things that do not last, which is a "chosen" and voluntary commitment for your whole life. If some regret at times appears in your mind for what you have renounced, overcome it at once, recovering your joy in full. And be proud of your vocation! Proud with the kind of pride Paul had, when he reasoned: yes, it is true, I could have (in fact, I have already had, and abundantly), what the others boast about. But all those things, compared to Christ, I no longer consider a gain, but rather a loss! Everything, indeed, is loss to me, compared to the extraordinary knowledge of Christ Jesus. It is to gain him that I have deprived myself of everything and considered everything rubbish. I prize only the justice that comes from faith in Christ and imitating Christ, and if only I could seize him, as he seized me on the road to Damascus! Unfortunately I have not yet arrived at this goal, but I long for it, like the runners in the stadium long for the goal and the prize! (Phil 3:115).

To become true pastors of souls, therefore, you must be friends of Jesus. And what do you do to be friends of Jesus? You must practice the virtues that Jesus asks of you, and, first, you must have a robust faith, which makes you see things through the eyes of God himself, with a new perspective, that often reverses the old viewpoint and turns it upside down.

It is this kind of faith, according to St. Paul, that gave strength and courage to the heroes of the Old Testament. Through this faith "Abel offered God a greater sacrifice than Cain's," and Enoch "was seen no more because God took him" and "Noah prepared the ark with holy fear," and "Abraham, called by God, left without knowing where he was going, offering Isaac in sacrifice . . . convinced that God is able to bring the dead to life;" and Moses "wished to be ill-treated together with God's people rather than enjoy the temporary rewards of sin." Through the same faith "others endured mockery, scourging, even chains and imprisonment; they were stoned, sawed in two, put to death at sword's point, they went about garbed in the skins of sheep or goats, needy, afflicted, tormented . . . they wandered about in deserts and on mountains, they dwelt in caves and in holes in the earth." These were all people who had faith in the word of God, men who kept "looking to the reward" that they had been promised, though knowing that that it was in the distant future, who felt that they were only "strangers and foreigners on the earth" (cf. Heb 11:140).

These people, therefore, open the way for us to a generous way of working; still more does Jesus open it for us. It is true that in him (man, but also God) there cannot be faith; but he does "inspire and perfect our faith." And in fact, being able to choose between joy and suffering, he chose the cross; heedless of its shame, he bore all hostility against his person by sinners. In this way He says to us: "Look at things with new eyes. And courage! Do not allow yourselves to become discouraged! Do not lose heart!" (cf. Heb 12:15).

Mingled with this faith must be our hope. The Lord has already placed very precious things in our hands, but he says to us: "These are only a beginning, a down-payment; afterward will come the best part! We are God's children now, but what we shall be later has not yet come to light (cf. 2 Pt 1:4; Col 3:4; 1 Jn 3:2). Wait!" Therefore we are waiting. We are waiting for the Lord, we are waiting for the wonderful transformations and the total renewal that he will work on us and on the whole universe; we are curious to see the new heavens and the new earth (Tt 2:13; Phil 3:2021; 2 Thess 1:10; 2 Pet 3:12). The Council dedicates a whole chapter to saying that we must be vigilant, on our feet, with our eyes turned attentively to this luminous future of the Church. In his first letter St. Peter urges us to be "always ready to defend yourselves confidently and respectfully, should anyone ask you the reason for the hope that is in you" (1 Pet 3:15). In other words, our "expectation" is a treasure; hope in what awaits us must become, at some moments, the desert or "place prepared by God," which the book of Revelation speaks of (12:6). The dragon comes, he tries to hurt us or disturb us; like the great lady, we will run to take refuge there and the dragon will not be able to get at us!

Mingled with hope must be charity. The older ones among you know that charity is the queen, the most important of all the virtues. So true is this that, when a person is to be canonized, the first thing that they examine, and with the greatest diligence, is whether this person has had a heroic love of God and his neighbor. Pope Benedict XIV, a "master" in this subject of canonization, explains the reason for this at length.[4] But our Lord had already alluded to it, by saying that those who were his disciples and Christians could be known by their fraternal love. St. Paul (1 Cor 13) ends his hymn to charity by speaking almost exclusively of the love of neighbor, and St. John writes: "If anyone says: 'I love God,' yet hates his brother, he is a liar, because one who does not love the brother he has seen, cannot love God whom he has not seen" (1 Jn 4:20).

Therefore in the seminary you must above all practice love toward your superiors, your teachers, your schoolmates and the service staff, although in different ways; by showing gratitude, avoiding complaints and criticisms, overcoming the little jealousies that spontaneously arise, bearing with faults, respecting the opinions of others, cordially offering your help, learning to discuss with noble courtesy, and knowing, if necessary how to refuse graciously, and contributing to giving recreation periods, conversations and walks a healthy joy. This is the rule of rules; it should be observed before the other rules; it must be the soul of all of them, especially in view of your future apostolate. In fact, love and mutual help among priests of the same diocese has always been a characteristic of the spirituality of the diocesan priest.

This love will always be better, because today pastoral action can no longer be individual. That is, a parish priest can no longer say: "I'm going to think about my parish, and that's it!" Your parishioners, dear Father, are now spending the major portion of their time outside the parish: at the factory, the school, the sports field, the movies and on tourist excursions. You can no longer take care of them all alone. You and the priests of the neighboring parishes must form a group of priests interested in the same problems, who establish a collective pastoral activity, who divide the work, each one taking the sector that is most suited to him, in which to specialize and work for the benefit of the whole inter-parish zone. These things will only be successful if we love each other, if we are used to working together, giving up our own viewpoint at times, and often replacing the irritating pronoun "I" with the more anonymous and less glorious, but more Christian and more beneficial pronoun "we"!

There is another virtue characteristic of the spirituality of the diocesan priest: union with his bishop, which is realized in the dual concept of the *Pontificale*:5 "obedience and reverence." Priests do not become obedient all at once; either they already become used to obeying during their time in the seminary or there is danger that they will no longer obey. For example, those who have been devoted to and passionate about "autos" from their seminary days, will always be for "autos." I am not talking about automobiles, but about the exaggerated affirmation of self which is expressed by the following words beginning with "auto": "autonomy": (I make the laws!) "autonomous government" (I know how to control myself), "autonomous decision-making" (I know what to do!), autonomous education" (that subject matter is worthless, I know!) "autonomous teaching method" (the right method is not the professor's, but mine!). Someone used to be an eternal grumbler in the seminary; he will also grumble as a priest. Someone is always late for class and for chapel; he will also be late for clerical retreats, with the offerings sent to the chancery office, with paying accounts at the store. Some are always out of their proper place; he was on the stairs while the others were studying; he cut out, glued, covered and painted, while he should have been doing his homework, reviewing, and learning his lessons. After he becomes a priest, the music, or rather, the discord, continues: he is rarely to be found in his office, he is a lover of art, or mechanics, or electrical engineering, a business manager, etc., everything except what people expect of him. And of course, he continues to say that it is not modern and progressive to chain yourself to a discipline; that "authority" (he doesn't like the "auto" in *this* word) is sacred, yes, but, before exercising it, the superior must listen to the subject, that is, come to terms with, make a deal with his subject.

My dear seminarians, I assure you that I have urged your superiors to introduce a family atmosphere in the seminary, to get you gradually used to a proper use of your freedom, to keep you informed, prudently, and in accordance with your age, about politics, sports, movies, everything that falls within your legitimate desires. Once this has been said to your superiors, however, I say to you: be docile, respectful and obedient; that will cost you sacrifice, but it will give you a firm, virile foundation, and training for future sacrifices. And have no fear of not being modern enough. We are always modern when we imitate Jesus Christ. For Christ obeyed. He was in the form of God, Paul says, with emotion, and yet he did not consider his equality with God a plundered object (that is, something guarded jealously and held on to at any cost). And he emptied himself (only in the external manifestation of his divinity, of course) and took the form of a slave, becoming similar to men . . . and he humiliated himself still more, being made obedient even to death, death on a cross (cf. Phil. 2:68).

Here, once more, it is enough to put yourself face-to-face with Christ, consider what he has done, and the difficulties fall away. I return, then, to what I said above: let us make friends with him, let us imitate him and we will be certain of being good shepherds of souls!

He wanted to be poor, he left his apostles poor, he taught them to be concerned even about little things ("gather up the crusts that are left over, so that nothing will go to waste" Jn 6:12). He did not think in the slightest that riches could help to save souls. Let us imitate him: the necessary, the reasonable (today in the seminary and tomorrow in the rectory) yes, the extravagant, the unnecessary, the wasteful, no.

And no dreams, either deliberate or welcomed, of greatness.

"What will become of me in the future?" Pope John XXIII wrote on being ordained a priest. "Shall I be a good theologian, or a famous jurist, or shall I have a country parish or be just a simple priest? What does all this matter to me? I must be prepared to be none of all these, or even more than all these, as God wills,"[6] And ten years later: "The habitual smile must know how to conceal the inner conflict with selfishness, which is sometimes tremendous and when need arises show the victory of the soul over the temptations of the senses or of pride, so that my better side may always be shown to God and my neighbor . . . Preoccupations about the future, which arise from self-love, delay the work of God in us and hinder his purposes, without even furthering our material interests. I need to be very watchful about this . . . Let whoever will pass before me and go on ahead; I stay here where Providence has placed me, with no anxieties, leaving the way clear for others."[7]

In 1919, after he had found and furnished an apartment: "I pledge myself especially to seek perfect poverty of spirit in absolute detachment from myself, never feeling any anxiety about positions, career, distinctions or anything else . . . Experience teaches me to be aware of responsibilities. These are solemn enough in themselves, if assumed under obedience, but terrifying for whoever has sought them for himself, pushing himself forward without being called upon . . . forward, forward, whoever wants to go ahead! I envy none of these fortunate souls."8

Jesus, who is most pure and chaste, posed, for the first time in this world, the question of freely chosen celibacy. He has said that there were three kinds of permanent renunciation of marriage: some cannot marry because of natural impotence; others, by violence and through the fault of others; others, finally, could marry, but by a free and carefully considered decision do not marry "for the sake of the kingdom of heaven," from superior motives, not without being supported by a kind of gift and special love from God (Mt 19:1112). This is perfect chastity, which many men and women practice, and to which many of you, I hope, will commit yourselves in a definitive way by the subdiaconate, looking on it from now on as the "jewel of the Catholic priesthood" (Pius XII).

But first you must properly understand the words "for the sake of the kingdom of heaven." We do not choose celibacy because we feel a kind of contempt for marriage, which should actually be respected and venerated as something sacred and a sacrament; nor because we want to ennoble ourselves by acquiring a magnificent balance and control over our senses; nor to exercise at a high level the virtues of temperance and purity.

The question is much deeper. The question, for example, of being able to say: "Lord I want to love you very much, without any third person between you and me having a right to my special love, and without having to feel that I am *divided*, as St. Paul would say, between you and a wife" (1 Cor 7:32 and 43).

And again: "Precisely because I love you, Lord, I would like to have all the time possible at my disposal to make you known to others, to serve you in the persons of the poor, the sick, sinners, and children!" Or: "Lord, it is difficult to love you as I want to, 'with all my heart, with all my soul'! And to opt definitely, once and for all, for you, and to take away the means for having second thoughts about the decision I have made! And to leave secondary goods for superior ones! Well, I am vowing myself to perfect chastity and I will bear with your help generously and happily, the sacrifices that it involves; if you think best, make use of me as a sign, as a help, as an encouragement to my brothers who find it more difficult than I do to observe your law and who need to see one of your maxims incarnate in a person whom they can reach out and touch! It is an obligation, I understand, that of being a sign of you and your Gospel, but, I trust in your support in fulfilling it!"

We say all this, after having serenely examined even the objections that we often hear made. Yet they are far from new. St. Francis de Sales heard exactly the same ones in his time. It so happened that, when he was preaching in Chablais, an old Protestant woman gave up, one after the other, all the difficulties against Catholicism, except this one: why do Catholic priests not marry? This one remained fixed in her head like a nail, in spite of the saint's repeated explanations. One day he thought that he had finally convinced her, and then he saw her come the next day with the old objections and some new ones as well. And then he began to repeat his explanations again, always calm, always patient, without regretting the precious time that was passing, until he happened to put forth a simple but fitting argument: "Madame," he said, "suppose that I were married and that today I had a wife and children. Do you think that I would have had so much time to listen to you and to talk with you?" His listener was struck by this reflection, which was for her the argument that settled the question, or as Dante would say, the "seal to undeceive every man"!

Finally, Jesus was meek and humble; he could find the roar of a lion when it came to the glory of the Father, or defending souls, but he forgave, sympathized, pardoned, and let himself be led to death like a lamb. And he taught us: "Learn from me, take the last place; serve others, do not ask to be served!"

This is what the One who St. Peter called "shepherd and guardian of our souls" (1 Pt 2:25) wanted and desired shepherds of souls to be. This is what you, who are serving your apprenticeship in this sublime pasturing, should try to be in the coming school year!

+Albino, bishop

Notes

1 *Opera* 3:195-204.

2 The Secretary of Vatican II was Archbishop (later Cardinal) Pericle Felici, who was also, coincidentally, the cardinal who announced Pope John Paul I's election from the balcony of St. Peter's Basilica.—Trans.

3 All this refers to the government persecution of Catholics in Mexico in the 1920's.—Trans.

4 *De servorum Dei beatificatione* III, Rome 1748, pp. 322-336.

5 The *Pontificale* or *Liber Pontificalis* is a liturgical book containing the rites and ceremonies celebrated by a bishop, such as confirmation and Holy Orders.—Trans.

6 Pope John XXIII, *Giornale dell'anima*, English trans. *Journal of a Soul* (New York: McGrawHill, 1964), p. 154.

7 Ibid., p. 184.

8 Ibid., p. 193.

A Healthy Pluralism

Homily for the Feast of the Immaculate Conception
December 8, 1972[1]

The three biblical readings that we have just listened to have told us, at least by way of allusion: Our Lady is wholly pure and wholly beautiful, because she has been guided by God toward a wonderful destiny. We will, however, hear an almost complete list of Mary's titles to greatness proclaimed in the preface. Here they are: "Preserved from every stain of original sin"; placed by God "to mark the beginning of the Church"; the "virgin most pure" of whom was born "the Son, the innocent Lamb who takes away our sins"; the "advocate of grace and model of sanctity" for the people of God. These few phrases contain in a nutshell almost all of Mariology: that of the past, the present and the future, which, in substance, will remain unchanged, although with the progress and the adaptation required by a healthy and honest pluralism.

But when is pluralism healthy and honest? I will try to tell you, because many people today are asking for an explanation of these words: "Pluralism in the Catholic Church."

I. THERE MUST BE PLURALISM

Let's begin with an observation: There is a certain pluralism in things. We human beings resemble one another in the same way as do leaves from the same tree, but we are never the same in everything; we also differ according to time and place; we have different cultures and civilizations.

That's not all; if we set out to describe the phenomena and events that we observe, we find that language will serve us, yes, but only up to a certain point. Often we have to say: "And now let's look at the other side of the coin." Often – pluralists by necessity – we must repeat the first exposition with a second and a third one, revised and expanded.

Again: Catholic institutions and doctrines also have their plurality. And therefore they possess human and changeable elements beside their divine and unchangeable elements. And therefore, they can incorporate, little by little, according to the time and place, new values, following the motto of Terence: "nothing human is alien to me."[2] And therefore the same unchangeable element can be considered under new and varied aspects. Jesus himself adapted his doctrine and his conduct to persons and circumstances. He fled from the people who wanted to "come and carry him off to make him king" (John 6:15); in view of his imminent passion, on the other hand, he himself prepared his triumphant entry into Jerusalem, and to the Pharisees made envious by the "Hosannas," he said: "If they were to keep silence, I tell you, the very stones would cry out" (Lk. 19:40). To the leper who had been cured, he said: "See to it that you tell no one" (Mt. 8:4). To the man from whom the demons had been cast out, on the other hand, he said: "Go home to your family and make it clear to them how much the Lord in his mercy has done for you" (Mk. 5:19).

And then there is the Holy Spirit, who of course works in the Church to keep her united, but with a unity that is harmonious, varied, and dynamic. The Spirit, said Manzoni, is light;

It pours from one thing to another
and stirs up varied colors
wherever it rests."[3]

The Council was aware of this state of things: "The inheritance transmitted to the Apostles has been accepted in various forms and manners, and from the very beginnings of the Church, it has had a varied development in various places, thanks to a similar variety of natural gifts and conditions of life";[4] "in the investigations of revealed truth, east and west have used different methods and approaches in understanding and proclaiming divine things. It is hardly surprising then, if sometimes one tradition has come nearer than the other to an apt appreciation of certain aspects of a revealed mystery, or has expressed them in a clearer manner. As a result, these various theological formations are often to be considered as complementary rather than conflicting."[5]

The most significant words on this matter, I think, are those pronounced by Pope John at the opening of the Council: "From the renewed, serene, and tranquil adherence to all of the teaching of the Church in its entirety and preciseness, as it still shines forth in the acts of the Council of Trent and the First Vatican Council, the Christian, Catholic and Apostolic spirit of the whole world expects a step forward toward a doctrinal penetration and a formation of conscience; in faithful and perfect conformity to the authentic doctrine, which, however, should be studied and expounded through the methods of research and through the literary forms of modern thought. The substance of the ancient doctrine of the deposit of faith is one thing, and the way in which it is presented, conserving at the same time its meaning and importance, is another."[6]

No wonder, then, that we talk about pluralism. We have always talked about it. St. Augustine, for example, once came across Psalm 45, which describes the "rainment threaded with spun gold" and the "embroidered apparel" worn by a queen. "This queen," he explained, "is the Church; that garment embroidered with many colors is the doctrine the Church professes." And he continues: "There is an African language, a Syrian language, a Greek language, a Hebrew language, and others: these languages make up the many-colored embroidery of the queen's garment." But he immediately adds: "Just as all the variety of the garments harmonize in unity, so also do all the languages in a single faith; there can be variety in the garments, but not division in the faith."[7]

II. CONDITIONS FOR A JUST PLURALISM

1. Here is the first condition of a healthy pluralism: that it does not endanger the unity of the faith. St. Paul appreciated and exalted variety in charisms, but he was uncompromising in matters of faith. He wrote to the Galatians: "Even if an angel from heaven should preach to you a Gospel not in accord with the one we delivered to you, let a curse be upon him" (Gal. 1:8). He recommended to Timothy: "Take as a model of sound teaching what you have heard me say . . . Guard the rich deposit of faith with the help of the Holy Spirit who dwells within us and flee novelties" (2 Tim. 1:13). To avoid the danger that pluralism would harm the faith, the ancient churches used the creed, or "symbol" of the faith, which acted as an identity card among Christians. In fact, "symbol" was originally the name for an object that, after being divided in two, was entrusted to families bound by an alliance. With the passing of time and changing of generations, the verification of the alliance was made in this way: the two pieces were exhibited; if, when put together, they fit perfectly, those who exhibited them recognized each other as brothers and allies.

Today too the Church is concerned that there be an identity card for Catholics to hold on to with conviction and courage. And they should not consent, when a doctrine has been defined or presented as obligatory by the Magisterium, to submit it to a free examination, to subordinate it to the criticism of the secular sciences, to public opinion, to the current vogues in philosophy, or to the tastes and perversions of newspapers and magazines. It is too important a matter for us to be able to yield on this point. No fanaticism and ultra-conservatism, and witch hunts, but firmness is absolutely necessary. "Faith is the beginning of human salvation, the foundation and root of all justification."[8] When it is a matter of faith, says Chrysostom, we must imitate the prudence of the snake. It yields everything; it permits the rest of its body to be trampled, as long as its head remains safe. "The same with you," he concludes.

"Hand over everything, except for your faith: money, your body, even life itself, because faith is the head and the root."9

"But what about the Council?" they say to me, "didn't it speak of religious liberty?" Of course, in the sense that a person cannot be forced by any human power to accept the revealed truth if he does not want to. No one, however, outside of the Magisterium, can arrogate to himself the freedom to determine which are the truths revealed by God.

They have also told me that in regard to the truth we are all cripples; we are not allowed to attain to it; the pasture of human reason is the debatable, not the certain; no one can claim to have the truth in his pocket. That hurts me. As a man, I don't want to do God the wrong of supposing that he first gives me a mind hungry for certainty, and then takes away from me every certainty with a new torture of Tantalus. I don't feel I can state with Luther that reason is a drunken man on horseback, nor do I want to be sent back more than 2,000 years to the skepticism of the philosopher Pyrrho. He too said that we can be certain of nothing. One day, however, when he was being chased by a mad dog, he took to quick and desperate flight. He was, therefore, certain of at least two things: that that dog existed, and that his own life was in danger! As a Catholic then, I have the duty to maintain that the Pope, with the bishops united to him and also alone, is assisted by the Holy Spirit in order to be able to present to us without error those truths that have truly been revealed by God for our salvation.

2. Another condition for a legitimate pluralism: that it preserves charity and prudence. "Is it or is it not permissible to eat the meat of animals that have been sacrificed?" asked the Corinthians. "In itself, it is, there is pluralism," answered St. Paul. But he added, "Take care however, lest in exercising your right, you become an occasion of sin to the weak . . . if food causes my brother to sin, I will never eat meat again" (1 Cor. 8:9,13). Analogically, some priests ask me: "May we or may we not present freely to the

faithful an opinion that we find agreeable, and which is supported by learned theologians?" I respond with *Communio et Progressio*: "It is necessary to make a clear distinction between the field of scientific research and that of the instruction of the faithful. In the first the scholars are to have the freedom necessary to their activity, and a chance to provide others with the results of their research by the publication of articles in reviews and books. In the field of religious instruction, only those things should be proposed as doctrines of the Church which are recognized as such by the authentic Magisterium with the addition of those theological conclusions that can be stated with certainty."[10]

A timely directive. The "faith of the coal-seller" (Go ask the Pope what I believe!) by itself is not enough, especially today. But on the other hand, the faithful have the right to know without confusion and unwarranted mixture what has truly been revealed by God. When instead they hear one thing stated by the so-called "conservatives" on the right, which, on the other hand, is denied by the so-called "progressives" on the left, they are disoriented, they become discouraged, and their faith is choked and paralyzed by doubt. Those on the right want an irrational and anti-historical refusal to change. But on the left there is often exaggerated impatience. They would like a new reform every day, and a continual stream of changing experiences. Perhaps they speak of sharing and co-responsibility holy things but deep down, what they are imagining, at times, is a flat communitarianism with perfect equality of gifts, authority and responsibility for everyone: *todos caballeros* [everyone a knight]. The primacy of the Pope is usurped by the episcopal college; the infallibility of the Pope and the councils is replaced by Kunghian "indefectibility", which states: Pope and councils make mistakes; Christians, assisted by the Spirit, however, can find a way to correct those errors; research at the level of the human sciences takes the place of the supernatural meaning of the faith; Vatican I is declared to be suppressed by Vatican II; Chapter III of *Lumen gentium* is swallowed by Chapter II. All of this produces a very widespread confusion among those who belong neither to the right nor to the left. If there is a time when priests must not dissent from the pulpit, and must be "preachers of the certain, the essential and the whole essential," it is now, on pain of increasing the confusion.

3. Along with a healthy pluralism, there must also be love and an authentic sense of the Church. St. Paul differed from the other Apostles because of the special way he was called, and because, contrary to what they did, he baptized even those who were not circumcised. In order to defend this pluralism, he went with Barnabas from Antioch to Jerusalem and was not satisfied until James, Peter and John had approved his practices, and given him and Barnabas their hands as a sign of full agreement (cf. Gal 2:29). Shortly afterwards, in Antioch, seeing that Peter, out of fear, avoided those who had been circumcised, with the danger that the Antiochian community would be split in two, Paul reproved him frankly and openly (cf. Gal 2:1114). A champion of pluralism and of unity, but even more of impassioned love for the Church! Those who appeal to pluralism also protest that they want the good of the Church. But what Church? The Council has stressed that the Church is a communion. Some understand it as a *parathetical* communion, or a communion of equals. The Council, on the other hand, understands it as a *hierarchical* community, that is a community in ascending degrees: it has indeed said that the bishops must be "brothers among brothers," but it has added that the bishops "govern the particular churches entrusted to them as vicars and ambassadors of Christ. This they do by their counsel, exhortations and example, as well, indeed, by their authority and sacred power. This power they use only for the edification of their flock."[11]

Some tend to take the word "authority" only in its corrupt sense of "power" or "lust for power." "Today," says Paul VI, "the character of service in the authority of the Church is being stressed so much that it can have two dangerous consequences in our perceptions of how the Church itself is constituted: that of assigning priority to the community, recognizing in it effective charismatic powers of its own, and that of ignoring the authoritative aspect of the Church, to the marked discredit of the canonical functions in ecclesial society: from which is derived the opinion of an indiscriminate liberty, an autonomous form of pluralism, and an accusation of juridicialism against tradition and the normative practice of the hierarchy."[12] Authority and charisms are therefore not opposed to each other in the Church; the first is the vehicle and guardian of the second. It is to the Apostles alone and to their successors that the following words of Christ refer: "Full authority has been given to me both in heaven and on earth. Go, therefore, and make disciples of all the nations. Baptize them in the name of the Father, the Son, and the Holy Spirit" (Mat 28:18-19); "Whatever you declare bound on earth shall be held bound in heaven, and whatever you declare loosed on earth shall be held loosed in heaven" (Mat 18:18); "He who hears you, hears me. He who rejects you, rejects me. And he who rejects me, rejects him who sent me" (Lk 10:16).

To Peter, then, the office of binding and loosing was given personally (Mat 16:19 and cf. Mat 18:18; Jon 20:23), while he is established as the "rock" on which the Church is built, that is, as the "visible principle and foundation of the unity of both the bishops and the mass of the faithful."[13]

4. A healthy pluralism, finally, is respectful of the value of tradition. It is the thought on which Paul VI insisted when he spoke to us in the Basilica of San Marco and appealed to the "goodness and wisdom of the Venetian people."[14] "To receive and to transmit with fidelity and in integrity," the Pope said, "is the duty of our moment in history." In addition to doctrine, this also refers to "ecclesiastical discipline, worship and Christian piety, spirituality, asceticism . . . all values that are experienced, confirmed and guaranteed in various ways by the teaching and the directives of ecclesiastical authority, by the lives of the saints, and by the *sensus fidelium*." And he

continued: "What a very rich and precious patrimony! A patrimony which a certain conformistic, iconoclastic, secularizing and desacralizing mentality is now threatening to undermine and scatter. It is easy to take away and to suppress, but it is not easy to find a substitute, provided that you are not looking for just any substitute, but a substitute that has an authentic value."

Some people fear that love for tradition is ultra-conservatism. "On the contrary," answers the Pope, "it requires moral strength, discipline in thought and habit, solidity, profundity, and a capacity for resistance to the ephemeral fashion of the time; it requires, in other words, personality, that human and Christian personality that is so much discussed, but that is not so easy to form and to possess." True words, these words of the Pope, and illustrated by what we observe every day. And that is: meetings, conventions and assemblies are multiplying, all with the declared aim of renewing and protesting. But at these gatherings you always hear the same slogans, things go the way that a few people want them to go; stereotypical formulas are used. The same people who cover their ears at the very mention of the axioms of the scholastic philosophers and the dogmas of the Council of Trent appear decked out and wrapped up in pseudo-technical jargon and the neologisms that are appearing in the fashionable reviews. More conformist than the conformists!

The problem of tradition, the Pope also said, is similar to the problem of Venice: "to endure and to grow more faithful to itself." And he concluded: "How many great initiatives the Venetian church has been able to promote in the course of its history, in order to confront and to solve the problems of the time! What works and how many works has it carried out! And how numerous the ranks of its saints! All this shows, then that you know how to maintain drive and enthusiasm for a forward leap, while keeping your creative ability awake and renewing it in view of an adequate and farseeing solution to the problems of today and of tomorrow." In these last words is the true formula for pluralism: "A forward leap," "creative ability," looking at "today and tomorrow," but without rejecting whatever comes from the past that is good and of enduring value.

Notes

1 *Opera* 5:503-508.

2 Terence, *Heuton Timoroumenos* [The Self Tormentor] l. 77.—Trans.

3 *La Pentecost.*

4 UR no. 14 [545]

5 Ibid., no. 17 [553].

6 Pope John's speech opening the Council, October 11, 1962. See Abbott, *The Documents of Vatican II*, p. 715.—Trans.

7 *Enarrationes in Psalmos*, 44:24; PL 36, col. 509.

8 DS, no. 1532.

9 John Chrysostom, *Homiliae*, 33:12; PG 57, col. 390.

10 Pontifical Council for Social Communications, *Communio et Progressio*, May 23, 1971, 118.

11 LG, no. 27 [351].

12 Paul VI, Discourse to the Sacred Roman Rota, January 28, 1971.

13 LG, no. 23.

14 Pope Paul VI to the clergy and people in the Basilica of San Marco, Venice, September 16, 1972.—Trans.

Meditation at an Ecumenical Prayer Service

Basilica of San Marco,
January 19, 1971[1]

The first of the two readings (Acts 2:42-47, Rom 8:18-25), is a little picture of the first Christian community; the second traces the dimensions of our redemption.

1. What dimensions? Eschatological ones, in short. There is "a glory to be revealed in us," says Paul. It is this that we look to in the "sufferings of this present time." It follows from this that we Christians are a kind of a traveling caravan. We must strive toward the future as individuals and as a Church. As individuals we must continue to renew ourselves; the image of God, stamped in us at Baptism, is often clouded, soiled and disfigured; we must compare it again with the original, lift it up and bring it back to being a true and faithful image. As a Church, it is *"semper reformanda* [always needing to be reformed]: but, says Congar, "she advances through history constantly hesitating, almost stumbling through trials and tribulations . . . she advances by groping her way, although consoled by the grace of God."

2. In contrast with this weakness of the present, Paul broadens the horizons and gives a truly cosmic vision of redemption. The material and rational world, created for man, he says, follows his fate. It was cursed by sin, and now finds itself in an enforced state of servitude, in the absurd, violent and degrading situation of having to be a slave to corruption and death. But it will be liberated from this situation, when the body of man is fully clothed with all the glory of the resurrected Christ. Here it is then, this whole created

world, in "eager expectation" (*apokaradokia*), here it is, as though it were a person, standing, its head held tensely and straining to observe, its body trembling with impatient anxiety for renewal and redemption, its supplicating eyes turned towards man. And what does it ask man? "Not to deny the solidarity that unites them and associates them! "Help me in the work of liberation, in bringing forth the new universe that is waiting to be born."

3. This is the groan emitted by the world, not in a state of agony, but in the travail of giving birth. With it there is our "groan": "We too groan inwardly," says Paul. Our bodies, in fact, have not yet been transfigured in glory like that of Christ, our salvation can still be at risk, we are in the phase of hope. Fortunately, if we are faithful, our hope will not be disappointed, given that we have the "first fruits of the Spirit" (v. 23). It is a groan to which the Father will grant an answer.

4. Coming to the little picture described in Acts, we find that the first baptized people "devoted themselves to the apostles' instruction." Here we are talking about hearing the word of God in the religious sense, or faith, without which all Christian churches believe it is "impossible to please God."

I once thought that there were difficulties for the faith today only among Catholics. I now find that there is also serious alarm for the integrity of the faith in other Christian churches.

Let us be on our guard, said Karl Barth, against Protestant "Ottavianis" and Catholic "Bultmanns!"[2] He was joking, but Visser t' Hooft, the former secretary of the World Council of Churches, spoke in earnest six years ago, when he warned against syncretism. "It is syncretism," he wrote, "to state that the revelation given by God is not a unique phenomenon; that there exist many opposite roads leading to the Divinity; that all the formulations of religious truths or experiences are, by their very nature, inadequate to express these truths; that we must harmonize the various religious concepts among themselves as best we can in order to open the way to a universal religion, which proposes the benefit of mankind." It seems to me that the work *Foi en crise* [Faith in Crisis] by Max Thurian,[3] whose thought I will summarize very briefly, is a complete and at the same time, serene, treatment of the subject. Christians today, says Thurian, want very much to meet the needs of the world; therefore faith is obliged to confront new situations and new risks; this is the reason why not a few of the baptized, no matter what Christian confession to, they belong, have fallen into difficulties.

Let it be clearly understood, adds Thurian: in speaking of a "crisis," we must not always be dramatic, there are crises and crises. Any person who is growing experiences good periods and difficult periods; it is equally valid for individuals and for communities.

The present moment is a difficult one for the Church, which is in the process of growing; she has received a great legacy from the past, but she cannot enjoy it in peace, because we live in times in which everything is being argued all over again. Looking at the history of the past, from that excellent observatory that is Taize, Thurian says that there have actually been moments worse than this. The Christian faith moved from the Jewish culture to the Greek; the first with a highly concrete vocabulary, the second, all intellectualism: in this process, the faith risked being absorbed or transformed. It then passed from the theological speculations of the Greek world into the hands of the Roman civilization, which was completely founded on law: another difficult moment. Later on, there were Constantine, Charlemagne, and the crises of the fourteenth and nineteenth centuries.

Nothing new today then, except for the enormous development of the means of communication. Thanks to them, some simple working hypotheses, which the specialists have the right to know and the capacity to understand, are very rapidly popularized over a wide area among masses of non-specialists who understand them the wrong way or understand them imperfectly, which does great harm to the people of God. Researchers in biology and chemistry, says Thurian, have developed a kind of convention: "Let's exchange the results of our research in closed congresses, in reports that are crammed with formulas, in reviews for the initiated, but let's pledge ourselves to not put on sale medicines and drugs that do not offer sufficient guarantees." There seems to be a need, he continues, for theologians to do something similar: form a "team" and have enough pastoral sense not to popularize too quickly discoveries that are only temporary stages on the long road of research. A person is not a true theologian unless he has a sense of the spiritual edification of Christians, and unless he understands that the truth he is researching is the strength and consolation of the poorest people.

TRUE ECUMENISM

5. Acts continues: "They devoted themselves . . . to the communal life . . . Those who believed shared all things in common; they would sell their property and goods, dividing everything" (v. 42-43). It is loving each other, being a family, especially with the poor: it is love that cements the unity of the first Christian community. "That all may be one, as you, Father, are in me and I in you," Christ had prayed (John 17:21). Before praying this way, however, an ecumenist *ante litteram*, he had shown by his example the way to practice ecumenism. He had not come to abolish the religion of the Chosen People, but to complete it, working and moving in an atmosphere of troubling schism between Jews and Samaritans. In that atmosphere, he had shown very sensitive love, but also great courage and respect for the liberty of others. Courageously he stressed that the only one of the ten lepers who came to thank him was a Samaritan. In a marvelous parable he presented the "Good Samaritan" as a model to whom? To the Jews, for whom every Samaritan is worse than an excommunicated person. Towards the Samaritan woman, he used the greatest kindness, frankly breaking down the social barriers that had been erected between the two different religious confessions.

He is faced with still more sensitive divisions. After the discourse on the "bread of life," in fact, many disciples leave him, setting in motion a schism that places the existence of the *"pusillus grex"* [little flock] in jeopardy. He respects the liberty of all and asks those who remain: "Do you want to leave me too?" (John 6:67). At that moment, he allows the existence of the group to depend on the voluntary support of a few fishermen.

Later, surrounded by threatening and doctrinally aggressive adversaries like the Scribes, the Pharisees and the Sadducees, he does not impose his own doctrine by force, he does not impede the spreading of contrary opinions, he only "testifies to the truth", certain that "anyone committed to the truth hears my voice" (Jn 18:37).

6: Acts again: "They devoted themselves . . . to the breaking of the bread" (v. 42).

It is the technical phrase used to indicate the rite of the Eucharist. All Christians recognize that this rite constitutes – as the *Vocabulaire biblique* directed by the Protestant J. J. von Allmen says – *"un des marques de l'Église et comme un des piliers essentiels sur lequel elle a été edifiée"* [One of the marks of the Church, and as one of the essential pillars on which it has been built]. We know this: we are all in agreement on the importance of the celebration of the Eucharist, but the various Christian churches and communities differ among themselves in declaring the exact meaning of the celebration itself. Recently, however, Professor Von Allmen, working for the doctrinal Commission "Faith and Constitution" of the World Council of Churches, has revealed with some surprise that there was agreement on many points and that understanding can progress at least on the following points: *anamnesis* and *epiclesis* in the Eucharist, catholicity of the Eucharist, Eucharist and *agape.* [4] It is a sign, a small step, it is a little light of hope, which, along with other things, encourages us to continue the doctrinal studies and meetings that are the most difficult in ecumenism.

7. The first community, Acts says again, by its behavior, won "the approval of all the people" who were not yet baptized. This is being "for the world", being missionaries by our testimony, being saviors as well as saved. They said one day to Karl Barth, "Do you know that there are many non-Christians among your listeners?" And Barth, smiling: "It's all the same to me; in fact, that's all we need, for the Christian faith to become an agent of separation or discrimination among men! On the contrary, it is the most powerful motive for bringing them closer together and uniting them, and it is also the imperative of the Church's mission."

8. "They devoted themselves to . . . the prayers" (v. 42) ". . . They went to the temple area together every day" (v. 46). Here all the Christian churches are in agreement. And it would be a serious calamity, if they fall away from the practice of either personal or community prayer. Christ prayed alone, in seclusion and in the silence of the night, with his apostles, with the people in the temple and in the synagogue. It would be useless to reunite the various churches in unity with ecumenism, unless it is to better speak of God and to be more effectively heard by him. It is risky for discussion to increase out of all proportion in our churches, while prayer diminishes. On the other hand, prayer is the soul of ecumenism and of unity. This was understood by Luther, who in 1522 composed the following very beautiful prayer:

> Oh God of unity we pray to you and we implore you;
> Gather, by the Holy Spirit, all that is scattered:
> reunite and reconcile what is divided;
> Grant also that we may return to your unity,
> that we may seek your one and eternal Truth;
> that we may reject all discord
> in order to arrive at unity of feeling, will, and knowledge,
> spirit and understanding,
> according to Jesus Christ our Lord;

Then, with one voice, in perfect unity,
we will be able to praise you and celebrate you,
Heavenly Father, Father of Our Lord Jesus Christ, Through
the same Jesus Christ Our Lord
in the Holy Spirit.

Notes

1 *Opera*, 5:110-15.

2 Cardinal Alfredo Ottaviani became famous as one of the most conservative bishops at the Second Vatican Council, while Rudolf Bultmann was a very radical Protestant theologian and biblical scholar.—Trans.

3 Max Thurian, *La Foi en crise* (Taizé: Presses de Taizé, 1968). Max Thurian (1921-1996), a Protestant founded with Brother Roger Schutz, the ecumenical monastic community of Taizé in the 1940's. He attended Vatican II as an observer and consulted on the liturgical reform after the Council. He converted to the Catholic faith and was ordained a priest in 1987.

4 Anamnesis refers to the Eucharist as a memorial of Christ's passion, death and resurrection. Epiclesis refers to the calling down of the Holy Spirit on the bread and wine. Agape is the Greek word for "love," and refers to the effect of the Eucharist in binding Christians in together in love.—Trans.

Women in Church and Society

Homily for the Feast of the Assumption[1]

August 15, 1975

Today the Catholic Church celebrates the assumption of the Virgin into a glory which makes her, as Dante would say, "higher than any creature."

The climate of "neofeminism" which is manifested here and there, however, has prompted some people to say: "Yes, you praise *her* to the skies, but you have always kept other women in subordinate activities; you haven't known how to recognize the dignity of women; because of this, it is without the Church or against the Church that women today, after centuries of Christianity, are winning their own liberty and vindicating their own rights."

I would like to respond to this reproach, which is only partly justified, gathering some elements from the Bible, from history, and from the attitude of the Church today.

I. THE BIBLE

1. "God created man in His own image; in the image of God He created them; male and female he created them" (Gen. 1:27). It is the first biblical reference to women; it is apparent from it that men and women are a true image of God only if taken together; separated from one another, they are a partial divine image.

The second biblical reference is also significant. With a popular image Adam is presented as creator and master of the world, and yet he seems joyless, isolated among beings that are magnificent, yes, but inferior to him. But as soon as God presents the woman to him, Adam is astonished and ecstatically gives voice to the world's first love song: "This one, at last, is flesh of my flesh and bone of my bone . . . for this reason a man will leave his father and mother and the two will become one flesh" (Gen. 2:23-24).

Here, along with women, it also speaks of love and conjugal union. The love is such that it prevails over filial love, the union is such that, thanks to it, the personality of the man is completed in that of the woman, and the personality of the woman in that of the man.

A magnificent design, honorable for man as well as for woman; unfortunately, sin disturbs it. In fact, we hear God say, to the woman: "With pain will you bring forth children; your urge will be towards your husband, but he will dominate you" (Gen. 3:16). The woman is subject to pains and suffering that should not have taken place; in the man, to the damage of man himself, authoritarianism ("he will dominate you") will often take the place of sensitivity and tenderness towards his wife; often he will fail to understand all the wealth of giving and love that a woman is capable of.

2. Is the Bible "natalist"? That is, does it see a woman primarily as the mother of a large number of children? Certainly, God said to the first human couple: "be fruitful and multiply, replenish the earth" (Gen 1:28), and often fertility appears to the Jews as one of the greatest blessings (cf. Ps 127). However, it is also stressed that the important thing is not to have many children, but well-brought up children. "Do not yearn for worthless children. . . Even if they be many, do not rejoice in them if they do not have fear of the Lord" (Sir 16:1-2). Elsewhere it says that the worth of a woman is not in fertility, but in the woman herself. "Blessed is she who, childless and undefiled, knew not transgression of the marriage bed" (Wis 3:13). "He who finds a wife finds happiness; it is a favor he receives from the Lord" (Prov 18:22). Still elsewhere married love is exalted. In the Song of Songs, the beloved lets her passion for her lover burst out in ardent expressions that astonish us Westerners. Proverbs urges the husband: "Find joy in the wife of your youth; your lovely hind, your graceful doe, she will keep you company, let her tenderness inebriate you always" (Prov 5:18-19). "Too often," Pope Paul VI would comment here, "the Church has

appeared, quite unjustly, distrustful of human love. Because of this we wish today to say clearly: No, God is not the enemy of the great human realities; in no way does the Church disregard the values lived every day by thousands of families."2

3. The Old Testament, according to some, confined women to the home, segregating her from the public; only Jesus Christ had the courage to remove her from segregation. That is not completely accurate. People will reproach the "Praise of the worthy woman" in Proverbs because it exalts her only as the stay-at-home housewife. And yet, the woman of Proverbs is compared to "merchant ships, she secures her provisions from afar . . . She picks out a field and purchases it." Housewife, yes, but anything but shut up in the house. Nor was Deborah, the prophetess who sat under the palm tree to resolve the people's disputes, shut up in the house. In addition to wisdom, she possessed abundant courage, so much that she instilled it in that timid man who was the Judge Barak, and that she personally led an army to victory. (Judges 4 and 5). A prophetess also was Huldah, who, when consulted, was not afraid to goad King Josiah to reform with terrible and threatening words (cf. 2 Kings 14:20). Even stronger than Hulda was Judith, the widow who with force and firmness, decided, acted, and killed in order to save her own city, and who was afterwards received by the people in triumph.

4. Another accusation: The Bible gives a pessimistic view of women. I answer: it gives a realistic view. What good could you say of Potiphar's wife, Delilah, Jezebel, Atalia or Herodias? At the time of Amos the prophet, there are women who "oppress the weak, crush the poor and say to their husbands: "bring us a drink." No wonder the prophet branded them with the too heavy phrase "cows of Basan" (Amos 4:1). Among the biblical authors, the author of Sirach has been judged the most antifeminist. In reality, he sets side by side two pictures: over here, the hag-courtesan; over there the gentle and sensible wife. Of the first he says: "I would rather live with a lion or

a dragon than with a wicked woman" (Sir 25:15). Of the second: "A woman's grace gives joy to her husband . . . there is no compensation for a courteous woman" (Sir 26:13-14). The wise women of the Bible are legion: it is enough to recall the wives of the patriarchs: among them Rachel; to obtain her, Jacob served for seven years, and "they seemed to him only a few days, so great was his love for her" (Gen 29:30). Some of the women who strayed out of weakness were rehabilitated: for example, of the four women who appear in the Gospel genealogies of Christ, three were sinners: Rahab, a harlot, Thamar, who had committed incest, and Bathsheba, an adulteress. And Christ accepted them as his ancestors and allowed himself to be counted as their descendant!

5. A unique place in the Bible is reserved for Mary, chosen to be the Mother of God and to cooperate concretely in the Incarnation and Redemption. In the past, we stressed, as Mary herself did, the gratuitousness of the divine choice ("He has looked on the lowliness of his handmaid" Lk 2:48). Today we also stress Mary's response, her "yes," or her "free and active consent."[3] A responsible and courageous "yes" to a task as vast as the world, a "yes" that stimulates women of today and says to them: "If you want to imitate Our Lady, you must not be afraid to take on great tasks in public life."

6. Biblical passages that are difficult to interpret or to harmonize with each other can find a plausible solution. I will give an example. Paul proclaims: "There is neither Jew nor Greek, slave nor free, man nor woman, because you are all one in Christ Jesus" (Gal 3:28). Christ, on the other hand, appears to have entrusted the external guidance of the Church to the Apostles alone. The same Paul wills that "women keep silent in the Churches, because it is not permitted them to speak" (1 Cor 14:34). And he prescribes: "Let wives be submissive to their husbands, as to the Lord," (Eph 5:22), "Wives, be submissive to your husbands, as is fitting in the Lord.

Husbands, love your wives" (Col 3:18). How can these passages be reconciled? I will try to say.

First, the equality of men and women, of slave and free, is equality "in Christ," in having the same identical salvation from him, in having the same brotherhood with him. Along with this equality, which is an incomparable gift, there can also be secondary disparities in the ethical and social order, at least within the limits of a certain time and place.

Second: the priesthood and the leadership of the Church are given by God only in view of a service to others: those who receive them have the duty to use them correctly, not the right to boast of them as forms of preeminence or exploit to their own advantage.

Third, according to Paul, women could not speak authoritatively in the meetings; they could speak on the other hand, if invested with the prophetic charism. Paul himself foresees this possibility, asking that when prophesying, the women keep their heads covered (cf. 1 Cor 11:5); in Cesarea, he met four prophetesses, daughters of the deacon Phillip (Acts 21:9); he speaks with lively gratitude of Chloe (cf. 1 Cor 1:11), Priscilla, Triphaena and Triphosa, Persis and other women who have "worked for the Lord" (cf. Rom 16:34, 12).

Fourth: it is difficult to deny some kind of submission by the wife to her own husband; the submission, however, "can vary, in degree and in manner, according to the different conditions of people, place and time."4

I. HISTORY

When looking at the past, we must admit that there have been many inequalities that have disadvantaged women in society, which has been influenced by the Church, and in the Church itself. They can be explained in part by popular prejudice, by the philosophy and mentality that prevailed at the time, by male authoritarianism, by human passions, and by ignorance. However, women have received a great deal from the Church: as consecrated virgins, and as wives and mothers, they have been surrounded by the Church with respect and honor: gigantic progress, compared to the way they were treated under paganism; the very devotion offered to the Virgin has flowed over in part onto women. Have they failed to receive everything they have hoped for? It is true, but it is so difficult to go against interests, institutions and mentalities that took root centuries ago! In any case, it is only fair not to invent faults, and not to exaggerate those that may exist.

8. The Church, I have heard it said, has inherited the mentality of the Jews who, at the time of Jesus, believing women inferior to men, exempted them from morning prayer and from prayer before meals, and limited their participation in public prayer. The Talmud is used to support this objection. But the Talmud was written four hundred years after Christ: we cannot deny that it can help us in understanding the Gospel at certain points, but it is also true that it is full of fables and childish and bizarre things. We should not go along with certain ancient rabbis, who considered the Bible silver and the Talmud gold, going so far as to assert that God Himself reads the Talmud and that His favorite chapter is the one "of the red heifer"! We have Acts which, when it shows the first little Christian community in prayer while awaiting the Holy Spirit, says that it was composed of the eleven Apostles, and of "some women along with Mary, the mother of Jesus" (Acts 1:14). As for public prayer, it is enough to recall the biblical canticles of Miriam, the sister of Moses (Ex. 15:20), Hannah (1 Sam 2:1-10), Deborah (Judg 5:2-31), Jdt 16:1-17), and above all of Mary (Lk 1:46-55), very widely used for centuries in the Liturgy of the Church.

9. Expressions by theologians and the Fathers of the Church that are derogatory to women are cited. But one swallow, as Aristotle said, does not make a spring. Other Fathers and theologians praise women to the skies. I will cite St. Jerome, considered a misogynist

by those who have read him superficially. In the introduction to *Sophonia* he writes: "It would take whole books to tell everything that is great in women."[5] Again, he writes, "the weaker sex has conquered the world, the stronger sex has been conquered by the world";[6] "while the men were silent, Hulda, Anna and Deborah prophesied; and therefore in the service of God what is important is not the difference between the sexes, but the differences between spirits."[7] And for Jerome these were not just words: in Rome the noblewoman Marcella collaborated with him on the translation of the New Testament; in Bethlehem Paula and Eustochium helped him revise his translation of the Gospels and also aided in the very difficult task of translating the books of the Old Testament from the Hebrew.

10. It has been observed that there have been very few women canonized in comparison to men, especially bishops and members of religious orders; and few married women in comparison to nuns and sisters. The observation is just, but it is no surprise to those who know the *iter* of canonization. In the high Middle Ages, canonizations took place by popular acclamation; it was natural that the virtues of a bishop of an abbot would easily become known; the virtues of married women dedicated to home and children, on the other hand, remained hidden from most people. Later canonization required a difficult and laborious *iter*; it was tackled by those who were able to organize: dioceses and religious orders. As soon as the sanctity of married women emerged and was approved, however, the Church was very happy to grant them a cult. I recall, among the earliest such married women St. Monica, St. Margaret of Scotland, St. Elizabeth of Hungary, St. Elizabeth of Portugal, St. Hedwig, St. Bridget, and St. Frances of Rome. As for the sisters, it is obvious that the religious life is an aid to a holy life; on the other hand, I would not like anyone to forget what Pius XII wanted to recall, and that is: there are women and men who need marriage in order to maintain their equilibrium. A normal woman, however, if virtuous,

can preserve her equilibrium even without a husband and children; the state of virginity can permit her the full development of her own personality as much as marriage and more.

11. Has the Church despised women, keeping them away from study, and neglecting their intellectual and spiritual formation? I will cite only a few names and facts. There have been abbesses recognized by the Church who carried the pastoral staff, wore the miter, and ring and exercised for centuries an authentic authority over abbeys and parishes, analogous to that of bishops. In the branch of the Benedictine order dependent on Fontevrault, the abbess had administrative authority over the monks. A similar situation existed in the Order of the Most Holy Savior founded by St. Bridget of Sweden. The Cistercian abbesses of Huelgas and Conversano also enjoyed very ample privileges over parishes and ecclesiastical bodies. For Conversano, (*"Monstrum Apuliae"*) a document of the Sacred Congregation of the Council of 1709 recognized such centuries-old privileges, though it reduced them: miter and pastoral staff, yes, but deposited on a side table beside the abbess; a kiss, yes, but on the gloved hand; priests were not to genuflect before the abbess, but only bow.[8] These are exceptions; they prove, however, that the Church does not despise women.

In medieval monasteries for women study for girls was honored. At the time of the Carolingian emperors, the Duchess Dhuoda was able to compose a *"Liber Manualis,"* which was meant to be a manual for the perfect Christian and the perfect aristocrat. Shortly after Dhuoda, in Germany, Roswitha, instructed by the nuns, knew Greek, Latin, music and philosophy, and imitated Terence by writing dramatic works and legends in impeccable Latin verse. Catherine of Siena and Teresa of Avila figure among the greatest "Doctors of the Church." At the time of the Counter Reformation, Catherine Cybo learned Hebrew and Greek in order to know the Scriptures better. Francis de Sales, perhaps the greatest spiritual director that the Church has had, was director to a great many women. If the letters we still have from him were addressed to great ladies and nuns, it is certain that he listened to many women of the people, and peasant women: when the death of Annette Boutey, a country woman, was announced to him, he couldn't help weeping, knowing how great she was in the sight of God.

In his *Treatise on the Education of Young Girls*, Fenelon wanted them to be taught a little bit of everything, including Latin. He was anticipated Rousseau as a genial and open educator: Let the woman educator, he said, make herself loved in order to make herself obeyed without commanding; and let her inspire love for the subjects rather than impose them. In the great work of Henri Brémond (*Histoire littéraire du sentiment religieux en France*) there is a chapter titled "The Great Abbesses." It is about a large number of courageous and well-prepared women, of great spiritual stature, who in the 17th century, undertook and conducted nearly to its end an energetic reform of the monasteries. All of France was watching them: from the King and Queen to the bishops, to the most eminent men of the time, and to the humble people. With St. Vincent de Paul, the nuns were succeeded by the sisters. After the French Revolution, there has been no social misery or need that they have not devoted themselves to: Third World countries, those infected with cholera, the elderly, prisoners, orphans, the sick, babies, children, young girls in danger, prostitutes who want to change their lives. Strange! Certain priests today do not appreciate the strictly priestly functions; they say they want to "go over to the poor" and the outcast. At the same time, however, they accuse the Church of leaving the sisters behind the lines with the poor and not admitting them to the ministerial functions. The same jobs, if certain priests go there, are the front lines of the great battles; if the sisters remain there, they are behind the lines, the place for the draft-dodgers!

III. TODAY

12. In the last few years, notable progress has been made in the advancement of women. There still remain some disparities that

are unjust. If they are truly unjust, the Church invites everyone to eliminate them. Pius XII said to women: "You can and must make your own, without restrictions, the program of the advancement of women, which has aroused immense hopes in the innumerable multitude of your sisters, who we can see still submitted to degrading practices, or the victims of misery, ignorance of their own surroundings, and of a total lack of means to culture and formation."9 In the same line, Pope John, in *Pacem in Terris*, greeted as a "sign of the times" the fact that woman "every time more conscious of her own human dignity, now does not allow herself to be treated as an instrument; she demands to be treated as a human person, at home as well as in public life."10

13. We should avoid the danger of the "false equality, which denies the distinctions established by the Creator Himself."11 Men and women, in fact, although they are equal by nature, are not identical: they have the same faculties, but they exercise them in different ways. To equalize rights does not solve the problem, says Paul VI, "we must aim at an effective complementarity, so that men and women may bring their own forms of richness and their own dynamisms to the construction of a world that is not leveled and uniform, but harmonious and unified."12

14. Certain problems agitated on today in favor of women are felt only by a few elite groups, they do not interest the masses: sometimes they concern rights that are uncertain or that do not exist. To hammer away on these, while millions of women still do not enjoy some essential rights, or elementary forms of respect, does not seem wise. Such, for example, is the problem of women priests. Recently, one person complained to me because the Pope had removed the problem of "Ministries" from the International Committee for Women. I doubt that I convinced my illustrious "interlocutor," but I will tell you the ideas that I expounded to him.

15. "Ministry" means a "service" to the Church. There are many ministries: the good of the Church requires that they all be performed; it is not necessary, however, for each person to always perform the ministries that the others carry out; on the contrary it has been established that there should be a plurality and complementarity of ministries (cf. Eph 4:11-12). Some of these are tied to Holy Orders: the diaconate, the priesthood, and the episcopate. Other ministries are founded on Baptism. Women have been admitted to the exercise of these last with an ease that is always increasing; they teach theology and canon law at ecclesiastical universities, they work in parishes, organizations, dioceses and in the Holy See itself; a great many women are extraordinary ministers of the Eucharist.

16. The difficulties arise over ministries that are tied to Holy Orders. We ask ourselves: is it possible to ordain women?

The theologians are divided: "It is not possible," say some, because Jesus chose only men as apostles, and the practice of the Church has never admitted exceptions on this point." "It is possible," others answer. "Jesus excluded women only for that time, because because in his time women priests would not have been understood; today it is different." A third group makes some distinctions: "Bishops and priests, no, because there have never been these in the Church; on the other hand, there have been deaconesses, and ordained with a special rite. Therefore it can still be done."

The question is not an easy one. Most theologians are in the first group; a number follow the third, very few the second. The Church does not abandon a long tradition unless it is presented with very serious studies to the contrary; it would be counterproductive to agitate about it on the basis of slogans. While waiting for further studies and possible decisions, it is a good idea to suspend judgment on this point,[13] and, in the meantime, to fight for the more urgent problems of women. "The hour has come," says the Message of the Council to Women, "in which the vocation of women will be carried out in its fullness . . . women filled with the spirit of the Gospel can do much to help humanity."

It is also a good idea not to take for progress and a conquest for women what is simply novelty. For example, go into the churches and museums of Venice and look again at the various Madonnas and women saints painted there: the Asssumption of Titian, the Madonna di Torcello, the Marian canvases of the galleries, the St. Ursula by Carpaccio, the St. Barbara of Palma il Vecchio, and thousands of others. Then compare them with the women on the advertising billboards. The ancient over here, the modern over there. Women as they were represented at one time, and as they are represented now. I strongly doubt that the comparison will favor the moderns in the matter of their estimation of women! The sublime greatness in which religion places Mary and the saints has flowed over onto women, and, in spite of everything, made an impression on men!

Notes

[1] *Opera* 7:139-48. The sermon was delivered partly in the basilica of San Marco in Venice and partly in the basilica of Torcello.

[2] Discourse to the *"Equipes Notre Dame,"* May 4, 1970.

[3] Paul VI, *Marialis Cultis*, no. 37.

[4] Pius XI, *Casti Connubi*.

[5] St. Jerome, *Epistles* 120.

[6] St. Jerome, *Epistles*, 122.

[7] St. Jerome, *Epistles*, 120.

[8] Cf. Pie DeLangogne, "Abbesses" in DTC, col. 2021.

[9] Pius XII, To the World Union of Catholic Women's Organizations, September 29, 1957.

[10] PT no. 41.—Trans.

11 *Octagesima Adveniens*, no. 13.

12 *L'Osservatore Romano*, April 19, 1975.

13 Luciani wrote this before Pope Paul VI released his Response to the letter of Donald Coggan, Archbishop of Canterbury (November 30, 1975), which rejected the idea of women priests; later the Congregation for the Doctrine of the Faith released "*Inter Insigniores,* on the Question of the Admission of Women to the Ministerial Priesthood" (October 15, 1976) to the same effect.—Trans.

The Pope

The Rock of All Catholics

Homily for the Feast of Saints Peter and Paul
June 29, 1974[1]

I am not the first patriarch of Venice to speak about the Pope from this chair in San Marco. Let me read to you some sentences chosen at random from among the writings of my predecessors.

The future Pius X wrote in his pastoral letter from Mantua to the people of Venice (November 5, 1894): "The first truth that a bishop must proclaim in these times is faith in the vicar of Jesus Christ."

Cardinal La Fontaine: "The unity of the Church has its center in Rome . . . whose bishop is the successor of the Fisherman to whom Christ repeats three times: feed my lambs, feed my sheep."

Cardinal Piazza: "It was said to Peter: 'Everything will be loosed and bound even in heaven' . . . The vicar of Christ writes in the great book of consciences, whose pages are turned in eternity: every page is countersigned by the authentic signature of Christ in characters of blood."

Cardinal Roncalli [Pope John XXIII]: "We stand with the promise of Jesus, who assists and protects his vicar in a special way, and we venerate in the Pope the living word of our Savior, his mind, and his heart."

Cardinal Urbani: ". . . the duty of obedience (to the Pope) does not regard only the truth of the faith . . . it would be absurd for obeying to be limited to the theoretical sphere of principles and not to be expressed in the practice of daily life."[2]

I am very small in comparison to these illustrious predecessors of mine, among them a canonized saint [Pius X] and two whose cause for beatification is in progress! I can nevertheless assure you that my faith and the feelings of my heart in regard to the

Pope are identical to those they have expressed. We are living at a moment when the temptation to a centrifugal movement away from Rome lies in wait for not a few of the faithful: it is my duty, I think, to point out that, in separating ourselves from the Pope, we are putting the unity of the Church in danger. In order to remain in the framework of reality, I will sum up for you some friendly conversations I have had recently with various persons.

One of them appealed to the Council in order to justify distancing himself from the Pope. "Excuse me, you are not well informed," I told him. "The Council, after recommending the assent of Catholics to their bishops, wrote: "This religious obedience of the will and mind must be given in a special way to the authentic Magisterium of the Roman Pontiff even when he does not speak *ex cathedra*, so that his supreme Magisterium is acknowledged with reverence, and the judgments he expresses receive sincere assent."[3]

Another person said to me: "What need is there for so much fear? We all know that the Church is indefectible and eternal!"

"True," I answered, "but it is the universal Church that is indefectible, not the local church, not the individual Christian. Which means: this or that person among the faithful may end up outside the Church. The single local community can undergo painful abandonment or shrinking or even disappear completely. The Africa of St. Augustine was a whole forest of dioceses: with the coming of the Muslims not a single diocese, a single Christian, remained down there."

A third person made an objection to me, an enormous one: "The primacy of the Pope means the humiliation of the bishops, the local churches and the whole grass roots of the church!"

I pointed out to him that even Vatican I thinks the contrary. It declares expressly, in fact, that Christ instituted the primacy of the Pope "so that the episcopate . . . might be one and undivided,"[4] and therefore, he instituted it in service of, not to the detriment of the bishops. If even Vatican I excluded that the cause of the infallibility of the Pope is the consent of the Church,[5] that is because only Christ, with the assistance of his Spirit, con produce this effect! It is not excluded, however, that the Church can, even must, in one way or another, be heard by the Pope before teaching. In other words, the preservation from error comes only from God and is granted in certain cases to the Pope alone in favor of the Church and not separately from the Church, or to the humiliation of the Church!

A fourth person said to me: "Pope means laws, limitation of pluralism, doctrine imposed from on high: people no longer accept these things, which offend the human person."

I answered, "If we were to fully accept your way of reasoning, everyone would become a church to himself, would make the law to suit himself; among the truths he would choose with an eclectic criterion only those that suit him. We would be in ecclesiastical anarchy, and would risk no longer being the Church of Christ."

"But I want to remain here, in the communion of the Church," he replied.

"I'm glad to hear it, but it is one thing to say you are in communion, another thing to really be in communion. You talk to me about the human person. It has its own great dignity, of course, but also its limits and deficiencies. Once we admit then, that Christ placed the Pope at the top of the Church with some precise duties, we do Christ a serious wrong if we suppose that he did it to humiliate us; he did it only to help us remain united, to have a fixed point of reference and a sure guide. In other words: when we follow the Pope, we have a guarantee and security; when we separate ourselves from him, we wander around in uncertainty and confusion. By working with him, we are builders of the Church; by working against him or without him, we risk being destroyers of the Church!"

I continued: "You talk to me about pluralism. There are two kinds: first, *genuine* pluralism, which the Church has always admitted, and which it now intends to apply to larger and larger sectors, favoring a unity that is not uniformity. Then there is *equivocal* pluralism. I mean the kind that begins with the good intention of helping modern people better understand the Christian message, and ends up losing the very content of the message. Today, in fact, it is not rare to hear people say: "We must adapt ourselves to other people's ideas" and then they end up losing their own ideas on the way; they start out hoping to convert, and are converted in reverse. To adapt yourself, to go to meet our time is good; what is not good is to accept indiscriminately all the ideas and fantasies of our time. It is the Gospel that must enlighten the world, not the other way around.

"You tell me you are allergic to laws, to everything that comes from on high. I understand your modern sensibility and your distrust of authoritarianism. Authority, however, is another thing. Instead of listening to me, I would like to have you listen to the voice of two others: Bossuet and Lenin. Listen to Bossuet: 'Where no one commands, everyone commands; where everyone commands, no one commands.' And that means: 'Take away the observation of the laws and you will have chaos.' Now listen to Lenin: 'In this philosophy of Marxism, which has the solidity of a single piece of steel, none of its fundamental premises, none of its essential parts can be separated from the rest.'"6

My brothers and sisters! These last words are revealing. The adversaries of the Church want for themselves the solidity of a steel bar and then put it into practice with commitment and evident success. On the other hand, some among the children of the Church are committing the extremely irresponsible act of compromising their solid unity. Think about it! "The Roman pontiff," says the Council, "as successor of Peter, is the perpetual and visible principle and foundation of unity both of the bishops and the multitude of the faithful."7 Let us also recall the words of Christ. It is of the Pope that Christ was thinking when he said to Peter: "On this rock I will build my church" (Mt 16:18). Then let's not separate ourselves from the rock! Let us pray for the rock and for remaining with the rock of all Catholics!

Notes

1 *Opera* 6:371-74.

2 All of these quotes are from the *Rivista Diocesana del Patriarcato di Venezia.*

3 LG, no. 25.

4 DS, no. 3051.

5 DS, no. 3074.

6 Lenin, *Opere*, 12, p. 267.

7 LG, no. 23.

Pope John XXIII

The Announcement of His Death[1]

June 3, 1963

My esteemed priests and beloved faithful, today at 7:49 p.m., Pope John XXIII died piously and serenely after 81 and a half years of life and 4 years, 7 months and 6 days of "humble service" as Pope.

This "service," in a very brief space of time, was in reality very dense with generous works for the benefit of both the Church and the whole world. "Humble" on the other hand, was the attitude of his spirit. Placed on a high cathedra, he presented himself to the world, saying, "I am one of you, I am your brother Joseph!" While working, teaching or approaching people in small groups or vast crowds, he repeated without ever becoming tired: "Let's seek what unites us!" "Let's have faith in God and mankind!" "Let's love one another!"

Simple, abandoned to the "good providence" of God, smiling and full of sensitive kindness to everyone, but resolute and tireless, right at the dawn of his pontificate he launched the daring idea of an Ecumenical Council, which he patiently prepared for and courageously initiated, and for the success of which he repeatedly offered his life.

Never, perhaps, has a Pope been so loved as has John XXIII, by the whole world, even non-Catholics, and it is surprising to observe how, in his simplicity and without trying to, he made an extraordinary impression on every kind of person. This leads us to meditate on and imitate his example of goodness, humility and robust faith in God.

In the meantime, however, we have the filial duty of supporting his pious soul with prayer, all the more so since, before becoming Pope, he was for five years our most beloved and venerated metropolitan Patriarch.[2] I myself cannot forget that I was consecrated a bishop by his august hands. And therefore with the soul of his son and your brother, at his moment I invite you all to pay him your respects and offer prayers for his soul.

His Vision for the Church [3]

Homily in the Cathedral, Vittorio Veneto,
June 6, 1963

The idea of Pope John that has made the greatest impression on my soul is this: "*Ecclesia Christi, lumen gentium!* [The Church of Christ is the light of nations]."[4] The Church must shine not only on Catholics, but on everyone; she belongs to everyone, we must try to help everyone get to know her better.

When the Apostolic Delegate Angelo Roncalli arrived in Turkey at the beginning of 1935, he felt a pang in his heart: there were dozens of priests and thousands of faithful there, but almost none of them had bothered to learn the national language of Turkey; the Catholics were somewhat closed within themselves; they formed an island. He tried to remedy the situation as best he could: he ordered that the official acts of the Delegation be written in Turkish; before each of his sermons he had the Gospel passage read in Turkish and ordered that the "Blessed be God" be recited in Turkish at the end of Mass. There was amazement and criticism and some people asked: "What are these novelties for?" He answered, "They are for both the Catholics and the Turks. To the Catholics I would like to say: 'Come on, come out of your isolation! Give up the French and the other things that hinder you, and get to know these people who are your hosts and who are also made for the truth!' To the Turks, I want to say, 'Dear Turks! We cannot give away a single point of our creed, but we want to let you know that the creed itself obliges us to show you our liking for you, our sincere esteem for the good you have been able to create, and our desire to walk together with you when it comes to things that are good by their nature.'"

It was, on a small scale, the program that he applied on a large scale as Pope: to build bridges to the world.

The Council is one of these bridges. In an audience for us bishops of the Veneto, he told us how the idea had come to him. "One morning Tardini[5] came here with his usual stack of papers. We reviewed them, then we examined the world situation. So many problems, so many difficulties! We said, 'What can the Church do to help?' I had not thought about it before, but at that moment a word flashed into my mind, and I said, 'It would take an Ecumenical Council!' When the word was said, I almost surprised at having pronounced it and I looked at Tardini. Right away, he placed the papers on the table; I saw his eyes shine behind his glasses, and I heard him say, 'Holiness, that is a great idea! Yes, it would take a Council!' I am accustomed to following with simplicity what seem to me to be inspirations from the Lord. I did so then, and you know the rest."

And you, my faithful, know it too. You have heard John XXIII speak on every occasion about the Council. He saw it as an examination, a self-criticism by the Church in order to improve herself, to beautify and renew herself and in this way to present herself as more attractive, convincing and welcoming to the separated brothers and to the rest of the world. No sermons would even be necessary, he said once, quoting St. John Chrysostom, if our faith really shone in our lives!

And in his famous speech at the opening of the Council, he was also thinking of the world. "Don't forget!" he seemed to be saying in his precise Latin, "I don't want a Council-museum, that limits itself to gathering and cataloging antiques; the Council must be instead a forge that brings forth doctrines that are unchanged, but in new forms, with a new spirit, in view of new needs. Today the Church must be a mother to everyone, kind, patient, and full of mercy, even towards the separated brothers; the great medicine of today must be mercy."

Mater et Magistra can also be considered a bridge to the world. The problems treated in it are of interest to everyone: it speaks, among other things, of the imbalances between advanced and underdeveloped nations; it deals with decolonization, with world population, which is growing in the face of meager means of sustenance. And it concludes: we are responsible for the underdeveloped countries; we must help, both as private individuals, and as nations!

In the encyclical, the principles remain firm: the well-known unfortunate ideologies are called "incomplete and erroneous," it speaks of Christians who "have been savagely persecuted for a number of years" in many countries, and of the "refined cruelty of their persecutors"; Catholics are warned "not to compromise" when "the integrity of religion or morals would suffer harm." Once this has been said, however, "a spirit of understanding" is recommended, Catholics are invited to "join sincerely in doing whatever is naturally good or conducive to good," and for the first time, in an encyclical, there is explicit praise for secular institutions like the International Labor Organization and the FAO.[6]

Pacem in Terris, on the other hand, is the first encyclical in which a Pope addresses not only the bishops and the faithful, but "all men of good will" on whatever side of the boundaries of the Catholic Church. Even here a single iota of doctrine does not fall. The peace of which it speaks is Christian peace, founded solely on the fear of God, love for mankind, and on liberty. Considering the phenomenon of refugees, it says clearly that "there are some political regimes that do not guarantee for individual citizens a sufficient sphere of freedom . . . in fact, under those regimes even the lawful existence of such a sphere of freedom . . . is denied."[7] But then it observes: we must not "confuse error with the person who errs; the person who errs is always and above all a human being, and he retains in any case his dignity as a human person; and he should always be regarded and treated in accordance with that lofty dignity."8 Absolutely nothing is conceded to error, but a step is taken towards those who are in error. Meetings between Catholics and non-Catholics on questions of a practical order are possible under certain conditions, and those are: that we be watchful in avoiding illicit compromises, that we be prudent, that there be an accordance with natural law, with the social doctrine of the Church and with the directives of ecclesiastical authority.

This is not the place to enumerate all that Pope John has done for the good, not only of the Church, but of humanity: I would only like to stress the spirit in which he has done it.

I learned about this spirit from his august lips, seated in front of his desk, in a private audience that I will never forget, five days before he consecrated me a bishop.

He confided to me that a page from the *Imitation of Christ* that he had meditated on in the fervor of the very beginning of his priesthood had been providential for him and had served as an orientation for the whole course of his life. "Go and look at it for yourself," he said to me. "It's in Book 3, Chapter 23." But meanwhile he recited it for me from memory. "There are four things that will bring great peace. First: seek to do the will of others rather than your own. Second: always prefer to possess less rather than much. Third: always seek the last place. Fourth: desire always, and pray that the will of God be accomplished perfectly in you." I have always tried to put these four points into practice," he concluded, "and I have always been content, in joys as well as in sorrows; the Lord has helped me and blessed me."9

During these sad days, thinking again about his life, and rereading his letters and discourses, I have found that he told me the truth. He truly let himself be guided by the will of God, he did not seek success or greatness and he possessed great gentleness and patience. When he was named an archbishop in 1925, he wrote to his friends: "I feel nothing but shame and confusion; my spirit, however, is calm, and my soul is at peace. I obey, though overcoming strong repugnance at leaving certain things behind, and at venturing to do certain others, and I am putting aside all anxiety. Yes, 'obedience and peace': this is my episcopal motto. May it always be so."

As apostolic visitor and then apostolic delegate in Bulgaria for nine years, he encountered trials that were neither small nor of short duration. The Catholic community there, which is in dire straits, has enormous needs and places great hopes in the delegate, but he is forced to admit his own inability to provide for everything, and to fulfill the hopes that had been cherished. Then comes the unfortunate affair of King Boris' marriage with Giovanna of Savoy; the delegate carries on the negotiations, he assures Rome that the august groom appears sincere and willing to fulfill his obligations, but instead Boris repeats the wedding ceremony, which has already been celebrated in Assisi in the Catholic rite, in the Orthodox rite, in a way designed to cause a sensation, and later has his daughter baptized by the Orthodox. The delegate hears that he is being criticized in the Secretariat of State, where his nomination, due solely to the Pope, is already not liked; he sees his faithful humiliated, the Orthodox exultant, the royal court irritated by the loud and clear public allusions of Pius XI; he must take difficult steps, he confesses that the affair has caused him "more troubles than there are hours in the day." But he writes: "I hope that the Lord will help me and not allow the desire for a change to issue, even once, from my lips or from my heart." And later: "I am in the condition that St. Francis de Sales calls the state of perfection: that is, I ask for nothing, and I refuse nothing. The Lord knows that I am here. That is enough for me." And still later: "We often suffer from impatience for great and sensational successes. We want to see and experience them every day . . . we are deceiving ourselves." And again: "I pay no attention to what the world says of me; the testimony of my good conscience and the knowledge that the Holy Father is happy with my modest work is enough for me."

From Bulgaria, he is transferred to Turkey and Greece. It is anything but a great promotion, all the more so because the newspapers had spoken of him as nuncio to Romania. But he writes: "Many people on both the European and Asian banks sympathize with me and call me unfortunate. I don't know why. I carry out the obedience that is asked of me and nothing else . . . Perhaps there are some bad days and painful situations in store for me. But I do not cease to look above and to look far."

Here is a phrase that becomes familiar to him: "To look above and to look far." Along with this one, he likes to repeat others. For example: "*Gutta cavat lapidem* [The drop of water wears away the stone]" Or: "*Dabo frontem meam percutientibus* [I will turn my face to those who strike me]" (cf. Is. 50:6). Or: "*Omnia videre, multam dissumulare, pauca corrigere* [See everything, overlook much, correct little]."[10] Imbued with this spirit of patience, detachment from the things of the world, and faith in God alone, he faces the difficulties of the Nunciature in France and the diocese of Venice and also the great problems of his pontificate. After being named to Venice, he writes from Paris to the vicar of the cathedral chapter: ". . . in this nomination of mine, there is nothing of my own; therefore I will be very glad to come." In Venice, again, facing some lively reactions to his project of removing the screens in front of the altar of the basilica of San Marco, he wrote: "If they told me that to succeed in my intention I would only have to kill one ant, I would not kill it." It is impossible to explain his strong and gentle patience in his very long death agony without the patience that he exercised through his whole life. "There are four things that bring peace," the *Imitation of Christ* had said. He constantly tried to put them into practice, and experienced for himself the truth of what the *Imitation* adds: *Ecce, talis uomo ingreditur fines pacis et quietis* – "The man who does these things enters the kingdom of tranquillity and peace."[11]

Now that his mission has been completed, he has gone to the Lord. Down here there remains the good that he has done, there remains, as a stimulus and a consoler, his luminous example. There also remains his exalted teaching, and it is this: Extend the area of the Church! Truth alone is not enough, we need love too! Look above and look far! Walk on the paths of obedience to arrive at the kingdom of peace!

Let's welcome the warning, and let's translate his example into firm convictions and solid virtues! Let it not be said of us that the passing of Pope John has only lightly touched our hearts. Let it be said: "That great and good Pope has impressed them, convinced them, and has transformed their ideas and their lives!"

Notes

1 *Opera* 3:43.

2 Before becoming Pope, Angeolo Roncalli was Patriarch of Venice from 1953 to 1958. Vittorio Veneto is one of the suffragan sees under the authority of the Venetian patriarch.—Trans.

3 *Opera* 3:44-48.

4 *Lumen Gentium* was also the title of the Council's Constitution on the Church.—Trans.

5 Domenico Cardinal Tardini was Pope John's Secretary of State.—Trans.

6 MM, nos. 212, 216, 239, 103.—Trans.

7 PT, no. 104.—Trans.

8 PT, no. 158.—Trans.

9 This account of the Pope's words is almost word-for-word the same as the one in Luciani's recently-discovered private notes, made immediately after the audience; they were published by Stefania Falasca in *L'Avvenire*, June 5, 2013, p. 3.—Trans.

10 The last phrase is from St. Gregory the Great.

11 *Imitation* Bk. 3, Ch. 23, v. 7.

"I Will Be Called Paul"

Homly in the Basilica of San Marco,
August 9, 1978[1]

"By what name do you wish to be called?" he was asked fifteen years ago at the end of the conclave. He said: "I will be called Paul." Those who knew him would have sworn to us that this would be the name he would choose. Cardinal Montini had always been a passionate lover of the writings, the life and the dynamic energy of the great Apostle of the Gentiles. And he lived his "Pauline quality" fully and to the last. Last June 29, he spoke of the fifteen years of his pontificate, and he made his own the words that Saint Paul, also near his end, had written to Timothy, "I have preserved and defended the faith" (2 Tim. 4:7).

That the faith should be preserved and defended was the first point of his program. In his coronation address, on June 30, 1963, he had declared: "We will defend the Holy Church from the errors in doctrine and morals, which, from within and from without her borders, threaten her integrity and dim her beauty."

St. Paul had written to the Galatians: "If an angel from heaven should preach to you a Gospel not in accord with the one we have delivered to you, let a curse be upon him" (Gal. 1:8). In our day we might think of culture, being modern, and being up-to-date, as "angels," and these are all things which Pope Paul cared about very deeply. But when they appeared to him to be contrary to the Gospel and to sound doctrine, he said *no* inflexibly. It is enough to mention *Humanae Vitae*, his "Credo of the People of God," the position that he took in regard to the Dutch catechism and his clear affirmation of the existence of the devil. Some people have said that *Humanae Vitae* was suicide for Paul VI, the collapse of his popularity, and the beginning of savage criticism. Yes, in a certain sense, but he had foreseen it and again, along with St. Paul, he said to himself: "Who would you say I am trying to please at this point, man or God? . . . If I were trying to win man's approval, I would surely not be serving Christ" (Gal. 1:10).

St. Paul had also said of himself: "I have been crucified with Christ" (Gal. 2:19). Paul VI confided: "Perhaps the Lord has called me to this (pontifical) service, not indeed because I had any aptitude for it, or so that I might govern the Church and save her from her present difficulties, but so that I might suffer something for the Church, and that it might be clear that He, and no one else, guides her and saves her." He has also said, "The Pope has the difficulties that come first of all from his own human weakness, which, at every moment, is faced with, and almost in conflict with, the enormous and immeasurable weight of his duties and responsibilities." At times that can even become agony.

The Corinthians made the following evaluation of Paul: "His letters are severe and forceful, but when he is here in person, he is unimpressive and his word makes no great impact." (2 Cor. 10:10). We have all seen Paul VI on television or in photographs embracing Patriarch Athenagoras: he looked like a little child, disappearing between the arms of a giant with an imposing beard. Even when he spoke, his voice was rather somber; rarely did it reveal the conviction and enthusiasm that were boiling inside him. But his thought! But his writings! These were truly clear, penetrating, profound, and sometimes finely sculpted. "Today the peoples in hunger," he has written, for example, "are making a dramatic appeal to the peoples blessed with abundance. The Church shudders at this cry of anguish and calls on each one to give a loving response of charity to his brother's cry for help." Development, yes, but the full development "of every man and of the whole man." "Every man," and not only the fortunate class, "the whole man," meaning that man must have the means to develop and progress, not only in the economic dimension, but also in the moral, spiritual, and religious dimensions. "To do more, know more, and have more, in order to be more."[2]

But St. Paul was above all the Apostle of the Gentiles, of those who then were considered outsiders to the Jews. He fought for them, in spite of the perplexity of the other apostles, and he traveled and suffered so much on their behalf. He wrote: "Five times at the hands of the Jews I received forty lashes less one; three times I was beaten with rods; I was stoned once, shipwrecked three times; I passed a day and a night on the sea. I traveled continually" (2 Cor. 11:24-26). Like him, Paul VI has traveled 80,000 miles by air: Palestine, India, the headquarters of the United Nations, Fatima, Turkey, Colombia, Africa, and the Far East, have been the principal stages of his travels. All of these travels, perhaps, have not obtained any conversions, but they have created a feeling that the Church is close to the peoples of the world and their problems.

Another type of closeness or better *rapprochement* that Paul VI has sought, is that of contacts with governments that profess themselves atheist. A sensitive point, this: the Pope has been criticized on it by some. Undoubtedly, there was a risk. But a limited and calculated risk. Limited, because he did not give way on principles, on the basis of the Gospel saying *iota unum aut unum apex non praeteribit a lege* [not the smallest letter of the law, nor the smallest part of a letter, shall be done away with] (Mt. 7:18). Calculated, because, although with sometimes slender hope, he sought the advantage of religion. There is the problem of so many Catholics living under persecuting governments: the Pope really must send them bishops or try to obtain for them a few crumbs of religious liberty. The atheists themselves are a problem: there are so many, so many; can the Church shut itself off from them? St. Paul had written "I have made myself all things to all men, in order to save at least some of them" (1 Cor: 9:22). Why then, not admire the courage of a Pope who takes risks? When Pius VII was negotiating the concordat with Napoleon, he had open opponents even among the cardinals. "Negotiate with that criminal!" they said. "And sweep away from their dioceses all the old bishops, many of whom can be considered martyrs for the faith! And put in their place the bishops that the First Consul wants!" Pius VII, with anguish in his heart, asked the old bishops to suffer, or made them suffer, not only *for* the Church, but also *from* the Church; he made to the First Consul all the concessions that were morally legitimate in order to have, in return, tremendous advantages for religion. Naturally, the happy outcome of the negotiations were not seen immediately, but with time. History runs its course and repeats itself. So does the history of the Church.

In the patriarchal archives, there still exist some letters exchanged between Patriarch Roncalli and the deputy Secretary of State Montini. The Pope, Roncalli writes in one, wants a certain priest in Rome: granting this is a heavy sacrifice for Venice, but I am granting it, because in the Church "we must see broad and far." Thank you, Montini answered him; thank you for the priest you gave up, and for the "broad and far."

My brothers and sisters, no man is perfect; even Paul VI, who we mourn so deeply, may perhaps have done some things imperfectly. It seems to me, however, that, very cultured as a man, exemplary as a priest, as Pope he truly saw "broad and far."

All of us must lift our gaze beyond every boundary and all work in a truly evangelical spirit, beyond every limit, with the Church of Christ, in universal dimensions.[3]

Notes

[1] *Opera* 8:584-86.

[2] PP, nos. 3, 13, 34, 6.

[3] This part of the sermon is an addition to the prepared text that Luciani made as he spoke; it was supplied by someone who heard the sermon: Ermenegildo Fusaro, "La luminosa presenza a Venezia," in *Prospettive nel mondo*, no. 43 (January 1980), p. 176.

Catholic Social Teaching

The Brothers' Portion

Intervention at the Synod of Bishops Rome,
October 21, 1971[1]

It has been said several times in this hall that humanity indeed expects from the Synod a light of doctrine on the subject of justice, but even more an impetus to action and an example.

This is not an easy thing; however I dare to make two suggestions.

The first suggestion: We must form in the faithful a mentality and an increase in solidarity imbued with the spirit of *Populorum Progressio*. Agreed, but we should not underrate the means to this end that are small, but that are within the reach of everyone, every day and everywhere.

Hence:

1. For centuries the little code of the "Laws of the Church" has been placed before the Christian people. It is learned by children together with the Ten Commandments of the Lord. Wouldn't it be possible to revise this mini-code a little, giving great emphasis to the precept to practice concretely, by both prayer and works, solidarity with the Third World?

2. Even confessors, bit by bit, could give a hand in this conscious-ness-raising, by assigning good works to be done to benefit the Third World as sacramental satisfaction. Works, of course, that are varied, and adapted to the age and condition of the penitent, and which are to be carried out either in the form of prayer, commitment to action, or money. This last is to be prudently donated to reliable organizations.

3. In the Middle Ages pilgrimages for the Jubilee Year, to the Holy Land and to Compostella were honored as manifestations of religious piety. They were enriched with indulgences and spiritual benefits. The same spiritual benefits and a still more prestigious importance should be given to everything that is done for the Third World. Let it enter into the sphere of ideas that those who, with pious generosity, commit themselves to the Third World are truly modern Crusaders and pilgrims.

4. Our faithful are accustomed to showing their gratitude to God by "ex-voto" offerings given to sanctuaries. With perseverance and prudence, they should be led little by little to give to God, Our Lady and the saints in that sanctuary that is made not of stones, but of the souls of our brothers and sisters in need.

The second suggestion involves–I'm going to call it this a *self-taxation*, which the more fortunate churches could impose on themselves to give testimony of their good will. I have given the secretary of the Synod a proposal that the Episcopal Conference of the Triveneto prepared last May, in the presence of delegates of the priests, religious, sisters and lay people. Allow me to summarize it in the following three points:

1. Each of the 16 dioceses of the Triveneto reserves annually one per cent of all its income to benefit the peoples on the road to development. This includes the revenues of benefices, what is received from religious services, alms and the contributions of the faithful for church works and activities.

2. This one per cent (1%) will be called the "brothers' portion," and this will mean that it is given not as alms but as something that is owed. Owed to compensate for the injustices that our consumer-oriented world is committing against the 'world on the

way to development' and to in some way make reparation for social sin, which we must become aware of."

The "brothers' portion" is separate from the initiative "A Loaf of Bread for the Love of God," a form of "keeping Lent" which has been in use in the Veneto for some years, in imitation of the German Misereor fund.[2]

3. The money obtained in this way will be turned over to the organ set up by Holy See for the needs of the Third World.

*****

Note: Luciani later expanded on his suggestions in an interview: "I heard the proposal for a new international committee to study the problems . . . Great and magnificent new things, but still suspended in the future. In the meantime, I said, why not lead people to the solidarity proposed by *Populorum Progressio* through the means that already exist, humble, everyday means, but ones that can be quickly put into practice? Every day, priests hear confessions. Could they question their penitents every day about whether or not they have put justice into practice, and whether or not it was felt with the heart? Could they, instead of the usual three *Hail Marys*, impose, on those who can, but not excluding children, a monetary sacrifice for those of the Third World? . . . What if there were some papal knighthood or commendation for those . . . who make notable sacrifices for the Third World? The chief of staff of a hospital, who went down with me to Burundi, burst into tears in front of a leprosarium that lacked everything. When we returned to the diocese, he said to me: 'For me it has been a spiritual retreat!' and how much aid he has obtained since! I could cite similar cases of doctors, professionals, and of humble workers . . . If justice is the very urgent and serious obligation we say it is, if the catechism is the essence of the Gospel, we must make justice a part of the catechism and in a practical and effective way. We could actually make aid to the Third World one of the 'Laws of the Church.' And what about popular piety? It is beautiful for people to show their gratitude to Our Lady for graces they have received. How painful it is, however, to see golden necklaces and rings, even very valuable ones, hanging on a statue of the Virgin, and often the object of sacrilegious thefts, while so many people are dying of hunger! Isn't Our Lady also the Mother of the Chinese, the Africans, and the Vietnamese? The people should be told this. A row of white hospital beds in Burundi, a series of schoolrooms, a group of poor African children clothed and nourished by us, make the best crown for the Virgin's head!"[3]

Notes

[1] *Opera* 5:280-81.

[2] See the following selection, "We and the Third World" for an explanation of this initiative.

[3] *L'Avvenire*, reprinted in RD, Nov-Dec 1971, pp. 525-26.

We And the Third World

Lenten Sermon,
February 11, 1971[1]

My brothers and sisters,

For a number of years we have carried on the initiative "A Loaf of Bread for the Love of God," which the bishops of the Triveneto have proposed as a "new way of keeping Lent," and as an alternative to the severe fast of times past, which has become difficult in the present work and health situation.

"You do not fast, but you must make some kind of sacrifice— we are believers, but alas! also sinners. So you deprive yourself of something that is dear to you and you put away the *lire* thus saved for the poor, this year especially for the people of Ishiara in Kenya." This, in essence, is the Lenten alternative that I dare to propose to you. Naturally, it is valuable as a religious penitential action, if animated by sincere love for God and neighbor. If it is also able to increase in each one of us the awareness that our *lire* put together are a tiny drop in comparison to the immense needs of the so called "Third World," and if it helps us to have and to spread truly clear and deeply rooted convictions about the duties of rich nations towards poor nations, it will be worth even more. And here, if you will permit, I will try to help form these convictions with the following reflections of mine made out loud in front of you.

1. The "Third World" is said in reference to the "Third Estate" of the time of the French Revolution. The "First Estate" was the nobility, the "Second" the clergy, and the "Third" the bourgeoisie, to whom the Abbe Sieyès dedicated a famous pamphlet with this title: "What is the Third Estate? Everything. What has it been? Nothing. What does it ask? To be something." The situation

is being repeated on a gigantic scale. The majority of the population of Asia, Africa and Latin America, the Third World, to be precise, numerically makes up almost all of humanity. Economically, up to the present, it has been almost a zero, a whole group of "proletarian nations." Now, on the contrary, "it is asking to be something." More correctly, as Paul VI would say, "The peoples in hunger are making a dramatic appeal to the peoples blessed with abundance." No one is justified in keeping for his exclusive use what he does not need, when others lack necessities."[2]

2. "Peoples in hunger." And that is the truth: two out of every three people in the Third World suffer from hunger or else they are ill and unable to do any kind of work. And that is not all. There are 700 million illiterate adults; almost all of them live in the Third World. While in the United States only 12% of the population is devoted to agriculture and produces God's bounty by using machines and fertilizers, and by expending little effort, in certain countries of the Third World 70% of the people are peasants. And rarely do they work a piece of land of their own: In Latin America, for example, a small handful of owners possesses 52% of the arable land, while the 100 million peasants who work it almost always lack farm machines and labor with tremendous difficulty, using rudimentary methods and implements, but producing from their efforts only enough to keep from dying.

3. Then a process takes place which, at first sight, might be surprising: the more that is produced over time, the richer the rich nations become, and the poorer the poor nations become. The reason? One reason, Paul VI said recently to the FAO, is "the scandal consisting in the acquisition at minimal prices of the production of the poor countries by the rich countries, who, in turn, sell their products at a very high price to these poor countries." In other words: the poor countries are monoproducers; they lack industry, so they export raw materials and import finished products; but, while very

little is paid for the former, the prices of the latter climb sky-high. The rich countries, it is true, periodically give "aid" to the poor countries, but they later recover five times the amount of "aid" that they give, profiting enormously by it. The rich countries save 15-20% of their gross national product in order to produce still more; the poor countries rarely succeed in saving anything for new means of production. In addition, they do not have schools to prepare the people for more efficient methods; they are not acquainted with the organization and discipline of the new type of labor; they do not have banks to transfer the money to those who know how to invest it; they do not have the necessary "infrastructures" (roads, irrigation, aqueducts, dispensaries, means of transport, electrical generators). The field in which they perhaps participate most in the benefits of science is that of health care: a great good, but a good which, by helping to increase the population, creates new problems: In the year 2000, in fact, there will be 6 billion people in the world, almost double the amount there is today. This double amount, however, will belong almost entirely to the "peoples in hunger."

4. Another fact: The poor countries have always been poor, but they did not know it. Now they know: they have seen our well-being, they have heard, and they have made comparisons. They know that the means to remedy the inequalities probably exist, but that they are squandered insanely in exaggerated luxury and in military spending (the scholar Ruiz Garcia estimates that every year 185 billion dollars is spent on arms!). For this reason they agitate, and they are tempted to have recourse to the unfortunate remedy of violence, which, when it is used, risks leading them to an even worse situation. For this reason the Pope loves to repeat: If you want peace, aid in the development of the poor countries, by spending at least a small part of the money destined for armaments on works for civil progress! Practice more justice and more charity among nations! Resolve this social problem, which is the most important one of our time!

But does the Pope, does the Church, have the right to touch on these questions, beyond the generic call for justice and charity? I know: the Magisterium of the Church must limit itself to declaring what God has revealed. Now, God, by His revelation, has opened new spiritual horizons for humanity, but He has not directly proposed the solution to social problems. Jesus expressly denied being a social revolutionary; he urged us to be just and to share our substance with the poor, but he did not specify how society and property should be regulated in specific periods in history; he has said that people as individuals are the goal, the protagonists and the foundation of human institutions and activities (the Sabbath is made for man, not man for the Sabbath), but he did not descend to details in socioeconomic matters. The ecclesiastical Magisterium, therefore, can only touch on these questions indirectly, by expounding the principles of Christ and setting them beside the various concrete social situations. The analysis of these situations, on the other hand, is up to the experts, whose collaboration the Magisterium must humbly seek and accept. This might explain, for example, why private ownership of the means of production, although stated and reconfirmed as necessary to human liberty and dignity in *Gaudium et Spes* and *Populorum Progressio*, occupies a less important place than at one time. And why the Pope, among other things, calls upon the responsible authorities for suitable international laws and an international authority capable of making them respected by the nations. Following the Pope, I exhort you to give international dimensions to your thought and your charity. We are already used to thinking of charity among ourselves, of justice between workers and companies. We must become used to thinking of charity among nations, and of justice on a world scale, by studying the problems in depth, and by convincing ourselves and others that "changes are necessary, basic reforms are indispensable," and then by "striving resolutely to permeate them with the spirit of the Gospel."[3]

Our operation, "A Loaf of Bread for the Love of God" is only a very small beginning, a simple first step. May the Lord bless it all the same!

Notes

[1] *Opera* 5:143-146.

[2] PP, nos. 1, 22-23.

[3] PP, no. 81.

Populorum Progressio Ten Years Later

Homily for the feast of Pentecost,
June 6, 1977[1]

Today we are celebrating the descent of the Holy Spirit on the apostles. It was an inner, invisible descent, but one accompanied by outward signs. The tongues of fire signified light, strength, and warmth. The one language spoken by the apostles, but understood by people of many different languages, announced that the Church had been sent to all the peoples of the earth.

From that day on, the Holy Spirit has continued without ceasing His work in the Church. An inner, invisible work; some signs of this work, however, are sometimes also glimpsed on the outside. The encyclical *Populorum Progressio*, issued ten years ago, for example, was almost like a tongue of fire: it too put forth light, strength, and heat, it too was addressed to all peoples and treated the problems of all peoples. Many Catholics however, have forgotten it or are not acquainted with it at all. Many of them sincerely yearn today for the values of justice and fraternity contained in the Gospel, but they shut themselves off from the Church, and are hostile and allergic to her. This Church, they say, is tied to capitalism, and to men who are holding power, and remains attached to a culture that is out of date, immobile, without courageous initiatives, and with her face turned always toward the past and never towards the future. Perhaps they would modify this judgment if they were to read *Populorum Progressio* correctly. Allow me to recall to you here some of its salient points.

"Today the peoples in hunger are making a dramatic appeal to the peoples blessed with abundance. The Church shudders at this cry of anguish and calls on everyone to give a loving response to this brother's cry for help" (no. 3).

Thus says the Pope at the beginning of the encyclical, which is not a treatise or a lecture, but the document of a pastor who speaks courageously and from the heart about some very serious and urgent problems.

The first part of the encyclical is entitled: "For Man's Complete Development."

Economic development has interested scholars and politicians for about forty years: from the time, after the end of the war, when we found ourselves faced with the need to rise again from complete ruin. Here, on the other hand, says the Pope, we are concerned with *complete* development, that is, "of every man and of the whole man" (no. 14). "Every man," and not only a few of the most fortunate, "the whole man," not only in his economic dimension, but also in his moral, spiritual, and religious dimensions. "To seek to do more, know more, and have more in order to be more" (no. 6); here, says the Pope, is the urgent desire of mankind, and especially of the peoples "who have recently gained national independence" (no. 6).

But these peoples run across very great difficulties on their way to development.

First, the economic situation. The European colonizers have undeniably brought the countries of Asia and Africa some good things: schools, hospitals, streets, railroads, etc. But they have not enabled these peoples, little by little, to do things on their own, with their own technicians, with their own industrial plants, and with a commerce that is integrated with world commerce. They granted political independence, but not economic independence. Certain former colonial countries have gone no further than the production of simple foodstuffs, others have only a primitive agricultural production, others have the beginnings of industry, but cannot progress for lack of technicians and capital.

Another circumstance. These people were also poor before, but they did not know that they were. Now they know: they have seen, heard, and made comparisons, they have realized that there is an abyss between them and the super-industrialized nations. They are talking about injustice and exploitation, of organization among themselves; they are putting forward demands, and not having anything to lose, they have everything to hope for and to gain in a future revolution.

A third circumstance. A conflict often arises between the local Asian and African traditions and the new ones that have been introduced from Europe; at times between their tribalism and our individualism. In the conflict something breaks apart: "The moral, spiritual and religious supports of the past too often give way" (no. 10). The misfortune is not so much the conflict or the fracture; it is that other spiritual values are not substituted for the broken or fallen supports. Instead, lying in wait, and ready to make their entrance, are pseudo-spiritual values, the pseudo-prophetic or salvationist movements. In Africa, for example, during the last century, there was a whole swarm of *Mahdi* (Muslim prophets). "The resulting dangers are patent," says the Pope: "violent popular reactions, agitation towards insurrection, and a drifting toward totalitarian ideologies" (no. 11).

What has the Church done, and what does she propose to do for "complete development"? Up until now, she has above all evangelized. While evangelizing, she has also civilized, that is, helped to "develop." The missionaries have gained for themselves great merit in development, by constructing "hostels and hospitals, schools and universities . . . They have often protected the [local populations] from the greed of foreigners" (no. 12). "Without a doubt, their work, insofar as it was human, was certainly not perfect" (no. 12). This was also noted by an Asian bishop at the Council, who said: "You have brought Christ to us, but dressed in European clothes. It would have been better to bring him to us naked: we would have dressed him ourselves, in the clothes of our country!"

Nevertheless, the missionaries "were also able to cultivate and promote local institutions." The Pope recalls Charles de Foucauld, called by the North Africans the "Universal Brother," because of his charity, and for his truly wanting to be a *Touareg* among the *Touareg*. Others could be added, like Father Lebbe and Cardinal Constantini. In the last few years, there has been an effort to discover the original native culture and art, to enhance it, to allow it to flourish, and to make use of it in the liturgy (no. 12).

Now, however, we have arrived at immeasurably greater and more complex needs. The Church by herself can do little, but she offers what she has and what she is. "Sharing the noblest aspirations of men and suffering when she sees them not satisfied, she wishes to help them attain their full flowering, and that is why she offers men what she possesses as her characteristic attribute: a global vision of man and of the human race" (no. 13), something which can be a spiritual impulse toward future development. That is, she teaches: You must not only save your soul, you must also perfect this soul and allow it to grow, developing all of the gifts that God has given you. And this "growth" is "not optional" but obligatory; it must also occur with the growth of other men, present and future.

It is not only you, and you, and you who must advance; all of humanity must advance along the "path of history" (no. 17).

And it must advance in all areas. To desire well-being, indeed, is good; but to desire only material well-being, and with cupidity and avarice, is to regress, setting men against other men. To prepare technicians is also good; but what will happen if we do not also prepare men of thought, capable of reflection, love, friendship, prayer and contemplation? (nos. 15-20).

At this point the encyclical gets down to some "concrete" questions.

Private property? It is a right. Free trade? It is a right too. But, before these two rights, there is another more important right, on which the first two depend, and that is for every man to be able to find on earth what he needs.

Hence: "private property does not constitute for anyone an absolute and unconditional right. No one is justified in keeping for his exclusive use what he does not need, when others lack necessities." In cases where a conflict arises, "it is the responsibility of public authorities to look for a solution" (nos. 22-23).

And here are some very practical cases.

Sometimes there are private holdings which cause considerable damage to the interests of the country and to collective prosperity. And that is because they are too extensive, because they are exploited little or not at all by the owner, and because they are the cause of misery in the population. Well then, the common good justifies their expropriation.

There are citizens who derive an abundant income from national activities and resources and who transfer a considerable part of it abroad, to their exclusive personal advantage, without any consideration of the evident wrong they are inflicting on their country. This unjustified evasion of capital "is not admissible" (no. 24), for the precise reason that it takes place, in a considerable measure, out of selfish speculation and because it must be replaced by conspicuous interventions of foreign capital, with the resulting danger or harm to these people's own country.

To set aside capital and then to invest it in industry is a good. It is also "a sign of development and contributes to it" (no. 25), and "one must recognize, in all justice, the irreplaceable contribution made by the organization of labor and industry to what development has accomplished" (no. 26). Not counting the fact that industrialization stimulates man to force nature, little by little, to give up her secrets, to place a discipline on his own habits, to develop "a taste for research and discovery, an ability to take a calculated risk, boldness in enterprises, and a sense of responsibility" (no. 25).

Unfortunately, there has been, and sometimes still is, the other side of the coin: "unchecked liberalism," which leads to "the international imperialism of money"; "a type of capitalism" which has been "the source of excessive suffering, injustices, and fratricidal conflicts." The Pope is not speaking here of capitalism or of economic liberalism in themselves (and in no way of political liberalism), but of the excesses and abuses that have turned a system that is passable or good in certain historical situations, into a "woeful system." Why? Because it "considers profit as the key motive for economic progress, competition as the supreme law of economics, and private ownership of the means of production as an absolute right that has no limits and carries no corresponding social obligations" (no. 26). These words condemn profit, but in as much as it is considered "the *key* motive of progress"; competition, but considered as "the *supreme* law of economics"; private ownership of the means of production, but considered "as an absolute right, that has *no limits* and carries no corresponding social obligations."

There is the other side of the coin for work too. On one hand, by his labor man continues the work of God, by placing his own spiritual mark on the world, and by developing his skill, his genius, and his spirit of invention. He feels that he is a brother to and united with others, with whom he shares hope and suffering, ambitions and joys. On the other hand, when carried out in certain situations and under certain conditions, work risks dehumanizing the worker, and, by promising money, pleasure and power, "invites some to selfishness and others to revolt" (no. 28).

Some people have observed: Does the encyclical note the defects of liberalism alone? Given the nature of the letter, with its simple style, which aims to persuade and not combat, it looks not for the name of Marxism, but for its substance. It says: "The Christian cannot admit [the doctrine] which is based upon a materialistic and atheistic philosophy, which respects neither the religious orientation of life to its final end, nor human freedom and dignity" (no. 39) It says: The state is not to develop the programs by itself, but together with private and intermediate bodies; and that is in order to "avoid the danger of complete collectivization or arbitrary planning, which, by denying liberty, would prevent the exercise of the fundamental rights of the human person" (no. 33). "Pluralism . . . of trade unions" is therefore called "admissible, and . . . useful," because by them "liberty is protected" (no. 39).

How many problems are involved in development! On one hand, it seems that they must be resolved immediately; on the other, sudden haste could bring ruin: an improvised agrarian reform, or a headlong rush to industrialization could disturb structures that are still necessary, generate social miseries, and cause a turning back instead of a push forward (no. 28).

A revolutionary insurrection could cause new disasters: what is needed instead are bold and profoundly innovative changes, conducted on the basis of programs and planning, with the agreement of everyone, and with public powers taking the lead. Education in literacy must have a place in the program. "Hunger for education is no less debasing than hunger for food: an illiterate is a person with an undernourished mind. To be able to read and write, to acquire a professional formation, means to recover confidence in oneself and to discover that one can progress along with the others" (no. 35).

Another programmatic point: the family, which remains the primary cell of society, monogamous and indissoluble, the place where "the various generations come together and help one another to grow wiser" (no. 36). But often "an accelerated demographic increase adds its own difficulties to the problems of development: the size of the population increases more rapidly than available resources, and things are found to have reached apparently an impasse. From that moment the temptation is great to check the demographic increase by means of radical measures. It is certain that public authorities can intervene, within the limit of their competence, by favouring the availability of appropriate information and by adopting suitable measures, provided that these be in conformity with the moral law and that they respect the rightful freedom of married couples. Where the inalienable right to marriage and procreation is lacking, human dignity has ceased to exist. Finally, it is for the parents to decide, with full knowledge of the matter, on the number of their children, taking into account their responsibilities towards God, themselves, the children they have already brought into the world, and the community to which they belong. In all this they must follow the demands of their own conscience enlightened by God's law authentically interpreted, and sustained by confidence in Him" (no. 37). It should be noted that these last phrases, which have not always been understood as they should be, speak of "appropriate" information, of measures that are "suitable" and that are "in conformity with the moral law," and of "decisions that are taken before God," "enlightened by God's law authentically interpreted, and sustained by confidence in Him."

In addition to the family, other structures are to be considered: professional and union organizations, cultural institutions and political groups. Those who direct them must make them serve not only to defend specific interests, but to spiritually elevate the members who are enrolled. "True, man can organise the world apart from God, but 'without God man can organise it in the end only to man's detriment'" (no. 42).

Development must be promoted by all of humanity, like mountaineers together on the same rope, like passengers in the same boat.

This means that it will not happen, as long as a *few* rich peoples help a *few* poor peoples through "occasional aid, left to individual good will" (n. 50) or by "scattered and isolated" efforts (no. 50). No, says the Pope, it is necessary that "all available resources be pooled, and thus a true communion among all nations be achieved" (no. 43), in a way that will "allow all peoples to become the artisans of their destiny" (no. 65). All these are things that cannot be improvised, but for which agreed upon programs are necessary, preceded by "careful study, selection of ends and choice of means" (no. 50). And he adds: this is the concern of all peoples, but "especially of better-off nations" (no. 44). This is for three reasons.

The first reason: *solidarity*. This solidarity, if valid among private individuals, "exists also for nations" (no. 48). Two little children from the same family cannot be allowed to go through the streets, one hungry and in rags, the other well-fed and elegantly dressed. Well then, in the human family, on entire continents, "countless men and women are ravished by hunger, countless numbers of children are undernourished" (no. 45).

Abbe Pierre has said: "Two thirds of mankind are badly off because they eat too little, the other third badly off, because they eat too much." The two-thirds are the people of the "Third World," also called the "Southern World" or the "developing world." But what kind of "development" can this mean, even if some of it is put into effect, if it is far below the increase in population? From 1951 to 1966 the average annual income in the United States changed from $1,900 to $3,200, and in Italy from $270 to $850, and in India only from $58 to $72.

How are we acting in this situation? We have given some aid, but given the greatness of the need, we are talking about very tiny crumbs thrown from afar to a poor and hungry Lazarus covered with sores. The encyclical says: this is no longer enough! We must see to it that little by little, "the poor man Lazarus can sit down at the same table with the rich man" (no. 47) "Every nation must produce more and better goods," both to improve the standard of living of its own people, and "also to contribute to the common development of the human race" (no. 48).

In the present situation, it would not be exceptional and extraordinary, but normal, for an evolved country to dedicate a part of its production to the meeting of the needs of underdeveloped countries (no. 48). And that is not all: we need to establish a worldwide common fund with money obtained especially by cutting down on the enormous sums now invested everywhere in weapons. There is in fact, "public and private squandering of wealth . . . prompted by motives of national or personal ostentation," expenditures that are "the result of fear or pride" (no. 53); and every exhausting armaments race becomes an intolerable scandal" (no. 53).

Receiving aid from a worldwide fund which is a little bit from all nations, the peoples who are the beneficiaries would be impelled to put away the rancor of the past and to become less suspicious. They fear the so-called "neocolonialism." That is, they fear that the aid given by a specific country is aid given for a political or economic end. "The gift or the loan that this country is giving us" they think in the Third World, "is a snare to trap us or to take advantage of us."[2] This common fund would succeed in establishing "a fruitful and peaceful exchange between peoples" (no. 51), it would give a little respite in paying debts, and with it, the lending states would have better guarantee of the good employment of the money lent, and those in the debtor country of being able to regulate their affairs without outside political interference.

A second reason: *the grave obligation of justice in commercial relations*. Here we come to "the scandal of international commerce." Every year the countries of the Third World export minerals, coffee, bananas, cacao, peanuts, cotton, rubber, jute, etc, to the industrialized countries, and import manufactured or finished goods: automobiles, textiles, etc. But what happens? The prices of the manufactured goods constantly increase, while the prices of raw materials constantly fall. Thus, "the poor nations remain ever poor while the rich ones become still richer" (no. 57). In 1954 Brazil would give 14 bags of coffee to purchase an American-made jeep; in 1962 it had to give 39 bags of coffee for the same jeep. In 1960, when Cameroun exported a ton of cacao, it imported in exchange 2,700 meters of raw textiles; five years later, the meters had been reduced to 800, while the ton of cacao stayed the same.[3] The phenomenon all its causes have not yet been completely determined makes an impression; economists, in studying it, have proposed various remedies. Among them is to use a differentiated system for international commerce between rich and poor nations. Up to now, the principle of *free exchange* or free commerce alone has been used: the two contracting countries, whether they are more or less equal in wealth, or whether they are far apart from one another in wealth, the rule is always this: "Let's stay with the market price!" Instead, say some economists, we should find a special rule for the special case of the rich country that trades with a very poor one, limiting free exchange, when necessary, "regulating certain prices, for guaranteeing certain types of production, for supporting certain new industries" (no. 61).

The Pope is not an economist, he does not say that the formula outlined is the best or the only one; he states, "without abolishing the competitive market, it should be kept within the limits which make it just and moral" (no. 61), for the formula, he defers to the experts who have proposed it, in fact, he writes, humbly: "We make bold to ask you earnestly, 'seek and you shall find'" (no. 85). He limits himself to shedding the light of the Gospel on economics. "The rule of free trade," he writes, "is an incentive to progress and a reward for effort," when the states involved are of more or less equal economic power (no. 58); but "the situation is no longer the same when economic conditions differ too widely from country to country" (no. 58).

Leo XIII had said in *Rerum Novarum*: Let it not be said that the contract is just, because the worker is free to accept it or not. The freedom of a worker, threatened by hunger or by unemployment, protected neither by the State or by unions, is very different from the freedom of the boss, who has, (as they say) the upper hand: in this case, there are not two equal freedoms facing each other, but a weak man facing a strong one. Paul VI says something similar for contracts between nations. The free exchange in certain cases is, in reality, not free. Facing each other are the state with a former colonial economy and the highly industrialized country: the first can usually offer only the products of a primitive agriculture, exposed to the highs and lows of climate and the market; the second offers products which are the fruits of a labor organized to perfection and protected in a hundred ways; a quintal of coffee in Africa has cost a great many hours of painful labor; a truck made on an assembly line in America, has cost little human labor. "Conditions are too disparate and the degrees of genuine freedom available are too unequal. In order that international trade be human and moral social justice requires that it restore to the participants a certain equality of opportunity" (no. 61). It is "a long term objective," says the Pope: in its path, along with other difficulties, there are nationalism and racism. But it is absolutely necessary to strive for this goal.

The third reason: *The grave duty of charity*. This is exercised in the rich countries by the warm fraternal welcome and the example of a wholesome life given to the emigrants from poor countries, whether they are students in pursuit of higher education, or workers seeking a salary (ns. 67-69).

The same charity should be exercised in the poor countries by industrialists, businessmen, and the heads or representatives of large companies, as well as by the experts sent on "development missions." The first must carry with them, along with work and industry, loyalty and a sense of justice in contracts; the second, friendship along with competence: "A people quickly perceives whether those who come to help them do so with or without affection, whether they come merely to apply their techniques or to recognise in man his full value" (n. 71).

In conclusion, Paul VI stimulates us to think and work with moderate and realistic optimism. Our hopes should not be judged "utopian" or impossible he says (nos. 79 and 55).

A realist is not someone who believes that it is possible to continue as before, but someone who perceives "the dynamism of a world which desires to live more fraternally" (no. 79); someone who is aware that "the very life of poor nations, civil peace in developing countries, and world peace itself are at stake" (no. 55). "Development" the Pope loves to repeat, "is the new name for peace." A realist is someone who remembers that obstinate greed could call down on them, not only the judgment of God, but "the wrath of the poor, with consequences no one can foretell" (no. 49).

Certainly, enunciated principles, pious exhortations, or even solid convictions, are not enough. International laws and a world authority capable of making them respected by nations, are also necessary. "Who does not see," says the Pope, "the necessity of thus establishing progressively a world authority, capable of acting effectively in the juridical and political sectors?" (no. 78).

I wanted to summarize the encyclical in some detail: what has actually happened is that so many people cite it, so many people talk about it, but very few people read it. When it appeared, there was an attempt on the left to exploit it by excerpting some passages and intentionally ignoring others; on the right there was an outcry that the Pope was in collusion with the Marxists. The correct judgment, on the other hand, was given by a secular-minded person, Luigi Salvatorelli, who stated: the encyclical indulges "neither in anti-capitalism and anti Americanism nor in a De Gaulle-style paternalism."[4]

Today, some "scholars" look down on the encyclical. "Development," they write, "is now an outdated concept: on the clock of history, it is now the hour for 'liberation' and 'revolution.' It is anti-historic to stay any longer with the 'middle way' between Marxism and capitalism pointed out by the so-called social teaching of the Magisterium."

On the contrary, this social teaching, though of necessity brought up to date with the new situations by *Octagesima Adveniens*, is still valid. Rereading *Populorum Progressio*, we Catholics should make an effort to think in new dimensions. Before, we did it by talking about charity between us and our neighbors, and of justice between workers and employers; now we must also think and speak about charity between nations, about justice on the international and world level. We must convince ourselves and others that "changes are necessary, and profound reforms are indispensable" and that we must "commit ourselves resolutely to imbue these reforms with the Gospel spirit" (no. 81). Just a few hours ago, speaking to the people in St. Peter's Square, the Pope expressed the hope for results that are concrete, long-lasting and acceptable to all the participants in the "Dialogue between North and South" in progress in Paris. Participating in it are representatives from the industrialized countries, the oil exporting countries, and those from developing nations. "Our prayer," Paul VI said, "is with all those who are working for a world in which all men, together, like true partners associated in the decisions that regard everyone, can find peace and justice." It is *Populorum Progressio* all over again.[5]

Notes

[1] *Opera* 8:143.

[2] The case of Switzerland, which has been anything but colonialist, is classic. In 1959 it destined 5 million francs for technical assistance for poor countries. But at the same time it profited 40 million francs due to the diminished price of cacao that it imported for its chocolate industry: "It has taken away from us with its left hand what it had given with its right!" they commented in Africa. (P. Gheddo, story in *L'Avvenire d'Italia* and *L'Italia*).

[3] Piero Gheddo, story in *L'Avvenire d'Italia* and *L'Italia*.

[4] *La Stampa,* April 2, 1977.

[5] At the conclusion to the original text in the diocesan bulletin of Venice, Luciani, referring to the increasing "scandal of international commerce" and its progress in the ten years since *Populorum Progressio*, appended an article by Arturo Bocchini from *L'Osservatore Della Domenica* (May 22, 1977), which described the increase in the international arms trade, and the consequent harm to Third World countries. It is too long to include here, but is a sign of the keen attention Luciani devoted to this problem.—Trans.

Marx and the Theologians

Homily for the Feast of the Epiphany,
January 6, 1974[1]

This morning I ventured to compare theologians to the Magi. I really do think that the writings of St. John Chrysostom, St. Augustine, and St. Thomas are gifts that are just as useful to the Church as the gold, frankincense and myrrh were useful to Jesus. To the above-mentioned writers should be added many others, ancient and modern, provided that they are writings of an authentic theology. For me, such is not the "theology of secularization" I spoke about this morning, nor is the "political theology" that I am going to talk about now.

The most advanced representatives of this theology accept the Marxist analysis of society, which is based on the following foundations:

1. Human life is a forest of the most disparate kinds of activities: religious, moral, esthetic, philosophical, scientific, technical, political, and economic. The principal activity, however, according to Marx, is economic activity: producing goods, making them circulate, consuming them, this is what corresponds to the principal need of man.

2. It is not just a question of a primacy of honor. The economy, according to Marx, influences, dominates and directs every other activity: it is the basic structure, the "infrastructure" of society; the others are only "superstructure." According to him, the world actually goes forward on the power of economy, not on the power of ideas: it is, at bottom, the need to eat, to clothe themselves, to feel that they are defended, protected, and enjoy well-being that guides us: religious and philosophical ideas either do not guide at all

or guide badly in that they are "ideology" or a mask cleverly used to hide economic interests. What, for example, is the future life, heaven? An ideology that the capitalists use to keep the poor well-behaved and calm. What does it mean to insist on the salvation of "my soul?" It means making yourself the echo of a capitalistic society. In capitalism, the individual, property and private initiative are privileged to the complete detriment of the mass. When, therefore, the priest preaches "save your soul" he give exaggerated importance to my miserable "I" to the complete detriment of class solidarity.

All this is done to stay with reality, to say things as they are, affirms Marx, to create a science that will suggest a method of action, and to stop the things that are in the way, ideological rubbish that gives a deformed and mistaken idea of the world. Religion not is attacked by Marx in as much as it is false, but in as much as it is used, according to him, to benefit the interests of the powerful.

A science, if it is a science, must lead to action; if not, it is not good for anything. And it is action, praxis that Marx wants. The philosophers, he said, wanted to interpret the world; it is not a question of interpreting it, but of transforming it. For him, theory and praxis are inseparable; no theory without praxis and not praxis without theory. The praxis, then, is not one of palliatives, but a rigorous, powerful one: it is revolution.

I do not intend here to speak badly of Marx. I know very well that a large part of his attack on capitalism was just and right on target. Here I intend only to give a brief account pointing out the way some theologians today connect themselves to him.

The first link between the theologians and Marx: the de-privatization of religion, the ironic criticism of those who still dare to put the accent on the personal dimension of faith. They no longer talk about the salvation of the soul, but about the liberation of the world. The Bible, they say, is to be read in a new way. St. Paul says: "Every one of us will have to give an account of himself before God" (Rom 14:12). Christ says of the foolish rich man: "You fool! This very night, your life shall be required of you" (Lk 12:20). There is no need, they continue, to give weight to these passages. Look at the Old Testament: it is a whole people that is liberated from Egypt; it is a people that is brought back from exile. Look at Revelation: it says there that there will no longer be a temple but a *city*: therefore a political community! What to say? I am in complete agreement that every human being is inserted as a part in a whole and no man is an island, that the salvation of my soul is linked to the environment in which I live, to my parents, to the teachers who have educated me, to the souls who have been entrusted to me, that I must concern myself with the salvation of others, call them community, class, people, mass, whatever you will. But does belonging to Christ require a personal decision, that I alone must take and carry out throughout the course of my life, or doesn't it? When I die and appear before the Lord, will I die alone or in company? Will the Lord give me an individual grade or a group grade? The word of God, as interpreted for two thousand years by the whole Christian people, leaves no doubt in this regard.

A second link between theologians and Marx: *Horizontalism.* The French bishops, in their letter to the so-called "critical Christians," including some from Italy, who gathered together in Lyon last November 17 and 18, have written: "We refuse to identify the political, economic, and social liberation of which you speak with salvation in Christ, we note a confusion. . . between the final end of man . . . and the earthly future of humanity and a reduction of the first commandment of the love of God to the second, of love of neighbor . . . the origin of this confusion is the substitution of political analysis for faith."[2]

Much has been said concerning those who proclaim themselves theologians, but on the plane of the things of God, slip down and remain on a purely human level. We have heard of young people educated in this theology judging the faith from the angle of social utility, not of truth. Why admit the most Holy Trinity, they say, which is not useful to anyone on the social plane? Why talk about the individual mortal soul, if that provides grist for the capitalist mill? Why remain in a Catholic Church which has never approved of any revolution, neither the French revolution, nor the one in Russia in 1917, nor the one in Spain in 1936? Often these theologians talk about hope, but not the traditional trust that, through the merits of Christ and good works, we will arrive at eternal life and pardon of our sins. Alves, a Protestant theologian, but one read by Catholics, says: this kind of hope is "the illusory fulfillment of a desire. The language of faith, entirely centered in history, does not speak of a super-terrestrial region, where desires come true and suffering is abolished" but stops at "history" and regards only the liberation of man in this world.[3] Is the Eucharist admitted? Yes, of course, but as a symbol of solidarity, which unites men in the struggle against injustice and every kind of oppression of man by man. Of this type was the "wild-cat Eucharistic concelebration" in Paris on Pentecost 1968. Participating were priests, brothers, lay people, Protestant ministers, and Jewish rabbis. Obviously, the thought of the body of Christ actually represented in sacrifice on the altar by means of special priestly powers was absent from that concelebration.

A third link between theologians and Marx: praxis. They say: the Pope and bishops, it is true, continually urge peace, justice and reconciliation. But they are pure and abstract exhortations, which in reality act as coverings for injustices and aid in the preservation of order, rather to the "established disorder." In this situation, they continue, it is up to theology to become practical and active: it is theologians who must roll up their sleeves and proceed to organize peace and justice in society; today that constitutes their primary task; the rest can wait. And they set the schedule for the action that the popes and bishops must especially carry out.

The first stage is criticism of contemporary society. And what is criticized above all is "capitalistic civilization"; socialist society," on the other hand, seems to "political theology" very close to the one traced out in the Old Testament and the Apocalypse.

Second stage: criticism of the Church by the Church, which must recognize that it has failed in its task, that it has been exploited by capitalism. The hour has come, they say, for the Church to atone by making specific choices, joining the side of the forces of the people, who are fighting for peace liberty and justice and breaking every tie with "established power."

Third stage, participate in the revolutionary struggle, which will change, violently if necessary, the unjust social and political conditions. It is the desire of Christ, who lived, they say, above all to transform society from an unjust one to a just one, and who calls everyone to revolution.

These last statements are truly gross. Christ a politician? That his religious teaching and political repercussions is certain; it remains, however a teaching that is exquisitely religious; it establishes rather for the Christians the duty of effectively combating every injustice, but does not indicate the practical means to use; these must be chosen from time to time by Christians in the light of good sense. Much less does it indicate the means through the application of Marxist analysis. Christ a revolutionary? Certainly, in remitting sins in the name of God, curing the sick on the Sabbath, letting himself be approached by publicans and prostitutes, making the Samaritan appear in a good light in contrast to the very bad light on the Jewish priest and Levite, Christ appeared to his contemporaries like a revolutionary. But revolutionary in his ideas, in religious ideas and that's all. Already the beginning of the public life of Jesus is presented as an appeal to integrity, to penitence. "The beginning of the good news of Jesus Christ, the son of God, writes Mark. And he continues. "John appeared in the desert and baptized and preached a baptism of repentance for the remission of sins" (Mk 1:1, 4). Then there are the three famous choices made by Christ in the three temptations in the desert. As Dostoevsky points out in *The Brothers Karamazov*, with those three choices, Christ made it understood that he would not seek in any way the political domination of the world. His would be a combat, but a spiritual, interior one, against those powers about which he would say that they can be overcome "only with prayer and fasting" (Mt. 17:20; Mk 9:28).[4]

I must conclude. "Political theology," as expounded above, is not acceptable.

1. In a number of cases, it is not only not theology, it is not even Christianity. They start by saying: "Primarily we are Christians; then we take a few valid elements from Marxism." They end up by saying: "Primarily we are Marxists; then we take a few fringe elements from Christianity: those that do not contradict Marxist analysis."[5]

2. "Political theology" reads the Bible in a biased and ingenuous way, clinging only to those few passages which, in its judgment, favor the thesis of de-privatization and revolution. It is true that the Bible, in the past, has been exploited too much to benefit the right. That is no reason to exploit it too much to benefit the left.

3. It is also true that, in addition to love, Christ commands justice to us. Love, however, remains. All men are still brothers, whatever race, religion or social class they belong to. I am still forbidden to hate any brother, even if I am forced to combat him to make justice triumph.

4. It is true that politics has its importance. But to privilege it in such a way that it absorbs by itself all of Christianity and all of theology, is too much. We must leave room for our personal relationship with God. We must recall that not all injustices depend on bad structures. It is a deceiving people to make them believe that when the structures are changed, there will be perfect justice on earth. As for the Church, it is true that she must help the world, She helps it, however, only if she remains an authentic religious Church and repeats the words of Christ: "Seek first the kingdom of God"

(Mt 6:33). "What advantage does a man have if he gains the whole world and loses his soul?" (Mt 16:26).

Notes

1 *Opera* 6:278-83; originally appeared with the title "The Most Advanced Form of 'Political Theology' is Unacceptable," RD, January 1974, pp. 51-54.

2 Cf. OR, December 30, 1973.

3 A. Alves, *Christianisme, opium ou liberation? Une theologie d'espoir humain* (Paris, 1972), p. 186. [Rubem Azevedo Alves (1933-) a Brazilian professor, is regarded as one of the founders of liberation theology.—Trans.]

4 The passage of Dostoevsky's novel Luciani is speaking about is Book V, chapter 5, "The Grand Inquisitor." The book was a particular favorite of his.—Trans.

5 Cf. Giulio Girardi, *I cristiani di oggi di fronte al marxismo*, mimeographed paper from the first Italian "Christians for Socialism" convention in Bologna, September 1973, pp. 5, 11.

Living the Christian Life

How to Pray

From a retreat for Priests of Vittorio Veneto
January 1965[1]

Allow me to say a word to you about your private prayer.

St. Teresa said: "let whoever wants to grumble, grumble, let whoever wants to murmur, murmur, let anyone say whatever they want, but I want to make a firm decision to be steadfast in prayer. I understand that unless I make a firm decision to pray at any cost, it will happen that I no longer pray. Because today it is the state of aridity of my soul, tomorrow it will be serious anxieties, the day after tomorrow it will be sins, for one reason or another, I will no longer pray. I must make a strong decision to pray."

Good for her! A true psychologist and especially acute is that accent on sin. At times we are in sin, and we say: "I don't have the courage to pray." This is very wrong; if there is a moment when we need to pray, it is precisely when we have sins. And the Lord, who knows these things, says: "That one, who has most need of all, poor man, prays to me too; he is waiting for me to help him!"

It is a great error to say, "I am in sin, I will pray when I've got my life in order." Pray, for heaven's sake! Even if your prayer isn't meritorious, in the sense that you are not in the state of grace, you can always obtain the help of God, and you can also make an act of perfect contrition.

Father McNabb, a famous Dominican who preached in London, used to say: "When I am in the confessional, I really clothe myself in the patience of the Lord. Whatever they tell me, I never feel agitated, even if there are adulteries or robberies. I say: the Lord will forgive, have courage, have courage! There is only one exception, when someone come and tells me he has neglected prayer. 'But you have actually never prayed?' 'No, Father, I have never really prayed.' Ah!" he says, "that is the time that I would gladly put my hand out the little window and give him a few sound boxes on the ear!"

How can we get along in this world, weak as we are, inclined to evil, with so many responsibilities, if we don't pray? It means that you have understood absolutely nothing. Without prayer you cannot go forward.

But what kind of prayer? I am not going to say that. Everyone has his preferences; prayer is not the same for everyone. It just has to be a well done prayer, not distracted, not superficial, not under your breath.

Prayer, when well done, is necessary for everyone. But for we priests, apart from our own spiritual life and our needs, it is still more necessary, because we will have to be masters of prayer to others. What, do you want to go teach others how to pray when you do not pray, or pray badly? These are things that if people don't know how to do them, they can't teach them either.

From this you can also understand why in many parishes the people don't pray: it is he, the priest, who does not pray. He does not insist. He hears confessions, but . . . he is careless, he doesn't give any attention to it. Instead our first duty is to teach the people to pray, because when we have put this powerful means in their hands, they too will also manage to obtain the grace of the Lord.

Therefore it is truly indispensable to pray.

I cannot offer a treatise on prayer, because for one thing, you may know more than I do. I will mention only a few things.

Perhaps we insist a great deal on petitionary prayer. "Lord, remember me, Lord forgive me!" Very beautiful! But when Jesus taught us the Our Father, he said to us: "Pray this way," and he divided his prayer into two parts. The first: "Hallowed be thy name, thy kingdom come, Thy will be done." This is the part that deals with our relationship with God. Only afterwards do we go on to the second part. "Give us this day our daily bread," etc. Therefore even in our own prayers we must follow this method: first comes the prayer of adoration, praise and thanksgiving and only afterwards the petitionary prayer.

In the epistles of St. Paul: "*Gratias agamus, Deo gratias, Deo autem gratias* [we give thanks, thanks be to God] . . . "These expressions (I haven't counted them), occur more than a hundred and fifty times. St. Paul gives thanks constantly. Even the *oremus* [let us pray]: the ancient *oremus*, not the modern ones, all have the praise, the compliment at the beginning: "*Deus qui corda fidelium Sancti Spiritus illustratione docuisti* [God, You who have instructed the hearts of the faithful by the illumination of the Holy Spirit] . . ." after giving a beautiful praise, *da nobis quaesumus . . .*" here comes the request. On the other hand: "*Concede nobis, famulis tuis* [Grant to us, your servants] . . . this is a modern *oremus*; it begins immediately asking something. The one who composed it hasn't understood anything, he hasn't understood anything.

But observe the other prayers as well: "Hail Mary, full of grace, the Lord is with you." Then come the requests: "Pray for us sinners." First we pay a beautiful compliment to Our Lady. We must be diplomatic: we give praise and then we ask.

And even the *litanies* to Our Lady. "*Mater purissima*," the praise, "*ora pro nobis*," the request. They are all like that. We must use this method in all our prayers.

You must also concern yourself a little . . . . The Lord has no need of our anxieties, but he is certainly pleased when we concern ourselves a little with him.

There is a very beautiful book by Father Faber: *All for Jesus*: it is not "high," but humble things, and it teaches precisely that we must concern ourselves with the interest of God, before our interests.[2] It seems to me that for we priests as well, who are dedicated to the Lord, this should be important and should truly enter into the essence of our private prayer.

What prayers and with what method? "You are teachers in Israel," you know that the most beautiful prayer, *per se*, is the passive kind where we are left to the action of grace. Imagine a boat with the sails unfurled; it is the wind that dominates. The boat goes forward even if the boatman stands with his arms folded. It is the wind that pushes it. This is how it is with some souls who are directly captured, formed, dominated, and sanctified by God. It is the so-called mystical prayer, of those who are given up to contemplation.

And about this I can say nothing to you, because, sincerely, I myself am not a mystic. I'm sorry, I would like it very much! I have even taught it at school, I have studied all the various systems, the various tendencies, the Carmelites here, the Jesuits there. Some say that we are all called to the mystical life. A little bit of charism, a little at a time, if we employ good will, it will come to us. On the other hand, some others say, "No," and I don't know yet who I think is right.

But St. Teresa, who is a very expert woman and truly a mystic says, "I now known saints, true saints who were not contemplative, and I have known contemplatives who had true graces of superior prayer, but who were not saints."

This means that, *salvo meliore iudicio* [for lack of a better judgment], contemplation is not really necessary to sanctity, although there are very famous authors who say, "Everyone, without exception, is called to contemplation."

In contemplation, then, there are: the prayer of quiet, the prayer of union, and way, way up, we are at last at transformative union. Things I cannot go into with you, because I'm sincerely not a good judge of them, even if I have read a few books. If one of you has these special graces, I tip my zucchetto and say to him: "I'm sending you back to your spiritual director, who, realizing that he has this privileged soul, will pull out the mystical works of St. John of the Cross and . . ." Not me, I'm not that far.

Therefore, I will stick with simple prayer, the prayer of simple souls.

Even here, not all authors are in agreement. I often explain myself with a very simple and practical example. Listen:

There is a father who is celebrating his name day;[3] at home they have organized a little celebration. The moment comes; he already knows what's going on, and he says: "Now we'll see what beautiful things they will do for me!" First comes the youngest of his children; they have taught him a poem by heart. Poor little one! He is there in front of Father, he recites his poem. "Bravo!" says the father, "I'm so delighted, you've done well, thank you dear." By heart.

Away goes the little one, and the second son presents himself, the one already in middle school. Ah, he is certainly not going to lower himself to learning a poem by heart. He has prepared a polished little speech, all his own, out of his own head. Brief, perhaps, but he considers himself an orator. "I never would have believed," the father, "that you would be so good at making a speech, dear." The father is very happy. "Just look, what beautiful thoughts!" All the same, he thinks, "It's probably not a masterpiece, but . . . ."

Third, the young lady, the daughter. This one has simply prepared a bouquet of red carnations. She doesn't say anything. She goes up to Papa, not even a word, but she is moved. She is blushing so much, it is impossible to tell which is redder, she or the carnations. And Papa says to her. "It's obvious that you love me, you are so red, and so emotional." But not even a word. But the flowers please him, especially because he sees her so moved and so full of affection.

Then there is Mama, the wife. She doesn't give anything. She looks at her husband and he looks at her: simply a look. They know so many things. That glance recalls an entire past, an entire life: the good, the bad the joys, the sorrows of the family. Nothing else.

These are the four types of prayer. The first—the little memorized poem—is vocal prayer: when I say the Rosary with attention, when I say the Our Father, the Hail Mary, then we are children, we are only beginning.

The second—the little speech—is meditation. A little something out of my own head too. There can be a book, but then the book is put aside. And sometimes even without the book, something of my own, I myself think, and I have my conversation with the Lord. Beautiful thought, and also profound affection, of course.

The third—the bouquet of carnations—is affective payer. The young girl who is so emotional and so affectionate. Here few thoughts are needed, it is enough to let the heart speak. "My God I love you!" If one spends only twenty minutes in affective prayer, it is better than meditation.

The fourth—the wife—is prayer of simplicity, of simple regard, as it is called. I place myself before God and say nothing. In a way, I look at Him. This prayer seems to be worth little, but on the contrary, it is superior to the others. And it is not so very difficult to arrive at either.

Consider for a while each of these forms of prayer.

Even the first. They say: "He is a child, he is only beginning." But St. Theresa writes: It is possible to become a saint even with the first type of prayer. Certain poor people have not learned to meditate, but say their payers well, from the heart, vocal prayer. It can be a prayer that does much good to souls.

And now allow me to recommend to you devotion to Our Lady, since I must mention the Rosary, which is in part a vocal prayer Never give up the Rosary, and recite it well. And have it said in the parish too. I am very worried about my faithful: There are still some of them who pray at home, but they no longer say the Rosary. At one time it was beautiful, you know. When the children in the family see Papa praying, praying together with everyone, this has an effect on their upbringing that our preaching will never have, be certain of that.

Therefore, on my pastoral visits, I also ask this question: "Do they say prayers at home?" In fourteen parishes, almost everyone has answered me: "Unfortunately, they pray little in common." Shame! Then I say it in church: "Do me a favor! You have to watch television, I understand, times have changed! But if you cannot say the whole Rosary, all five decades, say at least one of them, ten Hail

Mary's a single mystery, with the litanies. I recommend it to you so much, at least this." And you too, insist on devotion to our Lady.

One day they also asked me–they are curious, these pious souls– "and you, which Our Lady to you prefer? Our Lady of Mt. Carmel?" Because clearly I am devoted to Our Lady of Mt. Carmel. They are rather simple people, and I answered: "If you will permit me to give advice, I would suggest to you Our Lady of the pots, pans and soup."

You see that Our Lady became a saint without visions, without ecstasies; she became a saint through these little things. She washed dishes, she made soup, she peeled potatoes, or things like that.[4]

I meant to say: Much devotion to Our Lady. The Rosary, yes prayers to our Lady yes, trust in her, but above all, imitation of her virtues. Therefore, never tire of recommending devotion to Mary.

Regarding meditation, it is enough for you just to call to mind all the sermons your spiritual father in the seminary gave you and everything you have heard from preachers of spiritual exercises. There are so many methods, so many possibilities; but aim for the will.

You must warm your heart, move your affections, as they say, and never start only from the mind, but then you must decide, make some resolution, otherwise you will never bring anything to a conclusion.

Some say: At times, I'm a little lazy, I limit myself to reading. There is also reading with meditation on it, supposing that we're talking about the Gospel, [though] I would prefer the New Testament [as a whole] . . . I have recommended the Bible, but if you must substitute for mediation you should prefer the Gospel or St. Paul. There is the *Imitation of Christ*, there are also some other sacred writers; look for something solid in them, not those modern ones, because they have so much form and so little substance.

You read, you think whether there are some phrases that concern you, or the reading is transformed into prayer, mental prayer.

Let's suppose that the book says: "We must die." Stop there. It makes an impression on me. I knew it, of course, but it is good for me to remember that I must die. Lord see to it that I don't forget it, help me to prepare myself well, every day, every day. Then you go ahead, two or three sentences; you find another phrase that makes an impression on you, stop there again, with thought, then continue . . . it is a simple and useful way. There are certain spirits almost rebellious against a systematic mediation: instead with this reading made in the spirit of prayer, with some moments of pause and reflection, they derive more profit and also succeed better.

There cannot be a general rule in spiritual things. St. Ignatius teaches that we must involve our imagination, our memory, our senses, etc. Very well; someone who is made like St. Ignatius should use his method and it will be well. But we are not quite all alike in these things. I too get along well for a month in one way, then I get tired and I feel the need to change, also out of a certain curiosity: the important thing is to find a way of applying yourself, recollecting yourself in earnest.

And then: How long a meditation? Half an hour? Even here there is no fixed rule: the needs of souls are different. For example, the one who is meager in spiritual life, would have to pray more. I would be very rigorous with those who are superficial and dissipated.

A quarter hour is not enough for you. You have fallen into mortal sin; that isn't very much; you need to strengthen yourself in piety, be reinvigorated in grace. You must put more solid convictions in your head and have a more tenacious will. Another person, on the other hand, is rather advanced and pious, habitually united to the Lord: a quarter hour of meditation, twenty minutes, may be enough for him to preserve him in his grace.

I am rather for variety. Each person should feel and understand what his needs are in prayer, always speaking seriously, let me make it clear, without deceiving ourselves, in order to preserve ourselves, rather in order to progress in the spiritual life. We all know that prayer, if not the sole means, one of the most effective means for arriving at sanctity, as St. Alphonsus says in his very beautiful little book, *The Great Means of Prayer*, which we all should have read.

And work during meditation. St. Francis de Sales says: I know three little animals: the fly, the mosquito and the bee, which indicate to us how we can and must make our meditation.

Look at the fly: here and there, up and down, no sooner has he stopped than he takes off again, he flies away, he returns, even on flowers . . . but he brings home nothing: it is the meditation of the distracted, the superficial, the inconstant person, who doesn't know how to concentrate on anything; meditation doesn't help him at all.

The mosquito: a great noise, a great uproar, he continually beats at the windows, he keeps trying incessantly, he buzzes louder and louder, until you have to open the window for him and let him fly away. It is the meditation of the noise-maker, he enters, she stomps his feet, he blows his nose, he coughs, he clears his throat, he turns the page, he is a nuisance, we hope that he will go away. What you want is that he become more profound.

The bee: look at him, slowly, slowly, he is on the flower, and does not move until he has extracted, sucked out all the pollen; he stays there, he leaves again only when he is full and then he begins again with another flower. We must go slowly, stop, reflect, work in earnest. Then we will get something out of it. Even twenty minutes, for one who works in earnest, who really meditates, can be sufficient and fruitful.

Distractions are one great difficulty. It is the classic difficulty of every meditation, of every prayer. I don't know anyone who is not subject to them, we all have unstable minds. I don't know remedies for this difficulty, unless it is that of doing our utmost. If not even

St. Louis succeed in saying an Our Father without distraction, just imagine us! Stability of mind and recollection are only the fruit of many efforts, and great application. Courage! Of course we must create a zone of silence around us; and it will still not be enough because distractions will come just as much from the inside. It's a fine nuisance! At least twenty minutes, a fine meditation. I have gotten up early on purpose for the good of the soul, and the distractions come and carry me completely away.

But if we really want, even the distractions can be diminished, attenuated. I advise you to make your meditation when possible in the morning, with a serene and refreshed mind, because later we will be overwhelmed by the occupations and worries of the day. We never know what will happen to us: something we don't expect always happens. Instead in the morning, in church and perhaps even better, in your own room. In church, someone can come who wants to confess, some little old women, if they see the priest, cannot resist the desire to confess and then goodbye, mediation! Instead, in my room, early I am more certain of bringing it to a conclusion.

Correlative to meditation, I would also see *examination of conscience* . . . If in the evening I do not give a glance at the resolution made in the morning and unless I ask myself, "have I kept it or not? What has become of this famous resolution? And I don't make up for it in some way? What do I conclude? The resolution if it is not kept, is equivalent to orders that have not been carried out. It is not enough for the bishop and the pastor to give orders: they must then check to see whether they have been carried out. So in the morning: "*Dixi nunc coepi* [I said, now I begin] . . . "today, I begin, this is the work of the hand of God, I have really changed. In the evening I give a glance: Have I remembered my promises? And if I have forgotten, at least I am ashamed of it. Can you believe it? This morning I hit the ground running, and then I forgot everything. Lord, forgive me. It's up to me to begin again."

But the examination also requires a bit of a method. I am not going to complicate things. St. Ignatius has his good rules even for this. *"Gratias age, pete lumen, conscientiam discute, dole, propone,* etc. [Give thanks, ask for light, search your conscience, feel sorrow, resolve, etc].*"* Nothing to say. But I would put the accent on the *dole* [express sorrow] and the *propone* [resolve]. I would be rather quick with the glance: an attentive glance, active, firm at the morning's resolution, and the rest a pan shot if you will. But the *dole* and the *propone,* that yes. Then "tomorrow, Lord, you'll see, you'll see; you will be happier with me than you are today." Here we wake up in the morning determined to do something: in this way, life is made up of constant attempts.

Unfortunately, we have among our projects so many drawings, so many outlines, so many sketches, but few masterpieces. I don't know about you, but me, yes. The Lord will say: "Poor thing, if nothing else, at least you made an effort, you tried." And those who have nothing, not even sketches . . . let's do at least those.

Then there is *affective* prayer. At times I can fly a little bit above truths I have already meditated on, and sometimes I find myself in the state of feeling a great transport toward the Lord. Then I spend this half hour, this quarter hour in loving God, in protesting again my good will to begin again, to act, and it will be something very pleasing to God.

The *prayer of simplicity* or of simple gaze: sometime we can also avail ourselves of this; it is within everyone's reach and can give rise to some unexpected experiences.

Trying to improve your prayer is a truly fundamental thing for the spiritual life of a priest.

Our Lord recommends so many other things on prayer to us in the Gospels. The insistence: it is not enough to ask once. It is not like playing the piano: you touch the key and the sound comes out. "Lord, give me this grace." "Ready, here you are! Right away!" It's not like that. The Lord himself has said that it's not like that. "I want you to ask." He even told the parable. There was an unjust judge in a city. Nothing mattered to him, either God or poor human beings. A widow went to him every day. "Give me justice, give me justice." "Go away, go away. I don't have time, I don't have time." But the widow returned. Finally, one day the judge said to himself. "Even though I don't fear God and I have no regard for men, since this widow is always coming to bother me, and won't leave me in peace any more; I'm going to give her justice, so I won't have her under my feet any longer." The conclusion of Jesus Christ: "This is what an iniquitous judge does and for an egotistical motive, and your Father, when you insist in asking him to give you justice, will not your Father in heaven do it? So be brave, ask, insist a little" (cf. Lk. 18:1-8).

And we have already heard from the Council. We must pray always, pray without interruption. And why do we obey? Because it is a *praeceptum* [precept]. Do you want to pull out the sword to make two slices of your life, half work and half prayer? Father Suarez, who was a Jesuit had divided [the day] into three parts: eight hours of study, eight hours of prayer and eight hours of rest, that is, recreation eating and sleeping.

Eight hours of prayer: this is not advisable for anyone. And then our actions are not sanctified only because close to them there is a bit of prayer.

If you have read *The Adventures of Baron Munchhausen,*[5] you will recall one of the most improbable of them. There was a hare, the famous hare that no one could succeed in catching no matter how much they chased him. And do you know what the secret was? The hare ran for a certain amount of time with his four normal legs. Yes, because he had four other special ones. When he was tired, he turned over on his back where he had four fresh legs in reserve, and he continued his flight with those. Then the game would begin again to infinity.

Some people say; A little bit of prayer, then I will turn to do my other work. No, this the Lord does not want, it would not be the correct system. We don't run on alternating current in the spiritual life. This time of work has been sanctified because I have placed a period of prayer near it. No. the Lord wants all of our time to be sanctified.

Therefore we would need to learn the difficult art of impregnating all our actions, from the simplest to the most important, with the spirit of the Lord. Scalfaro, who – not now – but once came to visit me from time to time, told me, and later I also found it in his little book he had published, that one time he was talking with De Gasperi.[6] It is also edifying when men in government find time to speak of ascetic matters. De Gasperi said: "I too had many distractions in prayer, even during communion, especially the early period when I was prime minister." De Gasperi and one period of his life, went to communion every day. "America, and Russia used to torment my mind. At one point I understood what I had to do. Instead of saying: "Go away Russia at this moment, go away, America. I would say: 'Here, come here. Lord, you see, I had the head of government, but that Russia won't leave me be, it gives me a great many anxieties, see if you can help me.'" Instead of driving away the Lord by his anxieties, he wanted him to be concerned about them too. When speaking with the Lord he would enumerate them to him, along with his fears. Then, during his work, he would think: "I have put it under the protection of the Lord," and this thought would return to him often during the day. It is better to do it like this.

In the life of St. Bernard, written by the monk Geoffrey,[7] there is a beautiful expression. Now I don't know if I recall it exactly: *Totus quodammodo exterius laborabat, et totus interius soli Deo vocabat* [in some way he was totally absorbed in work on the outside and totally absorbed in calling on God alone on the inside]. St. Bernard, you know, traveled half of Europe, he was the advisor of popes, in fact, it was he who made popes at that time. Up and down, in England, in Germany, in France. A great organizer; he even preached a crusade, didn't he? And then the vocations. If you are looking for a saint to pray to for vocations, pray to him. He would go to Cologne or other cities, and return with thirty-five university students who entered his order, his convent. He even gathered a hundred, and more than a hundred sometimes! In the monastery of Clairvaux when he was elected abbot, I don't know if there were fifteen monks in the monastery: when he died, in the abbey there were seventy monks. In one of his biographies, there was a map with all the monasteries founded by him marked above it: well, Europe was covered with them!

And his biography says: "Just as exteriorly he was immersed in work, so interiorly he was immersed in God!" But also the biography of St. Ignatius of Loyola says of him: in *actione contemplativus*, he was immersed in contemplation, even when he was working. He worked, he worked, and while working he never took his eyes from the Lord. He introduced the Lord into his affairs, he united Him to them.

A happy art, to know how to do everything under the eye of God. And how do we do this? I am not capable of explaining it really well, but first, we must have the right intention in all things, and a great spirit of faith. What does it mean to have the spirit of faith? You must act according to certain principles, according to certain moral maxims suggested to you by the saints. Have them always present and never deviate from them.

For example: *Quod aeternum non est, nihil est,* what is not eternal is nothing. Be guided by this principle. You might be a canon, a monsignor . . . it counts for nothing. What is not eternal is nothing. You could get as much as fifteen thousand *lire* from that wedding . . . what is not eternal is nothing.

Without exaggerating, let's be clear, but when there are certain principles and we are walking in their light in such a way that they can direct our life, then there is the spirit of faith. Then it is easier to preserve ourselves in this state of mind, and to say: Everything that I do, I want to do for the love of the Lord.

I don't think I want to add anything else on private prayer. So many other things could be said, but the important thing is to put them into practice.

Notes

1 This except is from a longer talk on prayer, given during a retreat Luciani preached to the priests of Vittorio Veneto. The retreat was transcribed from an audio recording, and published in 1980 as *Il Buon Samaritano* by the Edizioni Messaggero in Padua. It was later republished in Luciani's complete works: *Opera* 9:330-41. Because of the more spontaneous nature of the source, sentences are sometimes incomplete; I have occasionally filled in some things in brackets.—Trans.

2 Frederick William Faber, *All for Jesus: The Easy Ways of Divine Love*, originally published in 1853 and available in reprints. Fr. Faber was a contemporary of Bl. John Henry Newman and with him a member of the Oratory.—Trans.

3 That is, his patron saint's feast day, which in Italy is often more important than a person's birthday.

4 To say that the Blessed Virgin "became a saint" may startle some Catholics, but cf. LG 8, 293: "the Blessed Virgin advanced in her pilgrimage of faith."—Trans.

5 A comical fantasy by Gottfried August Bürger, after an earlier work by Erich Raspe. It was one of Luciani's favorite works as a youth.—Trans.

6 Alcide de Gasperi, founder of the Christian Democratic Party, was prime minister of Italy from 1945 to 1953.—Trans.

Participating in the Liturgy

Homily for the Feast of the Madonna della Salute,[1]
November 1976

The feast of the Madonna della Salute falls this year two weeks after the convention on "Evangelization and Human Progress."[2] The seven representatives from the patriarchate have returned from this convention full of enthusiasm and fervor. They were particularly impressed by the way the various liturgies were celebrated during those days. "Those liturgies," they said, "were real epiphanies of the Church. In them, in fact, we felt: The people of God united with the bishops and the concelebrating priests by the bond of a charity at an incandescent level; A people striving to practice a new way of living fraternal communion, while recognizing and accepting that they have different opinions on things marginal to the faith; A people that perceives what value community prayer has for the glory of God and the good of humanity; A people that while they are resolved to dedicate themselves with all their strength to human advancement, feel at the same time that they are invested with the word of God and are convinced that in this matter, divine help is indispensable and that at the head of all forms of advancement comes the promotion of goodness and love." So say those who have returned from Rome. Neither they nor you nor I know yet what concrete applications to give to the convention. While awaiting the directions that the episcopate thinks fitting, a first introduction might be that of helping our liturgy approach the liturgy experienced during those days in Rome. The liturgy, according to the Council, is the people of God gathered together by the Risen Lord, it is a kind of unifying cement. Now, a more profound union and understanding among ourselves is the necessary platform for the launching of fruitful practical initiatives.

WHAT THE COUNCIL SAYS ABOUT THE LITURGY

1. It says that the liturgy is a continuation of the work of salvation. What Christ did then by preaching, suffering, dying and rising, he continues to do now in a new way, through the liturgy.[3] This liturgy, on one hand "day by day builds up those within the Church into the Lord's holy temple . . . The liturgy marvelously fortifies the faithful in their capacity to preach Christ"; on the other hand "to outsiders the liturgy reveals the Church as a sign raised above the nations."[4]

2. What Pius X had fortunately intuited, the Council has made explicit. That is, it has said: the first and most necessary source of the authentic Christian spirit is a liturgical celebration with the active, intelligent and responsible participation of all the people. The Mass, especially, is a great drama: everyone should carry out their proper part in it.[5] Not being present passively at the Mass; not singing *during* the Mass, but singing *the Mass*; feeling not like outsiders, passive and apathetic, but like actors, protagonists and joyous protagonists. An atmosphere of festive joy is essential to the Mass, because there we celebrate the Passover of the Lord, because the defining words are: grace, light, salvation and truth.

3. The Council has also profoundly reorganized the Biblical readings, through the richness of which the Holy Spirit kindles the desire to better know, understand, love and live the word of God.

Today the people listen to, express and sing these readings, like other liturgical texts, in their own language. Let's say it frankly: this has meant great progress, even though sometimes the translation of the Latin leaves a little to be desired. It is very important for the people to be able to nourish themselves in abundance, expressing themselves with ease in their language, the language of their emotions.

I note with joy that on the whole the liturgical reform in the patriarchate has been welcomed gladly, and is producing good fruit. So that it may produce more, however, it is necessary to avoid three obstacles that sometimes exist in the Church today.

THREE OBSTACLES

A first obstacle: superficiality and haste. Some people have not understood that the reform of the liturgy is something profound, intended to help the people of God grow in faith, hope and charity, and to reveal to mankind the new face of a younger and fresher Church. They are content to substitute the new rubrics for the old ones; they have not prepared their people by patient catechesis; they have not explained the significance and beauty of the new gestures.

They have asked their people for any old kind of participation, when what was needed instead was a participation at once personal and collective, full of conviction, and interior as well as exterior. They have forgotten that prayer is a difficult thing, and that, in order to help people encounter God, it is necessary to accustom them to detaching themselves a little from things, in silence and asceticism. They imagined that the reform could do away with effort and work. Thus it has happened that sometimes there has been, not a celebration of the true liturgy, but people who are, as it were, amusing themselves or exhibiting themselves on the pretext of the liturgy, or a seeking in the liturgy of esthetic pleasure or palpable emotions.

The *second* obstacle is more or less open rejection or hostility, due to various causes. Some, like Lefebvre, do not accept the Council; therefore they reject the liturgy, which is the soul of the Council directives, because the liturgy, by its nature, takes hold of the whole person. Others, confusing tradition with conservatism, do not understand that the Lord, precisely because he is always present in his Church, wants the secondary forms of worship to be constantly adapted to changing times and new needs. They appeal to the past, but they do not understand the past correctly.

In the very earliest times, in Rome, the liturgical language was Greek: when the situation changed, in the third century, Latin was substituted for Greek. The very oldest example of the Mass is the one described by St. Justin, but the Mass of Gregory the Great is very different from that of St. Justin; in his turn, St. Gregory VII introduced a number of changes in the Mass of St. Gregory the Great. They appeal to the Missal of St. Pius V; but Pius XII had already changed it before the Council as far as the Easter Triduum is concerned; Pope John himself changed the very ancient Roman Canon by introducing into it the remembrance of St. Joseph. It is true that for a long time, the black pall, the singing of the *Libera me, Domine*, formed the obligatory atmosphere of every funeral and, unfortunately, there were also different classes at different rates. Today the Council wants the ringing note of hope and certainty of the resurrection to prevail in the liturgy for the dead: black is replaced by violet, the *Dies Irae* by the *Alleluia*.

Rather than change, this is a different emphasis; instead of insisting on the fear of divine justice, which was stressed from the Middle Ages on, we are recovering the sense of trust that already shone very vividly through St. Paul and the very earliest Christian inscriptions. "May you live in God," said the inscriptions on the tombs in the catacombs. The Christians of Thessalonica, unlike us, all wanted to be present at the second coming of Christ, and St. Paul had to calm them, explaining that the time of the end of the world was uncertain. And as for the classes at funerals and weddings, that constitutes an intolerable different treatment that offends the poor and privileges the rich who aren't regular churchgoers to the detriment of those who aren't rich, but who are excellent Christians.

A third obstacle is the arbitrary control exerted by some on the pretext of a liturgy that is more suitable, more intimate, closer to the people or to a group. I read in Italian and foreign magazines that some priests actually celebrate in slacks and shirt sleeves; they ignore this or that part of the rites of the Mass or the Sacraments; they use formularies that have not been approved or even give way to improvisation outside of the cases provided for in the liturgical norms; they have the laity join in the recitation of the Canon; they invent new rites or transfer rites from their established place. These are illicit and dangerous attitudes. Illicit, because they are contrary to the Council, which has declared: "The regulation of the sacred liturgy depends solely on the authority of the Church [. . .] absolutely no other person, not even a priest, may add, remove or change anything in the liturgy on his own authority."[6] Dangerous, because they are an insult to the Christian people, who have the simple right to participate in a liturgy which is not that of a private individual, but the authentic public worship of the Church.

IT IS THE TIME OF UNITY AND CHARITY

At this point, I address a prayer to my brother priests: try to take proper advantage of the treasures of the renewed liturgy. And towards this end:

1. Hold fast to some theological principles that regulate the liturgy: the Mass is the most sublime act of our religion, the true sacrifice of Christ, not a mere convivial gathering and an opportunity to meet joyously together; as priests you are the envoys of Christ and not simply delegates of the community or group; Church with a capital C are the universal Church and the diocese; subordinately, and, until possible new directions, the parish: the groups, the "base communities" have a right in some way to call themselves Church and to carry out a useful role, if they are integrated into the parish and the diocese; otherwise they can become counter churches and do not celebrate legitimate liturgies.

2. You can see and hear: the world today is pleasure-loving but it is neither joyous nor tranquil; in its anguish it feels a need for God and, perhaps unconsciously, its appeal to us priests is: "Lord,

teach us to pray." (Lk 11:1). Let us teach them authentic prayer; let us not give stones to those who ask us for bread or a scorpion to those who ask us for a fish (cf. Lk 11:1).

3. Be faithful administrators and servants of the Word of God. For this reason: a) pay respectful attention to the Word itself in study, prayer, recollection, in the careful preparation of your homilies; b) respect the organization of the lectionary and have all three of the Sunday and feast-day readings proclaimed, at least as a rule; c) oversee the spiritual and technical preparation of the lectors; d) try to give homilies that are stimulating and concrete, but avoid making a secular platform of your pulpit; e) throw the light of the Biblical readings on the concrete situations of life, but also illustrate sometimes this or that part of the Mass, so that the Mass itself may become a speaking catechesis.

4. The "sense of the sacred" tends to diminish in a secularized society. Don't let it diminish through our fault; the gestures, attitudes, vestments and objects used during our liturgy should be a sincere expression of faith and love of God and should stimulate the "sense of the sacred" in the faithful. "Creativity" is suggested in certain cases as in the choice between one reading and another, between one rite and another, as well as in some established free interjections. Beyond certain limits, it is abusive and imprudent, because it compromises the principle of *lex supplicandi legem statuit credendi* [the law of prayer establishes the law of belief]. If any originality is desired, let it be that of the saints, who went to the altar and returned from it with their hearts full of the love of God each in their own way, and who appeared anything but facile with mechanical and standardized gestures. But let's avoid putting ourselves on display and of being too "creative" there, where the prevalent part should be left to the hidden work of God's grace.

My second prayer is addressed to the faithful. They too, up to a certain point, must feel responsible for a correct liturgical celebration.

They should agree to take an active and warm part in such a way that their fraternal communion is visible in the liturgy; they should, if prepared, be lectors; let them take part in the singing, which gives a supplement of soul to the prayers of the assembly and melds their hearts in unity. In acting in the liturgy, the laity exercise the common priesthood they received at Baptism; they should, however, try to exercise it decorously. As does not, it seems to me that soloist, Golden Throat, who, microphone in hand, turns toward the faithful, with movements and glances which scrutinize the audience and expect its approval, and acts like a singing star. A similar case, that of the *très jolie jeune fille* [very pretty young woman] who appeared onscreen on French TV: she was distributing Communion to the faithful, and every now and then, she would push her flowing hair behind her neck with a rapid, elegant motion of her hand.

At times I receive from the laity protests about certain liturgies that they regard as contrary to the norms. Everyone can write to the bishop, but generally, in this case, it is preferable for the faithful to speak to their respective priests: certain things can be smoothed out better by conferring directly. For instance, the Council has declared "The pipe organ . . . adds a wonderful splendor to the Church's ceremonies and powerfully lifts up souls to God." I signed these words with both hands; I cannot forget, however, that the Church asks the faithful to bring something of their own to their participation at Mass. Now if the Mass is for young people and the young people feel that guitars and modern music are their own, I accept that at times the organ will be silent. I only ask that the music and text of the young people not be unworthy of the temple and that they harmonize with the liturgy.

In conclusion, I return to the starting point. Does the church in Venice want to commit itself more to human advancement? *Ab*

Jove principium, as the ancient Romans said. Begin with God. Begin with liturgical prayer: this, if it is well done, unites us to one another, unites us more intimately to God and forms us for decisive and in-depth action.

May our Lady intercede for us and obtain for us full health (*salute*), that is both spiritual and temporal progress for the Venetian Church, which has invoked her for centuries with immense trust under this very title of the Madonna della Salute.

Notes

1 *Opera* 7:495-501. The title means "Our Lady of Good Health."—Trans.

2 This convention, held in Rome beginning in October 1976, focused on themes put forward at the 1974 Synod of Bishops and the Apostolic Exhortation *Evangelii Nuntiandi* by Paul VI (December 8, 1975).—Trans.

3 cf. SC 5-6.

4 cf. SC 5-6.

5 cf. Ibid., 28.

6 Ibid., 22.

The Saints: Filled With His Light

Homily for the Feast of the Epiphany[1]
January 6, 1973

We can find a guiding thread in the three readings for Epiphany. "The glory of God has shone upon us," says Isaiah. Paul continues: it shines on everyone now, even on the pagans. St. Matthew concludes: behold the Magi, behold the mysterious representatives of all the peoples of the earth, the first called, the first enlightened!

What is this divine glory that fills the whole world? The Council has written: "The Lord Jesus, the divine teacher and model of every perfection, has preached holiness of life to each and every one of His disciples, of every condition."[2] Christ is the *lumen gentium*, the light that is reflected, first and especially on the face of the Church,[3] so that he might then give light to the nations, that is, the world, by his teaching and his holy life. But he is too perfect to be imitated completely: each of us is completely fascinated by him, but we are each struck in a special way by this or that feature of his moral face. St. Paul was struck and won over by the fire that Christ brought to earth to set the whole world ablaze. St. Francis of Assisi admired Christ for his complete stripping at the cross. St. Vincent de Paul took from Christ his love of the poor and orphans; St. John Bosco, his love of young people; the Curé d'Ars, his seeking of poor sinners. The saints are people who allow themselves to be filled with the holiness of Christ, and who say to him: "Jesus, you are the only beauty; the Father himself is pleased with you; you have said to us: 'Follow me,' 'I am the way.' Well, here we are, we love you as no one loves a father or a mother, we want to imitate You, act in everything—although amid weaknesses and imperfections—as you acted."

Many people, in speaking of the Church, dwell on her defects; some Catholics indeed seem to be gripped by a kind of sadism and they constantly say: "Look how bad our Church is!" No, the Church, because she is made up of human beings, has defects and faults, but she is beautiful! Beautiful for many reasons. One is the "glory of God," the sanctity of so many of her children.

I have mentioned St. Francis of Assisi. Young, rich, attractive and enterprising, at the age of twenty-four, he strips himself of everything to wed "Lady Poverty," just as his crucified love had done. To a society of the proud, the predatory and the libidinous he proposed the three vows of poverty, chastity and obedience. He was followed by thousands of men. He carried out a great reform in the Church not by criticizing others, but by criticizing himself; and not with showy gestures, but with humble actions. For example, he became aware one day that an elderly friar was ill. There was no medicine. "If this friar were to eat some ripe grapes early in the morning," he thought, "I believe he would get better." One morning, then, he got up very early, without attracting attention. He called the friar and took him to the vineyard, which stood near the church. He spotted a vine from which some fine bunches of grapes hung, ripe for eating, and seated next to the friar, took some to eat, so that he would not be ashamed to eat alone. And while they enjoyed them, the friar praised the Lord God.[4]

Among the first Franciscan saints is St. Louis, the king of France. His many prayers did not keep him from being jovial and playful; rather they helped him govern the kingdom wisely and face the difficulties of his married life serenely. "He had married very young Marguerite of Provence, a provocative girl of fourteen. After a few years of flaming passion for his pretty wife, Louis was not slow to judge her too frivolous, too flirtatious, too little adequate to his own deep mystical aspirations. She was capable, yes, of showing herself a true queen, which was apparent during the drama of the Crusade, but also capable of little machinations, of half-betrayals, which could not fail to trouble him. And yet to this marriage, which at bottom was nothing a long and often painful misunderstanding, he remained completely faithful. In the eyes of God, in the eyes of men, not a single gesture on his part belied the motto which he had once had engraved inside his ring: 'In this ring is all my love.'"[5]

These two are only the beginning of a whole flowering of saints that would emerge from Franciscan spirituality. But Benedictine, Dominican, Carmelite and other forms of spirituality also gave numerous saints to the Church. More numerous still are the saints who do not belong to any specific ascetic tendency.

There are the young people: Agnes, a martyr at the age of 12; "Girls of her age," St. Ambrose wrote, "cannot manage to bear irritated looks from their parents; a pinprick makes them cry. Agnes offers her whole body to the point of the sword that the soldier brandishes over her in blind rage." There is Dominic Savio, one of Don Bosco's boys, a saint at 16. St. Joan of Arc ended her adventurous, mystical and military life at the age of 19. St. Bartolomea Capitanio, the founder of the Sisters of the Child Mary, died at the age of 26. St. Thérèse of the Child Jesus, called by Pius X the greatest saint of modern times, died at 24.

There are the lay people. Elizabeth, the daughter of the king of Hungary, married at 14 to Ludwig, the Landgrave of Thuringia, loved her husband with a marvelous love, and was loved greatly by him in return, but was left a widow at the age of 20, while she was expecting her third child. She died at 24, impressing all of Europe by her goodness and life of penitence. Blessed Contardo Ferrini, on the other hand, was married to science alone. When he received his degree in criminal law at 21, the judging committee found itself facing not a student, but a master. Mommsen said that "through the merit of Ferrini, the primacy in the study of Roman law passed from Germany to Italy." His friend Pius XI declared that his faith and his Christian life seemed almost miraculous in his job and at his time.

I am talking about canonized saints, but the amount of sanctity in life is much more extensive than sanctity that has been proclaimed officially. The Pope canonizes only authentic saints, true, but he does not claim, nor can he claim, to canonize all existing but unknown saints. And if we make a kind of selection here on earth, God does not do the same in heaven; when we arrive in heaven, we will probably find mothers, workers, professionals and students placed higher than the official saints we venerate on earth.

In fact, in order to be saints it is not necessary to accomplish extraordinary things, perform miracles, or be privileged with very special graces. It is also enough to perform ordinary works, though the commitment and love of God are not ordinary. St. Vincent de Paul astonished France by the greatness of the works that he was able to carry out in favor of the poor, orphans, and galley slaves, at a time of exceptional misery and calamity. But it was not the great works, but the great love that guided and sustained him in his works, that made him a saint. "Why," he asked, "must we be patient?" Perhaps because, all things considered, patience is useful?—Not only for this reason, Vincent answered, but above all for love of Christ, who has said: "Learn from me, for I am meek and humble of heart." "Why be sincere at any cost?" Is it perhaps because frankness and loyalty are beautiful things?—No, he answered, but above all in order to imitate Christ, who has said: "Let your words be 'yes, yes,' 'no, no!'" Some highly placed people accused him unjustly before the queen. "In your place, I would defend myself," the sovereign said.—"No, Majesty, our Lord did not defend himself from the accusations of the Pharisees." "The number of your missionaries is very few," he was told.—"No matter," he answered, "it is thus that we honor the small number of Christ's apostles." They didn't want him to concern himself with the poor who had mental illnesses, whom many of his contemporaries, out of prejudice and ignorance, believed to be possessed by demons. He said: "Our Lord wanted to be surrounded even by lunatics, demoniacs, the mad, the tempted, and the possessed: they brought them to him from every side, so that he might liberate and heal them . . . why are you reproving us for trying to imitate him?" And he urged the order of sisters he had founded: "When you go to see the mentally ill, say to yourselves: I am going to these poor people to honor the uncreated wisdom of a God who wanted to be considered (by Herod) as a madman."

St. Vincent is an authority for all of us: Christ, always Christ! Let's try to imitate him in everything so that at every step he is the golden rule of our life. He has said to everyone: "Follow me, learn from me, you are the light of the world, you are the salt of the earth." In his light all realities are immersed; in it even ugly things become beautiful, all small things grow larger, even banal things are elevated. Let us allow ourselves to be filled with his light and try to be not just mildly good, but very good—that is, saints.

Notes

1 *Opera* 6:14-17. The original title was "The Glory of God has Shone upon Us."—Trans.

2 LG, no. 40.

3 LG, no. 1.

4 *Assisi Compilation* 53.

5 Henri Daniel-Rops, *La Chiesa delle Cattedrali e delle Crociate*, (Torino, 1954), p. 345 [*Cathedral and Crusade: Studies of the Medieval Church, 1050—1350*, translated by John Warrington (London: Dent, 1957).—Trans].

Never Enough of Mary

Opening Address at the National Liturgical
Week in Bologna[1]
August 30, 1976

"De Maria numquam satis [Never enough of Mary]," it was
once said, and it was good, if we think of how much Our Lady
deserves to be honored; saving the intentions, on the other hand, it
was sometimes not so good and did not sound very fitting; when, for
example, Mariology and Marian devotion were turned into a
competition and a race as to who would say the most or say it most
lyrically, into an accumulation of more and more new titles and
privileges, into appeals and pressures on the Magisterium of the
Church to obtain new feasts and new pronouncements, with the risk
of creating difficulties with the separated brothers or with those
Catholics who had not first been properly prepared for the
innovation.

"De Maria nunc satis? [Enough, now, of Mary?]," some now
tend to say. It can be partially just, if we mean checking or stopping
the race mentioned above. It would be mistaken if we were to want
to arrest the study and deeper appreciation of Mariology and
especially the true devotion to the Virgin. Some years ago, during
his Christmas homily, the late Cardinal Döpfner declared: "Devotion
to Mary in its various aspects is part of Catholic piety. It is
impossible to conceive of the life of the Church without the Rosary,
the month of May, Marian feasts, Marian shrines and the many
images of Our Lady."[2]

Döpfner then enumerated some of today's questions: "Isn't
devotion to Mary isolated, separated from Christ and a conception
of the redemption inspired by Scripture and an essential, liturgical
piety? Isn't it an obstacle to the present liturgical renewal?"[3] He

himself gave brief and pertinent responses to the questions. Before he died, however, he was able to read the exhaustive responses of *Marialis Cultis*, in which Paul VI felicitously comments on and completes the chapter of the Council "On the Blessed Virgin Mary." We must hope that *Marialis Cultis* will open a new literary genre and a new period of Mariology, closer to salvation history and to the renewal of biblical and patristic studies, while Marian devotion is to be more centered on the liturgy. The privileges of Mary will still be recognized, but more emphasis will be placed on the poverty of the "handmaid of the Lord" and on her human qualities, such as her energetic readiness to come to the service of her neighbor. The unique perfection to which she attained through the privilege of God will unfurl like a banner and will say to all humanity: "Everyone is called to a similar perfection and will arrive at it more or less according to how each one more or less approaches the work and the person of the one Redeemer."

1. Salvation history? In order to speak of it we must begin with the Trinity, in which God the Father from all eternity transmits his own being and his own happiness to his Word, and through the Word, to the Holy Spirit. The Word, the perfect and coeternal image of the Father, in contemplating him, feels a thrill of joy, ravished by his beauty. The Holy Spirit, in his turn, from the mutual ecstasy of the Father and the Son, blazes forth like a fire of love. In eternity still, the three decide: "Let us create other beings and call them to join themselves to this joyous life of ours, within their own limits, by an act of our liberality that will elevate them in an extraordinary way!" This decision is the "plan of salvation" and it becomes "salvation history" as soon as it begins to be realized on earth through a long, continuous, and most merciful series of interventions by God in the lives of men.

I imagine these interventions developing on the two sloping sides of a roof. On the first slope humanity, impelled and assisted by God, climbs laboriously, with the Jewish people at its head, towards

Christ, the peak of the roof of human history. On the second slope, humanity, spurred on and assisted especially by the Holy Spirit, with the Church at its head, descends towards eschatological times, and when these times have come, over the present world, completely remade, will be pronounced the words "new heavens and a new earth" (2 Peter 3:13). Then the Church can be called in fullness "the people gathered in the unity of the Father, the Son and the Holy Spirit,"4 and the plan the mystery, St. Paul would say, first hidden in God, then revealed, then glimpsed, more than seen by us, will be stripped of every shadow in order to appear to us in all its splendor.

2. The peak of a roof is a poor image. With immensely greater effectiveness, St. Paul says "the fullness of time." There is the center of "salvation history," and there Mary should be placed. "When the fullness of time had come, God sent his Son, born of a woman" (Gal. 4:4). That woman, Mary, is called eleven times in the New Testament "the mother of Jesus" (Mt 2:10, 13:20, 12:46-50; Mk 3:3135; Lk 1:4243, 2:33-34 and 48-50, 8:19-21; Jn 2:23, 19:25-26; Acts 1:14).

Since Jesus is both man and God, we can also call Mary "the Mother of God." Out of love for Scripture and faithful to the Council of Chalcedon, Karl Barth himself states: "It is necessary to accept for Mary the title of 'Mother of God' if we want to touch the two aspects of the mystery: that is, that Jesus truly belongs to humankind, to our history, and that the son of Mary is identical with Him whom the Father has begotten from all eternity."5 Continuing, Barth says that being the Mother of God was Mary's great privilege, but a privilege granted to her in the working of the Incarnation. Agreed, but in its turn, the Incarnation is related to the salvation of mankind. Is Mary the servant of God only for the Incarnation or for the salvation of mankind too? In the beginning, God had touched the clay, and made of it a masterpiece: Adam. Did something similar happen with Mary? Touched by God, and used by him, but did she remain passive as that clay did? Or was she at once passive and active, in regard to that divine masterpiece, which is the salvation of mankind? That is the question. A beginning, or a hint of a response comes from the splendid way that God is accustomed to act towards man.

The psalmist says:

When I behold your heavens, the work of your fingers,
the moon and the stars which you set into place
What is man that you should be mindful of him,
or the son of man that you should care for him?
You have made him little less than the angels,
and crowned him with glory and honor . . .
putting all things under his feet. (Psalm 8:47)

So much trust, therefore, and so much power have been given to man that he becomes neither a passive being nor a simple bit player, but a great actor who works alongside the eternal protagonist, who really wants to see in man "a greater imprint of his spirit stamped on him by his creator!" Why could God not have found a way to give the Mother of God, already raised to cooperate in the Incarnation, the role of a great leading lady alongside the supreme protagonist of the redemption? Here the Council affirms: Mary, by her *yes*, "embracing God's saving will with a full heart . . . devoted herself totally as a handmaid of the Lord to the person and work of her Son. In subordination to Him and along with him, by the grace of Almighty God she served the mystery of redemption";[6] she was "used by God not merely in a passive way, but cooperating in the work of human salvation through free faith and obedience."[7]

The Council here treads softly and cautiously. "Free faith, obedience and cooperation" by the Virgin yes, but "by the grace of almighty God, under Christ and with Christ, as a servant, in the service of the mystery." Farther down, repeating the same concept four whole times, the Council will say: "The saving influences of the Blessed Virgin on men originate . . . from the divine will. They flow forth from the superabundance of the merits of Christ, rest on his mediation, depend entirely on it, and draw all their power from it." It adds: "In no way do they impede the immediate union of the faithful with Christ. Rather, they foster this union."[8]

For the Council, therefore, there is no danger of the person of Mary screening or shielding us from Christ, or of her creating a distance between Christ and believers!

3. We know: "One is the mediator between God and men, the man Christ Jesus" (1 Tim 2:5). Two lines below these words, however, St. Paul writes: "I have been made . . . herald and apostle . . . teacher in the faith" (1 Tim 2:7). Therefore the economy of salvation means that the only mediator for saving men makes use, with him and under him, of other men. Max Thurian stresses that "denying every other mediation outside of that of Christ, even if only a mediation in him, and by means of him, leads to . . . denying even the real mediation of Christ."[9] Neither are we to fear that admitting Mary's cooperation will lead to emptying God's grace of its value. Catholics, indeed, must remember that not even the beginning of, not even the desire for a meritorious action is in our power, unless God helps us.

The semi-Pelagians used to say: a sick man cannot get better by himself without the medicine and the doctor, but by himself he can at least begin his cure, by desiring it. We, on the other hand, say: in the supernatural field, by our efforts alone, we cannot even desire salvation unless God helps us, by stimulating a lively feeling for good, which has remained in us even after original sin. In every case, with St. Augustine, we affirm that in crowning our merits, God is crowning his own gifts. In one house, some of the children offer their father flowers from the garden for his birthday; they offer them to their mother and all the guests too. In this case, not only is it clear that the garden and the flowers belong to the father, but it is also clear that the father himself wishes and desires that the flowers be offered by his children. Our Lady is a favored daughter of God: if she acts generously and splendidly with men and with God Himself, she does it with the gifts of God and through the will of God.

4. But these considerations are, I would say, *theologumena*. Better to read Scripture and the Fathers. St. Luke, in his account of the Annunciation, presents Mary to us in such a way that she fills alongside Christ, the second Adam, the role of a new Eve. The angel calls her to faith as the serpent had called Eve to disbelief. Thus the obedience of Mary corresponds to the disobedience of Eve; her acceptance of being "the handmaid of the Lord" in her self-denial, contrasts with the will of Eve to assert herself and put herself in the place of God.

This theme, as the Council also notes,[10] was dear to the Fathers, who often contrasted the triad of Christ-Cross-Mary to the triad of Adam-tree-Eve; medicine-remedy-salvation contrasted with disease-corruption-fall.

5. St. Luke, again, stresses the presence of Mary in the midst of the Church which, still miniscule and not presented officially to the world, waits in prayer for the coming of the Holy Spirit. It is true that Mary had already had a first Pentecost of her own in the Annunciation. And, having received the Holy Spirit, she hastened to go to Elizabeth, impatient, as the apostles would also later be, to announce the *Magnalia Dei* [mighty deeds of God] by her *Magnificat* and with the active help of her cousin.

It is the presence of Mary in the upper room, however, that is emblematic. From that time on, Mary and the Church will no longer be separated in the minds of Christians and the Council has done well in including Our Lady in the Constitution on the Church. Shortly before the Council, Cardinal Journet, in his work *L'Église du Verbe Incarné*, dedicated a paragraph to the "Relationship of the doctrine on the Virgin and the doctrine on the Church,"[11] he stated that ecclesiology and Mariology *"sont faites d'une même étoffe, et portent sur le même mystère consideré d'une part dans sa réalisation* exceptionelle, *et d'autre part dans sa réalisation* commune [are made from the same fabric, and bear upon the same mystery, considered on the one hand in its *exceptional* realization, and on the other in its *ordinary* realization]." A little above, he had said: touch only certain nerve centers on grace, and on merit, and you will see: "*La doctrine catholique sur la Vierge, et la doctrine catholique sur l'Église, s'écrouleront simultanément.* [The Catholic doctrine on the Virgin, and the doctrine on the Church will fall simultaneously]."

In the Apocalypse St. John describes the woman clothed with the sun with the moon under her feet and on her head a crown of twelve stars. She gives birth in great pain to a boy destined to govern all nations, who is immediately caught up to God, while the woman flees into the desert (cf. Rev 12:16). It is probable that this woman symbolizes the Church of the Old Covenant, which, through Mary, gives birth to Christ and with him the Church of the New Covenant. The same John presents Mary to us at the beginning and at the end of the public life of Jesus. At Cana she appears as the one through whom one comes to Jesus and who exhorts people to have faith in him, saying: "Do whatever he tells you" (cf. Jn 2:1-12). This invitation by Mary is all the more effective, in as much as the one who received it had also had the opportunity to note how attentive she had been, with lovingly vigilant eyes, to the needs of two poor newlyweds and how she had then presented them with discretion to Jesus. At the foot of the cross, on the other hand, Mary is an example of how we must follow Christ until the end, even in the most painful experiences of life. We cannot deny, however, that the "Church-Mary" theme remains a rather complex one. The Church, in fact, not only has multiform aspects *in herself*, but she also has multiform relations with Mary.

Paul VI, who has declared Mary the "mother of the Church," also often calls her our "sister," while St. Francis de Sales calls her with tenderness "our grandmother," so that he might have the consolation of seeing himself as her grandson, who jumps with complete confidence into her lap.[12] In any case, the Church should look at her as a model. The Church should also feel that she is a "handmaid" par excellence close to the one great "servant" for the benefit of the people who are to be helped and saved. Mary, in turn, as the subject of ever greater study and devotion, should become in the consciences of Christians the one who has perfectly realized the vocation to which God calls all humanity; the one who is here and now preparing for and allowing us to foresee what the Church will be in her blossoming from this world into the world to come.

6. Meanwhile today's Mariology seems to be turning toward the near future. The so-called "devotional" variety seems less abundant than at one time, even though improved in quality. There is an increase, on the other hand, in learned Mariology, which I read as subdivided into biblical, historical, psychological, ecumenical, iconographic, cartographic, bibliographic, pneumatological, apparitional . . . An "Arab Muslim Marian literature" has even emerged. All good, as long as we keep in mind at least three objectives: not to lose contact with the past, not to end up on the dry ground of too arid a Mariology, not to neglect the *sensus fidelium*.

This is a kind of instinct or intuition, which the Holy Spirit gives to simple and good people concerning the things of the spirit, in order to help them to choose and discern correctly what is right. Ecclesiastical authority must verify and guide this *sensus*, of course, but it must also respect it and take in into account. I didn't visit the exhibit of the *ex-voto* offerings of Our Lady of St. Luke, organized in Bologna for the Centenary; they tell me that it's very interesting. A few weeks ago however, I saw the *ex-votos* hung in the corridors adjacent to the Marian shrine of Pietralba (Weissenstein): well, it is incredible how many people, and for how long and with what attention, stop to read these stories of faith and gratitude from the people; this means that even those little painted plaques have a voice and preach a sermon: a sermon from the people to the people. Last year in Brazil, in Santa Maria, a diocese in the State of Rio Grande do Sul, I participated in the *"romaria"* (pilgrimage) for Our Lady the Mediatrix: more than 200,000 people participated; after the concelebrated Mass, I congratulated the bishops who were present. "But you didn't see the *"romaria"* of the *Aparecida*, a month ago," they answered, "it was called a 'national flood.' Try to imagine it: a little town; without warning, 400,000 pilgrims arrive in 14,000 buses; the police who are keeping order no longer know which way to turn; it is impossible to find a glass of water or an orangeade, much less a dinner."

Dom Ivo Lorscheiter, the bishop of Santa Maria, added: "I used to be rather skeptical about these displays; then I saw that the people had them in their hearts; when they have been properly prepared and perfected, and when decades of the Rosary are interpolated during the procession, with liturgical songs, passages read from the Bible and brief explanations, and the whole is directed toward the final eucharistic liturgy, it becomes a magnificent occasion for catechesis and a form of worship offered with great decorum, as well as with great devotion." A majestic echo of Lorscheiter's words, it seems to me, is the mention made by Paul VI, in *Evangelii nuntiandi*, "of the values of popular piety, enriched through education that is directed toward evangelization."[13]

7. Besides bowing towards the people, in Mariology we must also bow toward the past, because all that has been said and done about Our Lady that is good and valid should not be lost.

In regard to Marian devotion, the Pope states that "the Church in every age has paid tribute to it with scrupulous study of the truth and always with careful nobility of form."[14] A timely and responsible statement, which does not exclude, however, the possibility of some deviations, exaggerations or superstitions in this or that particular church, or this or that individual little group which later, at the proper time, are renounced and corrected.

Typical of the Mariology of the past, for example, is *The Glories of Mary* by St. Alphonsus. Today it is very little read; but in the past, it went through 109 editions in Italian, 324 in French, 37 in

Spanish, 32 in English, 80 in German, 60 in Dutch, and 73 in other languages. We must admit that the numerous "examples" brought into the work are often ingenuous or legendary or historically false–at any rate not suitable for shrewd readers like us. The saint, however, used these examples not as proof but as a means of illustrating truths in a plastic way for people with very little education; in other words here we have a grownup resolving to use baby talk in order to make himself understood by children, a future Doctor of the Church who earns his laurels by teaching solid doctrine, but in the manner of an elementary school teacher. In this he can be an example to us: a theologian who not only talks about Mary, but who talks about Mary while constantly inserting very tender prayers. Let's speak and write a great deal about Our Lady, but in such a way that we make ourselves understood by everyone and touch hearts. Something that will not succeed unless we ourselves first have hearts that have been touched. St. Alphonsus did this when he composed songs for his poor illiterate people, sung afterwards for more than a hundred years throughout Italy, especially during the missions and the month of May. Don Bosco had his boys sing them. One, for example, begins:

> O my beautiful hope
> My sweet love Mary
> You are my life
> You are my peace.

Another begins like this:
> You are pure, you are merciful
> you are beautiful, O Mary
> Every soul knows
> There is no sweeter mother in all the world.

8. I realize that I have now entered the field of the heart. Sentimentality, what the Council calls "sterile and outmoded

sentiment"[15] is not appropriate, but it is appropriate for the heart, as well as the mind and the will, to be involved in the practice of Marian devotion. "Let the name of Mary not leave your lips," writes St. Bernard, "let it not abandon your hearts."

The Venetian Leonardo Giustiniani, in a lyric attributed to him, says:

> Tell me, sweet Mary,
> of the delight you had
> looking at your little Son,
> Christ my God . . .
> Oh what joy you felt, oh what good
> When you held him in your arms! . . .
> Oh, how many sweet acts of love you made,
> being with your gentle little Son! . . .

The person who wrote like that felt Mary near to him, and opened his own heart to her with confidence, which is also a human thing, or as they would say today, an "anthropological and psychological" thing!

Another observation. The Pope himself encourages us to new Marian studies, exhorting us to take them on with the assurance that we will arrive at new results. And we will: some aspects of Mary have yet to be studied or properly appreciated. It is good, however, to be on guard against calling new what is old, continually crying "discovery," "rediscovery," or "recovery."

I will provide a few examples. "Today, no more sentimentality, but actions," they say. But we have always said this. St. Louis Marie Grignion de Montfort judged severely the Christians who, while leading wicked lives, thought to save themselves with a few little devotions "under the mantle of the Virgin." "There is nothing more culpable," he wrote, "than this diabolical pretense."[16] "Let's stick to the essential," they say, but Newman, in his letter to Pusey, already distinguished between faith and devotion in regard to

Our Lady, writing: "We back up the devotion with faith; for us there is no risk of putting Mary in the place of Jesus, of making a divinity of the Mother of God."[17]

It is especially considered a great novelty to discover that Our Lady was poor and is close to the poor. But this too is something ancient. St. Luke had already noted that Mary was able to bring to the temple only "a pair of turtledoves," the offering of the poor (Lk 9:23). The Council has already described a Mary who "leads a life on earth common to all, full of family concerns and work."[18] That the poor have always felt privileged in regard to her is apparent from many prayers, the essence of which is "Intercede with God for me; I have a right to your intercession simply because I am poor." A prayer of this kind travels through the centuries; and parallel to it there travels a story on the poor people of Mary: it appeared in France in the 1200's, and has been passed on from age to age, told by popular preachers as an example, even written down by literary types like Anatole France and set to music by Jules Massenet in his little opera, *Le Jongleur de Notre Dame*.

The *jongleur* is Barnabé de Compiegne, so expert in his conjuring tricks that he leaves the people open-mouthed at the country fairs: and yet he remains miserably poor and hungry. And it is while suffering from relentless hunger on a night of freezing rain that he meets a monk on the road. "Friend," the latter says to him, "How did you come to be dressed all in green?" "Because I am a *jongleur* by profession, the finest trade in the world." "Friend," the monk replies, "take care what you say: there is no finer profession than to be a monk, because in the monastery we celebrate the praises of God, the Virgin, and the Saints." This was something new to Barnabé; on the invitation of the monk, he agreed to become a religious too.

But after a short time, he became dejected. He said to himself: "See, the prior composes treatises on Our Lady; Brother Macrobius recopies them on the finest parchment, which Brother Alexander then decorates with enchanting miniatures; other monks sing the praises of Mary; others compose hymns or sculpt statues in her honor; but I know how to do nothing, nothing." One day, however, slipping away from the community, he went to the chapel of Our Lady, and continued to do so every day, and he no longer appeared sad, but merry.

With two old monks, the prior decided to go and see what was happening in that chapel, and through the crack in the door, he saw: Barnabé, standing on his head, throwing some copper balls up with one hand, which he then caught with his feet with extraordinary dexterity. In honor of Our Lady, of course; not having anything else, Barnabé offered what he could. The two old monks cried sacrilege, the prior thought that good Barnabé was mad; all three made ready to drag him out of the chapel. But behold, they saw the Virgin descend the steps of the altar, go up to Barnabé and dry with her blue mantle the sweat falling in drops from his forehead. Holding their breath, the three monks stood still. "Blessed are the poor in spirit." said the prior. "Our Lady appeared to him, poor and ignorant, not to us, who are wise and learned!" said the other two. "Amen," responded the prior, kissing the ground.[19]

Begging your pardon for this last digression, I end with the following words once attributed to St. Augustine:[20] "I have spoken, not as well as the importance and greatness of the theme would have required, but as well as my meager preparation has allowed. If what is written is true, thanks to you, O Christ, that I have not been able to feel anything except what was pious and worthy of the Blessed Virgin, your Mother. If therefore I have written as I should, give me your approval, you and yours, I beg you. If on the other hand, I have not written as I should, pardon me, and may my readers pardon me" . . . and my listeners!

Notes

1 *Opera* 7:421-31.

[2] J. Döpfner, *La Chiesa vivente oggi* (Ed. Paoline, 1972), p. 227.

[3] Ibid.

[4] LG, no. 4.

[5] K. Barth, *Die Kirchliche Dogmatik*, 1, 2 p. 152.

[6] LG, no. 56.

[7] Ibid.

[8] LG, no. 60.

[9] Cited by P. Emonet in *Esprit et Vie* (1971), pp. 233-34.

[10] LG, no. 50.

[11] "Parenté de la doctrine sur la Vierge et la doctrine sur l'Église," cf. *L'Église du Verbe Incarné*, vol. II, p. 392.

[12] Cf. *Introduction à la Vie Devote*, ch. 16, *Oeuvres*, vol III, pp. 104-105.

[13] Cf. EN, no. 48, in AAS, 1976, pp. 37-38.

[14] MC, no. 15. [15] LG, no. 67.

[16] *Trattato della vera devozione* (Rome, 1963), no. 99.

[17] Cited in *Ésprit et Vie*, (1971), p. 500.

[18] AA, no. 4.

[19] The version that Luciani uses here was by Anatole France, "Le jongleur de Notre Dame," in *Etui de nacre* (1892). Massenet's opera was based on this version, but with some changes.—Trans.

[20] PL 40, col 1148.

Is the Rosary Outdated?

Homily for the Centenary of the Feast of the Holy Rosary[1]
October 7, 1973

What would happen during a meeting of Catholics if I were to invite the ladies and gentlemen to show what they had in their pockets or purses? I would certainly see a quantity of combs, pocket mirrors, tubes of lipstick, change purses, cigarette lighters and other more or less useful little items. But how many rosaries? Years ago, I would have seen more of them. In Manzoni's house in Milan today, you can see his rosary beads hanging at the head of his bed: he said the rosary habitually and in his novel *The Betrothed*, Lucia pulled out her beads and said the rosary at the most dramatic moments.[2] Windthorst, a German statesman, was once invited by some friends who were non-practicing Catholics to show his rosary. It was a trick: they had removed his rosary from his left pocket beforehand. When Windthorst did not find it in the left one, he put his hand into the right and ended up looking good: He always carried a spare rosary! Christophe von Gluck, a great musician, used to withdraw for a few minutes during receptions at the Court of Vienna to say his rosary. Blessed Contardo Ferrini, a university professor in Pavia, would invite his friends to say the rosary when he was a guest in their home. St. Bernadette assured us that when Our Lady appeared to her, she had a rosary over her arm, asked her if she also had one, and invited her to say it, while the Virgin recommended the reciting of the rosary to the three little shepherds at Fatima.

Why have I begun with this series of examples?

Because the rosary is contested by some. They say: it is an infantile and superstitious prayer, not worthy of adult Christians. Or: it is a prayer that becomes automatic, reduced to a hasty, monotonous and boring repetition of Hail Marys. Or: it's old-fashioned stuff; today there are better things: the reading of the Bible, for example, which is to the rosary as the wheat is to the chaff!

On this subject, allow me to give a few impressions as a shepherd of souls.

A first impression: the crisis of the rosary comes in second place. Today, in first place, there is a crisis of prayer in general. People are completely caught up in material interests; they think very little about their souls. And noise has invaded our existence. Macbeth would be able to repeat: I have murdered sleep, I have murdered silence![3] We have trouble finding a few little scraps of time for the inner life and the *dulcis sermoncinatio* or "sweet colloquy" with God. And it is a real loss. Donoso Cortes said: "Today the world is going badly because there are more battles than there are prayers." Communal liturgies, which are certainly a great good, are being developed: they are not enough, however; personal conversation with God is also necessary.

A second impression. When people talk about "adult Christians" in prayer, sometimes they exaggerate. Personally, when I speak alone with God and Our Lady, I prefer to feel like a child rather than an adult. The miter, the skullcap and the ring disappear; I send the adult on vacation and the bishop too, with the staid, serious and dignified behavior that go along with them, in order to abandon myself to the spontaneous tenderness that a child has for Mama and Papa. To be, at least for half an hour or so, as I am in reality, with my misery and the best of myself, to feel surfacing from the depths of my being the child I once was, a child who wants to laugh, chatter and to love the Lord, and who sometimes feels the need to weep so that mercy may be shown him, helps me to pray. The rosary, a simple and easy prayer, in turn, helps me to be a child, and I am not ashamed of it at all.

A third impression. I should not and do not want to think badly of anyone, but I confess that I have several times been tempted to conclude that this or that person thinks he is an adult just because he is acting like a judge, criticizing from on high. I feel like saying to him: "What do you mean, mature? When it comes to prayer, you are an adolescent in crisis, a disappointed and rebellious person, who has not yet gotten rid of the aggressiveness of the difficult age!" May God forgive me for my rash judgment! And now I come to the other objections.

Is the rosary a repetitious prayer? Father De Foucauld used to say: "Love is expressed in few words, always the same, and constantly repeated." A woman who was traveling by train had put her baby to sleep in the baggage carrier.[4] When the little one awoke, he looked down from the carrier and saw his mother sitting in front of him watching over him. "Mama!" he said. And the other: "Darling!" And for a long while the dialogue between the two did not change: "Mama!" from above, "Darling!" from below. There was no need for other words.

Don't we have the Bible? Certainly, and it is a *quid summum*, but not everyone is prepared to read it or has time to. For those who do read it, it will also be useful for them at times, while traveling, on the street, and in times of particular need, to talk with Our Lady, if they believe that she is our mother and sister. If the reading of the Bible is just beginning to be appreciated as mere study, the mysteries of the rosary, when meditated on and savored, are the Bible studied in depth, and made spiritual flesh and blood.

A boring prayer? It depends. It can be, instead, a prayer full of joy and happiness. If you know how to say it, the rosary becomes a lifting of the eyes to Mary, which increases in intensity as you go on. It can also turn out to be a refrain that springs from the heart and calms the soul like a song.

A poor prayer, the rosary? And what kind of prayer, then, would be "rich?" The rosary is a series of Our Fathers, a prayer taught by Jesus, of Hail Marys, God's greeting of the Virgin through the Angel, of Glory Bes, the praise of the most Holy Trinity. Or would you like lofty theological ponderings instead? They wouldn't be suitable for the poor, the old, the humble, and the simple. The rosary expresses faith without invented complications, without evasions, and without many words, it helps us to abandon ourselves to God and to accept suffering generously. God also makes use of theologians, but in distributing his grace, he makes use above all of the littleness of the humble and those who abandon themselves to his will.

There is another thing to be considered: the family should be the first school of piety and religious spirituality for the children. Religious teaching that comes from the parents, Paul VI has said recently, is difficult, authorized, and irreplaceable. Difficult because of the climate of permissiveness and secularism that surrounds us; authorized, because is part of the mission entrusted by God to parents; and irreplaceable, because it is in the most tender age that we develop the inclination towards and the habit of religious piety. The recitation of the rosary although in a shortened and adapted form in the evening by the parents together with their children, is a kind of domestic liturgy. The writer Louis Veuillot used to confess that the beginning of his return to God was the sight of the rosary that he saw being said with faith by a Roman family.

With these convictions in my heart, it has been a consolation for me to hear of the initiative of the celebrations of the past few days. The Dominican Fathers, already so worthy because of their spreading of the rosary in our city, and the "Gesuati," the parish of the rosary par excellence, are planning the re-launching of this great and pious practice. Hoping that their work may be blessed by God, I have come to this liturgy as to a joyous religious festival.

Unfortunately, the joy is deeply disturbed by the rumblings of the ominous and senseless war that broke out yesterday in the Middle East. When, oh when, will men stop hating each other? When will they be willing to sacrifice their wretched dreams of an unstable national supremacy to the supreme and stable good of peace? When will we finally see an international body furnished with real powers for avoiding the outbreak of such disasters? We cannot help thinking at this moment with profound consternation of the impending harm to individuals, families and entire nations; and of the anguish of so many of our brothers and sisters, who, for the most part, are helplessly suffering the consequences of decisions being taken at the top level of their nations. And the Middle East is also a tinderbox. We must pray to the Lord not only that the war, which has unfortunately broken out, may remain limited, but that it may be quickly put under control and extinguished. In the rosary we are accustomed to invoke Our Lady by her title of "Queen of Peace." Let us say to her fervently: *Regina pacis, ora pro nobis*!

Notes

[1] *Opera* 6:199-202 (title by translator).

[2] *The Betrothed*, chs. 20, 21.

[3] Cf. Macbeth, II, ii, 37, 42.—Trans.

[4] On Italian trains, the baggage carrier is a bag or net hanging above and in front of the seat.—Trans.

The Wings of Hope

An Essay for the New Year[1]
December 31, 1976

Do you recall that airy "fancy" that is the "Dialogue between a seller of almanacs and a passerby" by our Leopardi?[2] The "passerby," through a series of questions, each more deceptively good-natured than the last, leads the seller to conclude: if with the new year I could ask God for a new life, I would ask for this agreement: "just as God sends it, without any other conditions."

Not me. Writing at the New Year and making myself almost a "seller of almanacs" what kind of a seller would I be, if I peddled only a fatalistic pessimism that accepts things passively as they come, without trying to improve them? I intend, on the contrary, to sell authentic hopes, though tempered by the necessary realism. But as for the agreement with God, I would make it. Like this: "O Lord, continue to be close to me in the coming year. Keep your hand on my head, but help me always keep my head under your hand. Take me as I am with my defects and sins, but make me become as you desire and as I also desire." As you see, the first component of the hope that I propose is dialogue with God, the dialogue of a son with a father, of a poor sinner with the one who is infinite mercy; it is suitable for moments of joy as well as moments of sorrow; those who are not acquainted with the dialogue, or who have suspended or neglected it for a time, should take it up again as soon as possible.

Another component of hope: give more room to the better part of us, which we must know how to rediscover, cause to re-emerge from the depths and enhance. People today happily mythologize film stars, sports champions and successful people, and find role models in their lives. These people, you might say, are inspired by Carlyle, who thought of "heroes" as "superior men," who emerge to guide the peoples. Better to be inspired by our Giambattista Vico, for whom the "hero" is *qui sublimia appetit*, that is, who follows an inclination to higher things: to moral perfection, to union with God, to promoting, according to his own abilities, the advancement of every man and of the whole man. There is in truth greater hope in us when we feel burning in us most a nostalgia for an authentic human greatness. The kind, for example, that Hamlet attributed to his late father, saying:

> His life was gentle, and the elements
> So mix'd in him that Nature might stand up
> And say to all the world 'This was a man!'"[3]

Or the other greatness, of which a French poet speaks: *L'homme est un dieu tombé qui se souvient des cieux*," man is a fallen angel, homesick for heaven. We are a kind of angel who no longer has wings, but if we remember that we had them and if we believe that we will have them again, we will be transfigured by hope.

Third component, optimism. In one of his books Maxim Gorki recounts that one day on the seashore in the Crimea, he surprised the elderly Leo Tolstoy in dialogue with a lizard that was warming itself in the sun near him. "Are you happy" the great writer asked the little reptile. The latter did not answer, naturally, but Tolstoy, sighing and giving vent to his feelings, confessed to the lizard, "Not me." Sad words. I counter them with the thesis sustained in the novel *Fidelity is Simple* by Pierre l'Ermite.[4] And that is: Happiness is not complicated, made up of great and rare things, sought with extraordinary means, from far away. It is made up of little things; of inner peace maintained in the mist of the inevitable trials of life; of friendship with God, capable of compensating for the disappointments and betrayals of men; of knowing how to limit yourself in your desires. Of these last Teresa of Avila says: our desires are our tormentors. And Francis de Sales: what good does it do to build in our imagination castles in Spain if then we have to live in France?

Some people, in order to be happy, yearn to figure among the "greats" of this world. Good for those who do it. If someone arrives at that Olympus, however, he should not "keep his distance" from the people; Leopardi said that "men of great merit always have simple manners." At any rate, let him also keep in mind the advice of Goethe: "if you don't want the crows to screech around your head, try not to be the tip of the bell tower of your church." In plain words: the further up you go, the more you are exposed to criticism, the more you need to prepare yourself to be disturbed. High posts bring a certain happiness only if they are occupied to serve others.

People talk a great deal about pollution. There is also noise pollution from the frenetic and convulsive activity. Knowing how to carve out for yourself a space of silence, denying yourself the usual television, the usual radio, the useless chatter, the prolonged receptions, can also bring a measure of happiness.

I once saw at the station a porter: he had put a sack of coal against a column, rested his head on the sack and was sleeping. Trains arrived and departed, trunks were loaded and unloaded, passengers got on and got off; the strident voice of the loudspeakers alternated with piercing train whistles, but he continued to sleep soundly. He seemed to be saying "Go ahead and whistle, but I also want to belong to myself, as well as to others." I took him as a warning for myself: "Amid the noise of this world, also be yourself; don't let yourself be exploited; don't let yourself become the slave of opinions and fashions; for the good of your soul, assure yourself of a little bit of quiet; noise does no good, good makes no noise."

But the privileged place for quiet should be the home. "Hearth and home," people once said, when the hearth was almost the altar of the family and they gathered around it for prayer, to tell and listen to wonderful stories. Today, now that the fire is out, we have kitchens run by electricity and central heating; now that the stories are over, we have television. But the warmth of intimacy, finding yourself together with your family should not be lost. Calderon de la Barca thought that we are all actors on the "great stage of the world." But if we are ever actors, dressed in clothes not ours, on the stage, exposed to the audience, with our assigned parts, it is outside the home. At home, no; home is the place where we are truly ourselves, where we live the truest life, made up of affections, of mutual good example, of high duties, of spontaneity. A modern, functional and comfortable house is beautiful: but it is more beautiful still, if it is perfected and animated by healthy traditions, if it is the guardian of undying values.

At this point, some people will say: "But has this almanac-seller forgotten the very grave problems weighing on us? Doesn't he notice that the country resembles a steam boiler, the sides of which, under pressure, may burst from one moment to the next? And he finds the time to talk about these foolish trifles, when what we need are the great remedies for the economy, public order and the political sector." No, I have not forgotten, I too am awaiting the great remedies that, in an atmosphere of relative non-belligerence between the parties, those in responsible positions are preparing for us. I do say, nevertheless: those "great remedies" will be more effective, will be found in each of us, if we have already put into practice the "little remedy" of personal goodness, of a life lived under the eyes of God. Those who recall that they will have to render an account to God for their actions, in fact, do not deceive, do not rob, do not kidnap, do not engage in absenteeism, do not export currency illegally, do not enrich themselves at the expense of the poor; much less hijack airplanes and plant bombs that massacre the innocent and spread nightmares and terror. I think that for a happy 1977 we need the "great remedies" as much as the "little remedies." The Lord has said: "Do the one and do not neglect the other."

Notes

1 Originally published in *Il Gazzettino*, December 31, 1976. *Opera*, 7:540-43.

2 Giacomo Leopardi (1798-1837), Italian poet, philosopher, essayist and philologist. The dialogue cited here is from his *Operette morali*, completed in 1832.—Trans.

3 In reality, Mark Anthony says this of the late Brutus in *Julius Caesar*. —Trans.

4 Pierre l'Ermite was the pen name of Edmond Loutil (1863-1959), Parisian priest, journalist and novelist.—Trans.

The Bible and the Laity

Letter Announcing a Day Dedicated to the Bible[1]
January 24, 1967

As bishop of Padua, St. Gregory Barbarigo was also chancellor of that city's university. And in 1678 it was as chancellor that he found himself having to resolve the following question: can a young unmarried woman receive a degree in theology?

The question was not hypothetical, but real, because there was a real woman (as well as a virtuous, pious and learned one), Lucrecia Piscopia, whose father, the Venetian nobleman Giambattista Corner, was on fire to have his daughter receive the title of *magistra e doctrix* [teacher and doctor] in theology.

Cardinal Barbarigo wrote from Rome, where was staying at that time, "The answer is that such a thing cannot be done, because women are not capable of the doctorate . . . and because it would make the University of Padua ridiculous."[2]

Today, perhaps the great saint would answer differently. In the spirit of the Council, in fact, the theological faculty will soon be transferred from Venegono to Milan, where it will be intended, as a letter of the Pope says, "for the formation of lay and ecclesiastical teachers." It is not excluded that women will be among the lay people attending classes.

While we are still waiting for the doors of the theology faculty to be opened, the Council has opened wide to the laity the door to the soul of theology, the Bible, by taking away any limitations which, for some time and for legitimate reasons, had been placed on the reading of the Bible. Thus begins a new, more liberal period, which can be distinguished from a second, less liberal one and is more similar to a first, more ancient period.

During this first period, which goes from the beginnings to the twelfth century, reading of the Bible was recommended to all the faithful who had the capacity and for whom it was possible. From the Acts of the martyrs, in fact, it appears that lay people carried the sacred books with them. Some of them went to their execution with the Bible hung around their necks. St. Irene was burned because she did not want to hand over the Sacred Scriptures. St. Euplo was arrested because he was found to have a copy of the Gospels in his possession. The judge asked him: "Did you bring them here?" Euplo answered: "Yes, I was found with them." And the judge said: "Read them." Euplo opened the book and read: "Blessed are those who are persecuted for the sake of righteousness . . ." The judge said: "What is this?" Euplo answered: "It is the law of my Lord which has been entrusted to me." The judge: "Why didn't you turn in these books, which have been prohibited by the emperors?" Euplo: "It is better to die than to turn them in." "Then they hung the Gospels, which he had when he was arrested, around his neck . . . and after having again given thanks, he bent his neck, and his head was cut off by the executioner."[3]

In Rome, on the tomb of St. Petronilla, there is a fourth-century fresco showing the saint leading a Christian woman named Veneranda into heaven: the latter carries a round container with some books on scrolls; they are the sacred books that will open heaven for her.

Around 400, St. Jerome, directing Paula, Marcella, Leta and other Roman matrons of the so-called "Cenacle of the Aventine," exhorted them warmly to read and study the Bible. At almost the same time the poetess Proba, the niece, daughter and mother of consuls, retold in verse the principal episodes of the Old Testament up to the flood, and the New Testament up to the Ascension.

Two centuries later, Pope St. Gregory the Great wrote to Theodore, the emperor's doctor: "I have a scolding to give my illustrious son Theodore, because . . . dedicated without rest to the affairs of the world, he neglects to read every day the words of his

Redeemer. What indeed is Holy Scripture but a kind of letter from Almighty God to his creature?"

In the Middle Ages, the Bible was the "best-seller," the volume that was read more than any other. An English scholar, Edward Moore, had the patience to count how often Dante cited the Bible: it was more than 400 times.[4] The great poet had a marvelous knowledge of the Bible; he venerated it, he recalled:

> . . .the abundant rain of the Holy Spirit,
> which is diffused over the old and the new parchments
> (*Paradiso* 24:91-93)

All this refers, obviously, to those of the faithful who knew how to read and were able to procure for themselves either complete or partial Bibles. This applied to only a few people, because, since the printing press had not yet been invented, a copy of the Bible cost more than a horse.

The Bible was conveyed to the mind and heart of all the other uneducated faithful, apart from personal study of the text, through the liturgy, preaching and sacred art. The Catholic Church has always greatly appreciated Scripture, but not in the exclusive, almost fanatical manner of Luther, who used to repeat "Scripture alone!" The Bible is actually the inseparable companion of Tradition. Scripture and Tradition "are closely bound and connected to each other," the Council says they are two eyes, they work as partners and complement each other, so that we can see better.[5] When the illiterate faithful of the Middle Ages entered a cathedral and raised their eyes to the windows and the sculptures, they were not looking at puzzles; they knew, even recognized, those faces and those figures, they understood the language of the "Bible in stone" and the "transparent Gospel."

However, while during that time a growing number of people knew how to read French, German and Italian, they did not know

Latin. The translation of some parts of the Bible began in Germany, France and Italy, and the second period also began.

It happened that the zeal for translating the Bible was sometimes exaggerated. Peter Waldo had the Bible translated into French and in 1179 presented the text to Pope Alexander III, and up to this point, there was nothing wrong. The trouble began when his followers, simple lay people, brought anarchy into preaching, claimed to interpret the Bible without being priests, without having studied and as each one saw fit. The phenomenon was repeated, on a larger scale, with the Protestants, who insisted too much on "Scripture alone" interpreted as each person pleased. During the Council of Trent and afterwards, the Magisterium of the Church ran to the ramparts and said "I am the guardian of the Bible; I am its authorized interpreter! The simple faithful must pay attention to my teaching; if they do not want to do so, they will run into errors in their reading. And therefore, the simple faithful can only read the Bible in translation with my permission!"

From 1758 on, however, permission was given to everyone, if the translation was made by the Holy See with fitting explanatory notes. In most recent times, when circumstances changed, the Popes —especially Pius XII—greatly recommended to the faithful the reading of the Bible translated into the vernacular. During this time came the Council, which exhorted "all the faithful ardently and insistently, to learn the *divine science of Jesus Christ* through the frequent reading of Sacred Scripture. In fact, ignorance of Scripture is ignorance of Christ."[6]

As I said above, these words have opened a new period. I would like my faithful not to be the last to enter it. February 12, the first Sunday of Lent, will be dedicated to the Bible; priests are to make it understood what veneration it deserves; the faithful are to take on a new spirit, a new attitude toward it.

The Council says[7] that there are three ways to approach the sacred books: the sacred liturgy, pious reading, and suitable initiatives and aids. The liturgy, that is, the prayer of the Church, is rich with the Word of God taken from the Bible. The "new" Mass especially stresses the readings, and the priest who speaks at Mass has the duty of commenting on it in such a way as to make his listeners understand it and enjoy it. In the past, perhaps, the passage of the Bible seemed like a commentary on, or the servant of, the sermon. Now it should be the opposite: the sermon is a commentary on, and a servant of, the Biblical passage.

Reading is called "pious" because, as the Council says, "it is to be accompanied by prayer." While we read, there must develop a conversation between God and us: "we listen to him when we read the divine oracles."

It is not always an easy thing. Many parts of the Bible are actually obscure: the secondary authors of the holy books are human beings who wrote with a way of thinking and reasoning that are different from ours, speaking of times, places and things that we can often understand only in a confused way.

We can approach the Gospels immediately with a certain facility, because they have, at least in general, a simple vocabulary, clear imagery and teachings that are familiar to us. For the other books we will need to be initiated through classes or the study of some suitable book.

Among the "initiatives" recommended are the "daily Biblical readings." The liturgical commission, as it already has done for Advent, has prepared some of these readings for Lent. In the places where they have been put into practice for Advent, the faithful have showed that they enjoyed them.

But the knowledge of the Bible should be extended.

Mothers should tell their children Bible stories. There are some suitable books that will help them. By putting intelligence and heart into the telling, they can give their children "the sense of God."

In the elementary schools the Bible stories should have the lion's share, according to the principle: in catechesis the Bible is the queen, not the handmaid! Some people—unfortunately!—reverse this and make the "catechism" the jailer and the Bible the prisoner!

When the children are older, we should interest them in school, in the great Biblical figures: Abraham, David, Isaiah, Jeremiah, St. Paul, and above all, Jesus Christ, presented in such a warm and suitable way that they become friends and models.

It is a beautiful initiative for the Bible to occupy a post of honor in the home and for families to read a short passage together in the evening. Shortly before he died, John Kennedy appealed to the Catholic and Protestant people of his country to read the Bible as a "road map for life."

If a head of state can do this, shouldn't a spiritual head, a bishop, do it too?

Notes

1 *Opera* 4:23-27.

2 G. Rocco, *I luoghi di S. Gregorio* (Padua, 1961), pp. 243-45.

3 T. Ruinart, *Acta primorum martyrum sincera* (Paris, 1689).

4 *Studies on Dante* (Oxford, 1896), pp. 47-91.

5 DV, no. 9.

6 DV, no. 25.

7 DV, no. 25.

Evangelization and

Catechesis

Evangelization in Our Time

Intervention at the 1974 Synod of Bishops[1]

On the subject of the theology of evangelization, the following things, among others, are being said:

1. The community of the faithful is not only the subject, "*ad quod*" [to which] of evangelization, but also the subject "*a quo*" [from which] of it.

2. The community cannot suitably carry out the mandate of evangelization today unless it makes itself credible;

3. Unless it reproduces in itself the lifestyle of the primitive Church;

4. Unless it is sensitive to the demands of the people of our time;

5. Unless it uses simple and appropriate language in evangelization;

6. Unless it substitutes a truly pastoral charity for "structures";

7. And finally, unless it gets back in touch with the Old Testament texts on liberation dedicated to "human advancement."

All this contains some truth; however, we should guard against every exaggeration in order to avoid the danger of arousing excessive hopes to the subsequent frustration of the faithful.

1. It is true that the whole community has the task of evangelizing. This commitment should be stressed, but not in such a way as to almost deny the distinction between the "*munus*" [gift] of the community and that of the Bishops.

Indeed, the fashion is becoming more and more widespread of applying in the same sense to all the faithful the words of Christ which, as we know from tradition, must be applied in one sense to the Apostles and their successors and in another sense to the faithful. They are: "The one who hears you, hears me . . . Go therefore and preach . . . as the Father has sent me, so I send you."

According to some, the Church shines in her mark of apostolicity only in as much as she preserves the doctrine preached by the Apostles and not also because the Pope and Bishops are successors in the Church of Peter and the Apostolic College.

With a great deal of superficiality, many people are writing and speaking in the Church today as teachers, without any concern about receiving the approval of the Magisterium. Instead, these people, while they exalt their own teaching "*munus*," hold that the Pope and the bishops are a learning Church. This is true, in a certain sense, but it must not be said in such a way as to empty or attenuate the authenticity of the Magisterium.

2. The credibility of all the workers of evangelization is justly being demanded, but it must not be understood in such a way that the lack of it, whether real or presumed, legitimizes the disbelief or dissent of a few people.

It should not be forgotten what happened to Our Lord, who realized in himself the maximum of credibility, and yet many did not believe in him; rather, he became a sign of contradiction.

Not only this, but Our Lord predicted to the Apostles: "If they have persecuted me, they will also persecute you" (Jn 15:20) and again: "I am sending you as sheep among wolves" (Mt 10:16).

3. The admirable charity, the union of souls, and the communion of the primitive Church (cf. Acts 2:44-45, 4:32) are proposed as the goal to which the Christian community of today should aim as a meaningful exemplar.

However, in order not to go beyond the bounds of reality, we must also consider other events that took place in the primitive Church, such as, for example: the episode of Ananias and Sapphira (cf. acts 5:1-11); the murmuring of the Greeks against the Jews (cf. Acts 6:16); Paul's reproof of Peter at Antioch "in the presence of all" for having involuntarily divided souls (cf. Gal 2:11-14); the "*seditio non minima*" of Paul and Barnabas at Antioch against the Judaizers, in order to remedy which the Council of Jerusalem was called, where again "*magna conquisitio facta est*" [a great debate took place] (Acts 15:17); the divisions that emerged from the beginning within the Church in Corinth (cf. 1 Cor 1:1114); Paul's complaint that some people, out of rivalry and envy, had not preached Christ sincerely, but in a party spirit and with the intention of making his imprisonment even harsher (cf. Phil 1:15-18. Cf. also 2 Cor 1:8; 2:1-11; 2 Tim 4:16, 7:10; 3 John 9f).

This proves that the primitive Church had its imperfections and divisions: therefore it must indeed be taken as an example, but with caution, without proclaiming and demanding in too facile a way the miraculous fusion of souls in today's dioceses and parishes.

4. Not everyone asks the same thing of the Church, nor is the criterion of the request always authentic, nor is the request always advanced with exact information and with the right intention.

Therefore those who evangelize must be "all things to all men" (1 Cor 9:22), so that everyone can be saved; they must also be available, as far as possible, for every legitimate human aspiration and need; at the same time, however, they must say to themselves: "*se hominibus placerem servus Christi non essem*" [If I were to please men, I would not be a servant of God] (Gal 110).

At any rate, it is not approval that constitutes a yardstick and rule for the Gospel and its presentation to the people of God; on the contrary, the Gospel must be the norm for the behavior of men, even if when the Gospel is preached, it can cause the one who announces it "*sine glossa*" [without commentary] misunderstanding and persecution.

5. Simplicity and modernity of speech can never be recommended enough, but it happens with speaking as it does with food; even if it is prepared very exquisitely, it is no help to those who are unwilling or stubbornly refuse to nourish themselves.

The Apostle Paul preached excellently, but he sometimes had to realize that he was preaching to people who were "*spem non habentes et sine Deo in hoc mundo*" [without hope and without God in this world] (Eph. 2:12).

Perhaps the same thing is being repeated in our days. Perhaps, while preachers are being exhorted to use an appropriate language, we might suggest to critical hearers that they read the little book of the Jansenist Nicole, entitled, *How to Profit from Boring Sermons*.

At any rate, our trust must be placed first of all in the intrinsic strength of the Gospel preached and in the grace of the Holy Spirit, who evangelizes "*ab intus*" [from the inside]. "The Lord opened Lydia's heart to accept what Paul was saying" (Acts 16:14) Acts says. "Prophets can speak out loud, but they do not confer the Spirit; they speak well, but if you are silent, Lord, they do not kindle the heart; they give the letter, but you explain the sense . . . they show the way, but it is you who gives the strength to travel it."2

6. As for the "structures," it corresponds to the truth that they were few in the primitive Church. But that Church, in the number of the faithful and the diffusion and complexity of the problems, compared to the Church of our times, was like a small boat compared to a transatlantic liner. Therefore it is not at all strange that there are more structures in the present Church than in the ancient one. The structures of the Church that are not constitutive and that have at present fallen into disuse or have become useless should or can be replaced. It is not true, however, that at the beginning, the faithful were guided by merciful charity and charismatic gifts alone. At the beginning of the Church, the exercise of pastoral charity was often joined to precise commands and even to punishments. We have clear

examples in the first letter to the Corinthians (1 Cor 4:20-21; 5:5ff) and in the pastoral letters. Speaking of the Christian endowed with a prophetic gift, Paul wrote: "If anyone thinks he is a prophet or endowed with the gift of the Spirit, he should know that what I have written you is the Lord's commandment. If someone does not recognize it, neither is he recognized" by God (1 Cor 14:37-38).

7. The connection between evangelization and human advancement must, of course, be recognized. However, in this matter, reference can be made to the Old Testament only with caution.

In fact, some discrepancies exist between the Old Testament and the New Testament on the themes of salvation and liberation:

a) In the O.T. liberation has a temporal character, it regards the whole Hebrew people and only them, although a few times, as in the book of Jonah and in Isaiah the universal perspective makes an appearance;

b) Once they accepted faith in the resurrection, the Jews of the Old Testament see liberation or salvation fully realized in eschatological times;

c). In the O.T. it is always God and not men who has the initiative in salvation;

d). The central idea of liberation, although presented in a sociopolitical dimension, always consists of the covenant of the people with God; the liberation from slavery in Egypt culminates in the covenant and the worship of Mt. Sinai; the liberation from the Babylonian captivity with the reconstruction of the temple;

e) On the other hand, in the N.T. salvation and liberation are preeminently spiritual and universal. The invitation is addressed to all men. The essence of salvation is in the fact of being friends of God by free individual adhesion. It is the individual who lives in the divine life, who is reborn and incorporated into Christ. A life, rebirth and incorporation, which indeed begin in the present time, but which have their full development only beyond history in heaven;

f) In addition, in the N.T.–this does not appear in the O.T.–the Christological as well as pneumatological character of liberation stands out in a preeminent way.

It follows from all this that the liberation of the O.T. must be read with a Christian eye, seeing it as a pre-figuration of and preparation for the liberation of the New Testament. It cannot be isolated in order to see it through a solely political lens, much less a revolutionary one.

Notes

[1] *Opera* 6:457-61. This is Luciani's written intervention of October 28, 1974; he greatly preferred writing to speaking on the floor.— Trans.

[2] *Imitatio Christi* Bk. II, ch. 2.

Not Convention, but Conviction

Homily to the Triveneto Convention
of Communion and Liberation[1]
May 31, 1976

The theme you treated this morning is "Evangelization and Human Advancement." The same theme that has been proposed by the Italian Bishops' Conference and that will be the subject of the convention in Rome next November.

At that convention, the various components of the Italian Church will be separate, all of them with excellent intentions, but sometimes with different viewpoints, hopes, expectations and methods. Among the ecclesial components there is also your movement, which some people view with curiosity, others with sympathy, others with inexplicable animosity. The Patriarch of Venice looks at you with keen sympathy, if for no other reason than because you put into practice what Lacordaire advised young people to do: "Have ideas and know how to defend them." You defend them without provoking or attacking anyone, committing yourselves personally and at a great cost, giving an example of coherence and Christian courage in an environment that is sometimes one of widespread gray cowardice.

It is in the name of this sympathy that I permit myself to trace out a few lines in regard to "Evangelization and Human Advancement."

1. I would like, however, for you to prize "evangelization" over "advancement." To be Christians, children of God and brothers and sisters of Jesus, is, in fact, the greatest of good fortunes: more than being healthy, rich, learned or well placed in the world. Anyone who is persuaded of this cannot keep this good fortune only for

himself; he feels a need to communicate it to others. Here, then, is evangelization. "I speak to you about Jesus: I assure you that to follow him, imitate him and live His Gospel is beautiful and happy; true, it requires some sacrifice, but brings peace and happiness to the heart." But how will you tell them these things unless you live them first? People want witnesses rather than teachers; they accept teachers as long as they are witnesses.[2]

The first evangelization then is done not with words, but an honest and luminous life. We don't evangelize only what we know but above all what we are, by our constant efforts to conform our own lives to the maxims of the Gospel and the example of Christ. The one who evangelizes asks himself constantly: what would Christ do, if he were here in my place? I try to do it myself. I feel that I do not have sufficient strength; I ask it of him and I say: "Lord, take me as I am, with my faults, with my defects, with my temperament; but make me become what you desire me to be." Some people call all this right wing religious extremism. But then, St. Paul too would be a right-wing extremist, when he said: "For me, living is Christ" (Phil 1:21). "It is no longer I who lives, but Christ who lives in me" (Gal 2:20). Leon Bloy would have been a right wing extremist when he wrote: "there is only one misery: not to be saints."[3]

The disciples of Christ, fortunately, are not concerned over what people say about them, but what Christ thinks, Christ who has not commanded us to be a little bit generous, but very generous; he has not asked for a little bit of trust, but a great deal of trust in him. He has said, in fact: "Whoever loves his father and mother more than me is not worthy of me" (Mt. 10:37). In the middle of the storm he said to the apostles: "Why do you fear, men of little faith?" (Mt. 8:27); "courage, it is I, don't be afraid" (Mt. 14:27) and then to Peter: "Man of little faith, why did you doubt?" (Mt. 14:31).

I referred above to peace of heart. Manzoni also spoke about it in *La Pentecoste* and he says:

New, immobile in the face of terrors,
And faithless to allurements,
Peace that the world mocks,
But cannot snatch away.[4]

I like citing these words for you on this day of Pentecost.

2. The Christ whom we evangelize, however, is attached to the Church. The *Christus totus*, the whole Christ, said St. Augustine, is composed of Christ and the Church, of Christ as the head and the Church as the body. This was the first great truth that St. Paul learned during his conversion. "Saul, Saul, why are you persecuting me?" the voice said as soon as he fell to the ground. And he: "Who are you, O Lord?" "I am Jesus, whom you are persecuting" (Acts 9:4-5). But he was persecuting only the Church; he understood then that the two things coincided, and it was a truth he later repeated in his letters. But the Council has also said it several times and in several ways. Once it did so in a way that should please you in Communion and Liberation. The Church, says *Lumen Gentium*, is "a people gathered in the unity of the Father, Son and Holy Spirit." (LG no. 4). Here is a unique communion; it is not enough to form a group and union among ourselves; we must enter a group with the Father, Son and Holy Spirit. . . . Jesus prayed to the Father so that his disciples "may be one single thing . . . perfect in unity (Jn 17:22, 23). We, then, are just the receivers of unity and communion; the maker of the union, the one Christ asked it from, is God, who also involves us, drawing us into the circle of his own life!

But the Catholic communion also possesses an external reference point. Christ—the Council recalls—"established in the Pope the principle and visible and perpetual foundation of unity in faith and communion."[5] And it explains: "The principle and foundation of unity belongs to the bishops as well as the multitude of the faithful. The bishops, on the other hand, taken in isolation, are the viable principle and foundation of unity in their individual churches" (LG, no. 23).

There was a little island, Chesterton wrote, and the children used to go there to play ball. They played serenely and securely, because the playing field was completely surrounded by a high wall. One day some important people approached the little island and said: "knock down that wall: don't you see that it limits you and takes away your space? Away with it, more air, more liberty." They were listened to, the wall was thrown down. But now, if you go to the island, you find the children unhappy: there is no longer the same security as before; every so often a ball falls into the sea, and they waste time fishing it out; sometimes the waves carry it away. "Away with the Pope," some people say, "he limits you! More air, more liberty!" Sometimes they are listened to, but the consequences are under our eyes: without the Pope we lack a sure reference point, they slip in others to act like the Pope, and great insecurity, doubt and confusion are the result.

3. When we proclaim the Gospel of Christ, Paul VI has written, we must recall "the unceasing interplay of the Gospel and of man's concrete life, both personal and social." (EN 29). And he continued: we have "the duty to proclaim the liberation of millions of human beings . . . the duty of assisting the birth of this liberation, of giving witness to it, of ensuring that it is complete."[6] I stress this last adjective: liberation, yes, but total. To banish "famine, chronic disease, illiteracy, poverty, injustices in international relations and especially in commercial exchanges, situations of economic and cultural neo-colonialism sometimes as cruel as the old political colonialism," agreed, but also banish sin and the conditions that give rise to sin, in such a way that man can open himself more to the absolute, even to the absolute of God. To liberate every man and not only the most fortunate: but also liberate the whole man, in such a way that those who want this are not impeded or caused difficulties on the level of morality and religion.

I said: those who want this: a life lived in a religious way and in fact, honored, only if freely chosen, a religious life that is not chosen, but imposed would be a degraded one. *Nihil enim est tam voluntarium quam religio*" [For nothing is as voluntary as religion], Lattanzio has written. Jesus, on one hand, "wants all men . . . to come to knowledge of the truth" (Tm 1,2,3), and in spite of threats, wants "his servants to proclaim his word with complete certainty" (Acts 4:29). On the other hand he did not want to impose his truths with force: though he was unhappy about it, he did not impede the spreading of contrary opinions; he simply "rendered testimony to the truth," assuring "whoever is for the truth will listen to my voice" (Jn 18:37).

Like Jesus, we too are for liberty. We do not want a confessional state but a secular one: but we want the state to be secular, not secularist; it should not take away our right to defend and live the values that are dear to us. The Church has many enemies and adversaries: some in bad faith, others in good faith: however, the Church is not the enemy or adversary of anyone, even it she must combat error with peaceful weapons. In line with this spirit, we too must seek to take up the arms of strong religious convictions: no longer religious convention, but religious conviction; not a dozing and sleeping Church, but a wide-awake and dynamic Church; we want to respect the liberty of others, but also to have our liberty respected; not to disappear in the gray of the mass, but to emerge from the mass marked with our Christian originality. We want to follow the method of Christ and his saints. "I will proclaim justice," Christ has said, "but I will not contend, I will not cry out; the bruised reed I will not break, the smoldering wick I will not quench" (Mt 12: 18-20). "If someone puts out my right eye," St. Francis de Sales has said, "I will try to smile at him with the left one he has spared me; if he also puts out the left one, I will still have a heart to love him." Commmunion and Liberation follows this system: it may sometimes be beaten up by the world, but loves the world!

Notes

[1] *Opera* 7:360-64

[2] Cf. EN 41.

[3] Leon Bloy, *La femme pauvre.*

[4] Alessandro Manzoni, *"La Pentecoste."*

[5] LG no. 18.

[6] EN 30.

Catechesis and Christian Commitment

Intervention at the 1977 Synod of Bishops[1]

Catechesis must be concerned not only with transmitting the revealed truths, but with transmitting them in such a way that the one who receives them receives them with faith and is impelled to live them. Narrate and speak, yes, said St. Augustine, but in such a way that the hearer *Audiendo credat, credendo speret, sperando amet* [by hearing, believes, by believing, hopes, and by hoping, loves]." *Credat*: he glimpses God behind the catechist, who is the "postman of God." *Speret*: he rejoices, perceiving that he is before a doctrine that he will realize nobly as a human being and a child of God. *Amet*: feeling himself loved by God, he sets out, "shot," towards the good works to be done for God, for his neighbor, for himself.

In order to interest and engage young people especially, catechesis will dress itself in Augustinian *hilaritas*. They are not attracted to a life bristling with "no's," padlocked and chained, among barriers of every sort: don't do this, don't look at that, don't touch here and don't go there; this is bad, that is worse; they want to live, expand, conquer and be protagonists. In a catechesis in which they are only spectators and listeners, even worse if made up of nothing, or almost nothing but "can'ts," and "must nots," they will feel suffocated. Catechetical wisdom is to forbid to them only what really cannot be permitted and launch them into action. The motto of St. Catherine of Siena: "The style of acting always helps." Cardinal Ferrari used to say: "The surest way of fleeing evil is by doing good; if we throw young people headlong into goodness, evil will end up being reduced in their lives."

Some carefully chosen lives of the saints can be a great stimulus to the commitment of the young. "The saints are to the Bible what a musical composition executed by fine artists is to the written score: they indicate how this or that biblical teaching should be translated into daily life, into such and such circumstances, and they attract by their example."[2]

Also in the sense that young people are often the best catechizers of the faith, especially of the young, it will prosper, as a rule, only in the warmth of a Christian atmosphere in their daily lives; that the parents, above all, must consider themselves the first catechists of their own children, almost as the bishops and parish priests of their homes.

In the sense also that young people are the best catechizers of their peers, because the latter are looking for an advisor and a model for their lives close at hand, and want to live the life of the group to which, and to the charismatic leaders of which, they give the obedience which, on the other hand, they are tempted to deny to their parents and teachers. The ideal catechizing community, however, is the parish, if it is a true community; if other catechizing groups refer to it as to a center; if in it one breathes the fresh air of the diocese and of catholicity, with reference to love, respect and obedience to the bishop and the Pope.

Theologians are of great help in catechesis, if on one hand they place the fruit of their own work at the disposal of the Magisterium, and on the other, they popularize the documents of the Magisterium, by going deeply into themes and explaining them. For the redaction of catechisms then, their contribution, next to the very useful one given by experts in pedagogy, is, I would say, necessary, even if the last word on the text of the catechism belongs to the bishops. For this, it is necessary to urge on theologians a spirit of true ecclesiastical service and the cult of a theology that is a discourse not only *about* God, but *of* God. On the other hand, a *Professoren-Kirche* [Church of Professors] opposed in some ways to the "Church of the Pastors" would be a "Wound of the Church." George May, of the University of Mainz, made this clear. A Protestant church, which at first was crowded, gradually came to be almost always empty. "Why?" a priest from Trier asked the sacristan. And the sacristan answered: "First, a pastor came from Griefswald and said, 'Jesus was the Son of God.' Then one came from Rostock and said 'Jesus was simply a man.' Finally, one arrived from Tubingen and he said: 'Jesus never existed.' And so the people concluded: 'If they can't agree among themselves, we'd better stay at home.' And so they stayed at home."

Here, culture should be understood not in the classical humanistic sense of a fund of ideas possessed by a few and at a rather high level, but in the sense of the way different peoples have of speaking, dressing, playing, expressing joy and sorrow, celebrating feasts, etc.

In regard to this type of culture, two principles should be stated and put into practice.

1. Catechesis should try to make the faith penetrate into all these various cultural manifestations that are not in obvious conflict with the Word of God;

2. Catechesis should make use in the favor of the Word of God everything that is good in these cultures. That, for love of the Word of God itself, which must be able to travel by every means; this, without fear of facing some risk, and of introducing innovations. This, also, in the Spirit of Pope John, who in his speech at the opening of the Council,[3] spoke on one hand of presenting the truth in new forms, and on the other demanded a "dutiful, serene and tranquil adherence to all the teaching of the Church in its certainty and precision, which is still resplendent in the acts of the Council of Trent and of Vatican I."

We harmonize St. Vincent of Lérins with De Lubac and with Carnegie. The first said, *Noviter, sed non nova* [In a new way, but not new things]. De Lubac said: "Why insist on learning from the sunrise the colors of the sunset?" . . . Carnegie wrote: "I like fat strawberries with whipped cream. But when I go fishing, to attract the fish, I put on the hook not the strawberries I like, but the worms that they like."

As a goal, try to arrive at expounding all the truths of the faith. Proceed gradually however, in regard to didactics.

Hierarchy among the virtues? If they are truths of the faith, they must all be believed in the same way, in homage to God, who has revealed them; however, explicit knowledge of all of them is not necessary in the same way.

The hierarchy, instead, is in the fact that some truths are capable of illuminating others.

In expressing them, catechesis places in relief that the Gospel is News that brings happiness, and that Christ is at the center of the plan of salvation; Christ is like the peak of a roof with two sloping sides. The Old Testament mounts towards him, preparing for him: the New Testament, the Church which continues him and the Sacraments descend from him, leading pilgrim mankind from this passing world to the other, eternal one.

Morality should be presented as man's magnanimous response to God's love, a response which cannot be imagined without the help of God himself, and which gives happiness; not to him, but to us.

The dominant note therefore, must be joy; the fear of God, however, should not be forgotten. The Church and the Saints, referring to the Gospel (Mt 25:31-33; Lk 12:15ff; Lk 13:22ff), have insisted in opportune ways and times, on the salvation of the soul – the most important matter of all–the uncertainty of the hour of death and the obligation to flee occasions of sin.

Present to them the greatness and the responsibility of their mission; the obligation to make their own work authentic by being in communion with the bishops and by acquiring the necessary qualities.

Moral qualities: sanctity of life and piety (we don't teach only what we know, but what we are: if I am not good, of myself, in my person, I negate the words of goodness that come from my mouth), love for the Church and for the students, (Lacordaire: "We cannot do good to others unless we love them").

Intellectual qualities: knowing well what we teach; and in order to know it, constantly studying and bringing ourselves up-to-date. Huet, the bishop of Avranches, did not always receive the people of his diocese because he "had to study." The people wrote to the Pope: "Please, Your Holiness, next time send us a bishop who has 'finished studying.'" But there is no bishop or catechist who has "finished studying."

Pedagogic-didactic qualities: knowing how to adapt yourself, enlarging and compressing the scope of your discourse, according to the capacity of your hearers. And also adapting yourself as far as possible, to their desires and aspirations. If a catechist is able to sense and comprehend what the legitimate desires and hopes of young people are, it will then be easier for him to conduct and orient the young people themselves towards the interests and expectations of God.

Notes

1 *Opera*: 8:276-79; written intervention at the Italian small group (*circulo minore*) of the Synod.

2 St. Francis de Sales.

3 *Gaudete Mater Ecclesisa*, October 11, 1962.

The Tough Questions

On Reading the Encyclical "Humanae Vitae"

Pastoral Letter, July 29, 1968[1]

Dear people of the diocese:

On April 13, 1968, when writing to my priests, I touched, among other points, on the question of birth control, and I said: "Priests, when they speak and when they hear confessions, must hold to the directions given several times by the Pope, as long as he does not feel he can give a different judgment." And I added: "Let us pray that the Lord may help the Pope resolve this question. Never, perhaps, has there been one so difficult in the Church: because of its intrinsic difficulties, its many implications for other problems, and the acuteness with which it is felt by enormous masses of people."[2]

I must confess that I hoped in my heart, even though I didn't let it out in writing, that the very serious difficulties could be overcome and that the reply of the Teacher, who speaks with a special charism and in the name of the Lord, might coincide with the hopes raised in so many couples, especially after the establishment of a special pontifical commission to examine the issue.

I know for certain that concern for these souls in pain and an ardent desire to bring them light and comfort were the only reasons for the considerable delay in the coming of the Pope's answer. He has reflected at length, he has consulted countless learned and prudent representatives of the episcopate, the clergy and the laity, and he has prayed at length before putting aside his reservations. Now he gives his judgment, conscious that he is performing a duty, and with a spirit of great faith. He knows, indeed, that he is going to be the cause of bitterness in many people; he knows that a different solution would probably have brought him more human applause; but he puts his faith in God and, in order to be faithful to His word, he re-proposes the traditional teaching of the Magisterium in this very delicate matter in all its purity. The recent scientific discoveries? The social evolution of our time? The increased demands of "responsible parenthood?" All of these things are to be kept in mind, but they do not postulate a new doctrine. The doctrine that has always been taught, presented in the new framework of encouraging and positive ideas on marriage and conjugal love, better guarantees the true good of man and of the family.

The thoughts of the Pope and mine go especially towards the difficulties, sometimes serious, of couples. Let them not lose heart, for heaven's sake! Let them think that, for everyone "strait is the gate and narrow the path that leads to life" (Mt 7:14). That the hope of the future life should illuminate the path of Christian couples. And that God does not let his help be lacking for those who pray with perseverance! Let them try to live with wisdom, justice and piety in the present time, knowing that the scene of this world is passing away (cf. 1 Cor 7:31 and Rom 5:5). "And if sin still has a hold on them, let them not be discouraged, but let them have recourse with humble perseverance to the mercy of God, which is lavished in the sacrament of penance."

I would like these last words of the Pope to be stressed in a particular way by priests, to whom the Pope recommends "the patience and kindness, of which the Lord himself has given the example in dealing with men," hoping that "couples may always find in the words and the heart of the priest an echo of the voice and love of the Redeemer."[3]

I am confident that I have everyone with me in a sincere adherence to the papal teaching, and in this assurance, I bless and greet you.

Notes

1 *Opera* 4:198-99.

2 In this same letter, Luciani had also given two principles to help priests who were dealing with this problem in the confessional: "1. It is easier, today, given the confusion induced by the press, to find some married women [using contraception] who are in good faith; if this happens, it may be advisable, under the usual conditions, not to upset them. 2. Towards the penitent user of contraception who proves to be both penitent and discouraged, it is proper to use encouraging kindness within the limits allowed by pastoral prudence." (*Opera* 4:165).—Trans.

3 HV, no. 39.

Abortion: "Thou Shalt Not Kill"

Talk at a Pro-Life Gathering
in the Church of Santo Stefano, Venice[1]
April 2, 1977

Abel, Cain, God; these are the characters in the first reading. Of Abel, the Bible says: "His blood still cries to God from the ground" (Cf. Heb. 12:24). And of Cain: "Woe to those who have walked on his road" (Jude 1:11). Victor Hugo imagined the eyes of God gazing at Cain between the leaves of the thickest wood. Cain flees in order to escape from that gaze. In vain. The eyes flash at night in the sky; when he looks at the ground to evade them, they are before his steps; they appear in the waters of the ocean, at the back of caverns. To protect himself, Cain erects a city, surrounds it with walls, closes it with a gate and writes over it: "God is forbidden to look." No use: God still follows him with his eyes even there. And when Cain, desperate, digs a tomb and buries himself inside it, the eyes are still in the tomb looking at him.[2] This is the imagination of a poet, but it is God's peremptory, imperative and categorical taking of a position in the face of all violence and killing, the 'Thou shalt not kill" that the Bible repeats three times (Ex 20:13; Deut 5:17; Mt 5:21). "For your own lifeblood, too, I will demand an accounting: from every animal I will demand it, and from man in regard to his fellow man" (Gen 9:5); "You have been guilty of blood, and blood . . . shall pursue you" (Ez 35:6); "scatter the nations that delight in war" (Ps 68:31).

Comparing the situation of the world now with these texts, we discover to our bitterness that Cain has returned. He has returned with wars, racial and tribal massacres, inhuman torture and imprisonment for political motives; he has returned with kidnapping of people, ambushes set for the forces of order, the battles with traditional and non-traditional arms that bloody our cities and with the expeditions of piratical hooligans, which cause a huge amount of damage and spread tension and fear; he has returned with the drug traffic which mows down victims even among young adults and adolescents, with the carnal violence against young women assaulted by gangs of lowlifes, with the exploitation of male and female prostitution, with the "white deaths" due to insufficient protection of the life and health of workers. My brothers and sisters, it is humiliating for us to regress to Cain and to find ourselves in a Christian society set one against the other. We must be one for the other, one with the other.

Before the rage of Cain, Abel tried, perhaps, to defend himself. Against the exterminating rage of Herod, the little children of Bethlehem could only weep. The creatures enclosed in their mothers' wombs cannot even weep. But God sees them. God, who said to Jeremiah: "Before I formed you in your mother's womb, I knew you" (Jer 1:5), does not remain indifferent when they are barbarously and cruelly suppressed. Barbarity and cruelty are the right words. In Bethlehem the mothers attempted a desperate defense of their children; in abortion, it is the mothers themselves who become Herod's assassins; they conceive the child, then they accuse it of being their unjust aggressor and suppress it.

It is an abominable crime, says the Council.[3] Before the Council, Pope John had written: "Human life is sacred, and from the moment of its appearance it is a pledge of the creative action of God. Those who violate His laws offend against His divine majesty, degrade themselves and humanity and do nothing but sap the strength of the communities of which they are members."[4]

I know. They say that we are talking about the first few months—of beings that are not yet humanized. But biology and genetics are there and they demonstrate beyond doubt that the unborn child does not need to be humanized; it is already a human being.

They talk of freedom. The freedom to kill does not exist. A human law that grants that freedom tomorrow would not put so much as a scratch in the divine law, it would only create new divisions in a country already so divided. Over here, in fact, are the forces of those who accept the law; over there the forces of those, who, obliged by their conscience, will continue to proclaim loudly that abortion is a crime and the permissive state law a moral absurdity.[5] In families, on one hand, the parents will still have the task, so difficult today, of educating their adolescent children; on the other, the adolescents will be able to conceive and abort without their parents knowing anything about it.

In the hospitals, over here the doctors and staff who are conscientious objectors will refuse to take part in abortions in very large numbers. Over there we will have repetitions of scenes similar to the invasion recently carried out in the Mangiagalli gynecological clinic in Milan. In the case of Milan it could be demonstrated that the woman, who died of a heart attack, neither desired nor asked for the interruption of her pregnancy. Evidently, however, some people, while they were demanding the freedom for women to give death, were denying the doctor the freedom to defend life (Gen 4:2-10).

My brothers and sisters, it is a humiliation for us to have to dwell on such a painful theme. We were called to quite different heights. St. Paul said to us: "Chosen in [Christ] before the foundation of the world, to be holy and without blemish!" (Eph 1:4), our obligation is to "put off the old man" and "put on the new man" (Cf. Eph. 4:22-23). "If at one time you were darkness," St. Paul says to us, "now you are light in the Lord. Live therefore as children of light" Eph. 5:8). "Light," that is, a clean and holy life. That is, the Gospel teaching, proposed clearly and in its entirety. Now, what is our Christian life? Is it an almost extinguished votive light, faint and intermittent, or is it a beacon which cuts through the darkness and can be seen from afar? Let it not be, please, a life reduced to just a few prayers but in all the rest neither more nor less greedy for goods and commodities than the life of the pagans! Where are our works of charity and justice? Today we demand this justice from others, but do we practice it toward others? At the church of San Francesco della Vigna, some time ago, I noted the tomb of Fra Matteo da Bascio, a Franciscan, the founder of the Capuchins, a zealous preacher, but ready with invective.

They say of him that in Venice, towards the middle of the sixteenth century, he often entered the duke's palace; when he met people in the courtyard and the antechambers, he would say: "Those who do not render justice, those who allow the innocent to be oppressed, who do not provide for the poor, are headed for hell." The chronicler Paolo da Foligno writes, "And one time, he appeared at the hour of tierce, when the courts are full, with a little lighted lantern and a broom to sweep under the benches, like one looking for something he has lost. And when asked what he was looking for, he answered: "I am looking for justice." He clearly thought that there would be little of it. Without being pessimists like Fra Matteo da Bascio, let's try to bring about more justice; let's not remain passive and neutral in the face of today's problems.

And let's try to have the light of the Gospel shine more. Let's not bury it under a gloss, as St. Francis would say. "It is a mistake," Igino Giordani said, "for people to propose to souls a Christianity that is undernourished, depressed or dissimulated, so as to have it swallowed in capsules of ambiguity, diluted in the lukewarm water of compromise." The lukewarm, it says in Scripture, God will vomit out of his mouth. That saying and not saying, that hesitation between immanence and transcendence, between the world and the Church, generates a "no man's land," a desert zone, which the enemy overruns. The word of the Lord was always clear, like a blade, such that it earned him persecution and the cross when he was present among us and present in the Church.

Perhaps one of the impulses that has led whole masses of people to become alienated from the Church and content themselves with the residue of ethics and surrogates for theology, reduced to the impoverished state of a kind of paganism with ecclesiastical ethics, lies precisely in our having presented to people a religion that is a refining still that puts out an emulsifying brew, formed of concessions to fashionable errors and giving in to the same vices as always. Those who used to present dogma in this way perhaps believed they were updating the Gospel; and instead they were reshaping it, cutting off little bits at a time from the Magisterium of the Church, the statements of the Popes and the revelations of the saints. Those who have softened, embellished and extenuated the truth, those who have disguised the cross as a decoration, have taken from the people the beauty and power of the divine commandment, which asks us to give God our body, soul, everything, and to make a decision in the tremendous, all-important dialectic between Christ and Mammon, light and darkness; to continue to take a position for Christ, until we make ourselves into Him; and to live our mission on earth as the work of restoration of all things in Him. "Yes, yes, no, no," is what the Church teaches and the Gospel demands (Eph 4:17-19; 5:8-14).

The last four readings are all devoted to the love of neighbor, a central point of the Gospel. The expressions we have heard still echo in our ears. "Whoever hates his own brother is a murderer" (1 Jn 3:15). And who is this brother? Every man; not only our friends, our sympathizers and those who at least do not torment us, but also the others, those who speak evil of us and do wrong to us." Even if you will have to suffer for the sake of justice," says St. Peter, "blessed are you! Do not be afraid and do not be terrified with fear of them" . . . (1 Pt 3:14). "It is better to suffer for doing good, if this is the will of God, than by doing evil" (1 Pt 3:17). I believe that in this matter we can be happy; young Catholics have been struck, Catholic associations, headquarters of Communion and Liberation have been made the object of aggressive acts, the launching of Molotov cocktails, insults and calumnies, but we have never taken the initiative in attacking, have never responded to the attacks with violence. We are experiencing in a new and worsened edition the climate of 1931, when Pius XI wrote the encyclical *Non abbiamo bisogno* on Catholic Action; a climate of anticlericalism that is not only verbal but that goes out hunting Catholics. Young Catholics only have to profess their faith firmly, declare themselves peacefully in favor of Gospel morality on subjects that have not been open to debate for Christians for twenty centuries, such as divorce and abortion, and the new "action squads"[6] leave on their expeditions, and the press thunders. This press! It has shouted, blowing all its horns, that abortions were required at Seveso and the surrounding area, because the children conceived would be born deformed because of the dioxin. Now that all the babies, to the number of 87, have been born healthy and normal, that same press has not deigned to write a single line of reporting. How should we behave? The composed calm of Jesus before Pilate and the screaming crowd; his generous forgiveness from the cross of those who insulted him and the thief constitute for us the model to imitate. That does not mean that we cannot and should not peacefully defend ourselves. St. Peter has said to us; "Be ready always to answer, but gently and respectfully, those who ask you for a reason for the hope that is in you" (1 Pt 3:15).

On January 22, 1973, the Catholics of the United States rang all their bells in a death knell to recall the new massacre of the innocents decreed by the North American abortion law. We will not ring our bells. We will continue instead with all our efforts, to awaken consciences, to do our best in favor of motherhood when there is need for understanding and help, to intervene as best we can, where individuals and families find themselves in difficulty. Catholics have found themselves at times in exceptionally difficult situations, which they have faced with very great courage, respectful of the rights of others, but determined to defend their own rights. Now is one of those times. Trusting in the help of God, solidly united, avoiding growth in the force of others by our internal divisions, let's go forward with our program of justice and peace.

With Christian pride and humility, we will say with Montalembert; "We do not want to be feared, but neither do we fear

... amid a free people, we do not want to be oppressed like pariahs or helots. We are the successors of the martyrs and we do not tremble before the successors of Julian the Apostate!"[7] (1 Jn 3:13-17; 4:7-16; 1 Pt 3:13-18; 4:12-16; Jn 19:1-17; Lk 23:33-46).

Notes

[1] Originally published in *L'Osservatore Romano,* April 21, 1977; *Opera Omnia* 8:78-81.

[2] Victor Hugo, *Legendes des siècles* (Paris, 1878), p. 14.

[3] GS, no. 51.

[4] MM, no. 181.

[5] The law in legalizing abortion in Italy was first voted on in Parliament in January 1977; it was passed in one house but defeated in the other; it achieved final passage and became law in May 1978.—Trans.

[6] The original *squadracce* or "action squads" were an arm of the Fascist police state in Italy that took care of the regime's enemies.—Trans.

[7] The eloquent young Catholic nobleman, Charles, Comte de Montalembert spoke these words in 1831 in the French house of Peers against the liberal French monarchy's monopoly on education and in favor of the freedom of Catholic schools.—Trans.

The Church and Sexuality

Homily for
the Feast of the Presentation[1]
February 2, 1976

Today is the 40th day after Christmas. The Church takes advantage of it to have us solemnize the presentation of Jesus in the temple. A Jesus greeted by the liturgy as *lumen gentium*, the light of nations.

The Council opened the most important of its 16 documents with this very phrase. It added: "Yes, Christ is truly light, but a light which is reflected and 'brightens the face of the Church' which, in turn, illuminates all men and women,[2] first by the lives and works of its saints and the best among its children, then by its teachings."

The most recent of these teachings in the order of time is the document of the Holy See on "Some Questions Regarding Sexual Ethics."

I suppose all of you know about it, at least in substance. I declare that I support it from my heart, and I want to offer some reflections on it.

1. The day before yesterday I read in the Liturgy of the Hours the following words, spoken by St. John Bosco to one of the priests of his congregation: "Let's regard those over whom we have to exercise some power as our children. Let's put ourselves as though at their service, like Jesus, who came to obey and not to command. Let's be ashamed of everything in us that might make us seem like dominators, and let's only dominate them in order to serve them with greater pleasure."[3]

I can assure you that these same feelings guided the Holy See in the writing of the document in question. No lust for power, no mad desire to be a policeman or a controller of morals; only consciousness of a duty to be done, the desire to help especially the young people, and with full awareness of the unpopularity that it was going encounter. Advantage, convenience and love of peace suggested, "Remain silent!" But the Gospel ordered: "Speak!" Which Gospel? The one that says: "Woe to you when all speak well of you. Their fathers treated the false prophets in just this way" (Lk 6:26). This is the fate of the Church when it teaches: the day when everyone claps their hands would be a terrible day: it would indicate that the Church has become a church of false prophets.

2. Speaking of the Christian religion, Tertullian pleaded: *Ne ignorata damnetur*! (Don't condemn it in ignorance).4 I do the same for the document. Don't criticize it only from hearsay or from having read what the press has often written, either carelessly or deliberately; read the document attentively and without prejudice; you will find that, while remaining faithful to the doctrines of Christ, the Holy See professes great respect for individual consciences, and shows sensitive concern and understanding for the difficulties in which people are struggling. It judges some actions, which have always been considered sinful in Christians; but it does not judge the sinners. If anything, it reminds them that God loves them and how much he loves them, and how, in certain situations they may actually not be responsible. For example, in regard to homosexuals, it says that the Church does not hold that "all those who suffer from this anomaly are personally responsible," even though homosexuality remains intrinsically evil. Stress is laid upon the great value of mutual self-giving and love between the spouses, along with the end of procreation inherent in sexual acts. In fact, Paul VI has said: "Too often the Church wrongly seemed to look at love with mistrust . . . no, God is not the enemy of the great human realities: the Church

certainly is not lacking in appreciation for the values lived daily in thousands of homes."[5]

3. The great Mozart set to music *Cosi fan tutte* [everyone is doing it] by Lorenzo da Ponte, a poet from Vittorio Veneto and the court of Vienna. That was a comic opera, but alas! "everyone is doing it" is threatening to become a moral law, an ethical norm. People no longer distinguish between what is and what should be. "Now," they reason illogically, "Everyone is doing it, it has even been shown by opinion polls. Once it was considered illicit, but that was in the Middle Ages, in a peasant civilization. Today it is licit. We are in a new context of industrial and atomic civilization; therefore it is moral, therefore no authority can prohibit it or prosecute it."

Not only is this reasoning erroneous, it can become dangerous if we broaden it from sex to crime. "Now a great many people are robbing, assaulting, killing, it is the new morality. Therefore let's adapt ourselves to it, let's accept it, let's rob and kill without scruples, too."

We might go even further: "If what was true yesterday is no longer true today, and what is true today will no longer be true tomorrow, the truth is not something fixed, but relative to a given period, to a given human psychology. Therefore it is not truth at all. It is man who creates truth; first it exists and man then discovers it; he gives himself the law, he determines what is good and what is evil." In this way, goodbye to points of reference that are fixed and the same for everyone, goodbye certainty. Only doubt and confusion remain. Take the same thing, under the same aspect, and those who say it is white and those who say it is black are both right. Any kind of morality collapses.

The Holy See deserves praise, if for nothing else, for having put up a barrier against a trend which is threatening to dissolve the family, morals, society, etc.

4. Shortly before the Council, I happened to read at the same time two writings: one by Freud, the other by Gandhi.

Freud, as you know, gives an exaggerated importance to sex. In that writing, he said, among other things: there is a meeting; some among those present are making noise and causing a disturbance. The president intervenes and has them removed. But what is this? After they have been driven from the room, they make more noise than before. They bang on the doors, they throw stones at the windows, they force the meeting to break up. Freud concluded: Have you "repressed" or driven out your sexual desires? They leave, but they take refuge in your subconscious; from there they give you no more peace. They can disturb your whole psychic makeup, causing neuroses. Freud did not generalize: he was speaking only about sick people; he also admitted that sexual desires could be "sublimated." Others, who came after him, and did not have his scientific preparation, did generalize, speaking as if sex dominated everything and could not be regulated.

Gandhi, on the other hand, tells how first he, and later his wife, gradually realized that the time had come when their spiritual maturation required them to live in perfect continence, which they both did. I will quote some of the thoughts that guided him: "The man who has chosen truth for his bride cannot give himself to others." "Chastity, like all other rules, must be observed in thought, word and deed . . . those who dominate their bodies but harbor evil thoughts are striving in vain. When the spirit goes astray, the whole body, sooner or later, follows it."

Thus wrote, thus acted, a man who was not a Christian, but is considered by everyone as possessing the highest moral wisdom.[6] Gandhi is close to Christ, who loved and counseled virginity, though stressing that voluntary virtuous continence is not for everyone, but only for those who have the grace for it (cf Mt. 19:11) and who watch and pray (cf. Mt 26:91). But Christ made all his followers understand that while the Gospel is indeed "Good News", the source of inner happiness, it is not experienced by those who yield to every kind of pleasure, without measure and rule. It is the meaning of the words "narrow gate," "carrying your cross daily," "denying yourself," or "cutting off your hand," when this becomes an occasion of scandal. Christ also said: "Everyone who looks at a woman with lust has already committed adultery with her in his heart" (Mt 5:28).

The Holy See, obviously, thinks that Christians, and still more priests or religious, must compare their doctrine and their life with these words, or at least with the example of Gandhi. It seems, instead, that many prefer to talk, along with Freud, about "catharsis" and "sublimation," with Marcuse, about the "sexual revolution," and with others, about "emotional integration."

5. "It is the way they do it that offends us," one young man wrote about the document of the Holy See. "We are in a democracy; we young people might accept an ethical system, as long as it is developed together with us, after discussion and dialogue. We don't like commands raining down from on high, we are proud of our freedom. And we don't accept this linking of sex to sin, this idea of needing forgiveness in sexual matters."

There is some good in these observations. It is right to be proud of your own freedom, to want to obey with eyes wide open, to engage in responsible dialogue. But there is also something that should be clarified.

Human laws, we know, come originally from the "base"; the members of parliament who vote on them are in fact elected by the people. In our case, on the other hand, we are talking about divine laws: the Magisterium of the Church finds them already promulgated by God and limits itself to indicating them authoritatively and explaining them. Of course, not being able to practice democracy in the strict sense, it must at least behave in a democratic spirit, by dialoguing, and serving. But in our case, the dialogue has taken place in the long preparation of the document: contacts and consultations have taken place with experts in the areas of adolescent psychology, biology, and sociology. Care was taken to ascertain that no contradiction existed between the document and the scientifically uncertain data of these sciences. It was not possible, obviously, to take into account some of the hypotheses formulated by this or that science: too many of them contradict each other.

Again: in establishing his laws, God is thinking only of our advantage and respects our freedom. He does establish an obligation that is morally binding, on the pain of the loss of his friendship. But he does not physically force anyone. For example, he doesn't stand with a leveled gun, ready to shoot those who swear or commit robbery. The Christian who obeys, however, is conscious of obeying responsibly a father who loves him. Therefore it is the obedience of a son, not of a slave: even God doesn't like servile obedience.

Now we come to sin. Everything depends on how we conceive it. If it is an obsession, self-centered anguish, a guilt complex, those who refuse to admit it are right. But this is not the right way to look at it. When I find myself in sin, I do not feel at all like an abnormal being, or a shameful disgrace or someone pointed at with an accusing finger. I think that we all must sincerely say "Father . . . forgive us our trespasses." I do not even dream of saying to myself: "You miserable wretch, you should be ashamed of yourself!" I say instead: "It has happened to you again, it could be foreseen, given your weakness, but how could have have broken your covenant of friendship with the Lord again? Renew it as soon as you can. He is already there, waiting for you and offering his help. In fact he pleads with you. It's almost as if he is asking you to give him your repented sin as a gift!"

Asking for forgiveness does not mean freeing ourselves from an obsession, but something much more attractive: allowing ourselves to be found in our wandering by the Good Shepherd; resting on his shoulder, looking forward to the great feast that he will give us to enjoy as soon as we have returned to the fold. Sin is valid for everyone; still more so for those who have the most weakness in them. It is written in the Bible: "This is how we shall . . . reassure our hearts before him in whatever our hearts condemn; for God is greater than our hearts" (cf. 1 Jn 3:10-20).

Notes

1 *Opera* 7:258-62.

2 Cf. *Lumen Genitum* (the Constitution on the Church), no. 1.

3 *Epistolario*, IV (Torino, 1959), pp. 204-205.

4 *Apologeticum*, 1, 2.

5 May 4, 1970.

6 Cf. Gandhi, *Pensieri* (Vicenza, 1950).

Test-Tube Babies

Interview with *Prospettive nel Mondo*[1]
August 1978

Q. What is your opinion on the English baby girl conceived in a laboratory?

A. It is not easy for me to answer your question like this, on the spur of the moment, from the telephone in my hospital room, where I am now, without books that I can consult. And that is not the only difficulty. I have, in fact, read up to now only a few newspaper accounts about the "English test-tube baby"; in order to make a judgment, in addition to what is in the newspapers, I would have to be acquainted with the scientific data drawn up by the two doctors who are the leading actors.[2] That is not all: at this moment, I am not speaking as a bishop, but as a journalist consulted by a colleague; in such a very delicate and almost new matter, I am also waiting for what the authentic Magisterium of the Church will decide to say, after the experts have been heard. My answer to your question is therefore personal, at my own risk, and, I might say, in the form of a conversation.

1. I share only in part the enthusiasm of those who are applauding the progress of science and technology after the birth of the English baby girl. Progress is a very fine thing, but not every kind of progress is helpful to mankind. The ABC weapons (atomic, bacteriological, and chemical) have been a kind of progress, but at the same time, a disaster for mankind. Even if the possibility of having children *in vitro* does not bring about disaster, it at least poses some enormous risks. For example: the natural ability to conceive sometimes produces, as a result, malformed children; won't the

332

ability to conceive artificially produce more? If so, won't the scientist faced with new problems be acting like the "sorcerer's apprentice," who unleashes powerful forces without being able to contain and dominate them? Another example: given the hunger for money and the lack of moral scruples today, won't there be a danger that a new industry will arise, that of "baby-manufacturing," perhaps for those who cannot or will not contract a valid marriage? If this were to happen, wouldn't it be a great setback instead of progress for the family and for society?

2. From every side the press is sending its congratulations to the English couple and best wishes to their baby girl. In imitation of God, who desires and loves human life, I too offer my best wishes to the baby girl. As for her parents, I do not have any right to condemn them; subjectively, if they have acted with the right intention and in good faith, they may even have great merit before God for what they have decided on and asked the doctors to carry out.

3. Getting down, however, to the act in itself, and good faith aside, the moral problem which is posed is: is extra-uterine fertilization *in vitro* or in a test tube, licit? Pius XII, in speaking of artificial fertilization in marriage, made, if I remember right, the following distinction: Does the intervention of the technician or doctor serve only to facilitate the marriage act? Or does it help to obtain the child by continuing, in some way, an already completed marriage act? No moral difficulty; the intervention can take place. Does the device, on the other hand, not help or prolong the marriage act, but actually exclude it or substitute for it? It is not licit to use the device, because God has bound the transmission of life to marital sexuality. So said Pius XII, more or less; I do not find any valid reasons to deviate from this norm by declaring licit the separation of the transmission of life from the marriage act.

4. "But," I have read in some newspapers, "it is ridiculous to pose moral problems to those who are availing themselves of the magnificent conquests of science. And then there are the rights of the free individual conscience." Fine, but morality is not concerned with the conquests of science: it is concerned with moral actions, through which people can make use of scientific conquests for both good and evil. As for the individual conscience, we are in agreement: it should always be followed: both when it commands and when it prohibits; the individual must, however, strive to have a properly formed conscience. Conscience, in fact, does not have the task of creating the law. It has two other tasks: that of informing itself first of what the law of God says: then of judging whether there is harmony between this law and a specific action of ours. In other words, conscience must command man, not obey man.

Notes

1 *Opera* 8:571-72.

2 In fact, at the time of Louise's birth, the English doctors, Patrick Steptoe and Robert Edwards, had not yet published a description of their procedures in a medical journal, which made many members of the medical community decide to suspend judgment on it. This was also why Luciani said that he could not comment more precisely on the morality of the actual procedure used.—Trans.

Faith and Culture

A Healthy Christian Humanism

Homily for the Feast of the Presentation[1]
February 2, 1977

Up until 1960, today was a prevalently Marian feast in the West. In the East, on the other hand, it was always a feast recalling Christ's entrance into his temple and his meeting with his fellow Jews, represented by Simeon and Anna. Simeon, however, and the modern liturgy, celebrate Christ as "light of all the nations." February 2, the fortieth day after Christmas, is considered a second Epiphany, a manifestation of Christ to the entire world.

1. Let us ask ourselves once again: for what purpose has Christ been manifested to the world? Principally to save souls, of course. But what about the body, which is attached to the soul and shares its destiny? And what about the other realities of us poor creatures, who are embodied souls and bodies animated by souls? Is everything that is not the soul to be eliminated and thrown away? My brothers and sisters, exaggerations are to be avoided. Pessimism is not becoming to believers, to whom Christ says: "Blessed are you"; to whom St. Paul says: "Rejoice in the Lord always . . . Everyone should see how unselfish you are . . . Dismiss all anxiety from your minds" (Phil 4:46). The proper way of looking at the things of this world is indicated again by St. Paul: "My brothers, your thoughts should be wholly directed to all that is true, all that deserves respect, all that is honest, pure, admirable, decent, virtuous and worthy of praise" (Phil 4:8). "Those who make use of the world should conduct themselves as if they were not using it, for the world as we know it is passing away" (1 Cor 7:31).

The saints, who have translated the Bible into practice, as artists translate music written on paper into the sounds of voices and instruments, understand this. St. John Bosco chose as his program, and copied on a page which he always kept in his breviary the following words of Ecclesiastes (3:12): "I have concluded that there is nothing better than to be happy and to do good during life."[2] Being happy, therefore, but by doing good; doing good, but by being happy.

2. And what about the "theology of the cross"? And what about the words of Jesus: "Whoever wishes to be my follower must deny his very self, take up his cross each day, and follow in my steps" (Lk 9:23)? May God keep me from diminishing the force of these holy words. They have been, and still are, explained by some people, even saints, in the harshest sense. I would like to explain them, as others have done, in the always difficult sense of changing ourselves, of renewing ourselves inside. Self-denial, therefore, is in harmony with the "*metanoia*," the "change of heart," that Christ preached from the beginning: something that is not easy and must be begun again every day. This kind of renunciation, which requires effort, struggle, conviction and deep commitment, which does away with the kind of "religious puppets" who are moved by pure conventions, and forms a race of "religious athletes" who are guided by authentic convictions, is also suited to our psychological makeup. In each one of us there is an *I* and in the *I*, alas, is sin. As I fight within myself, for myself, I must not throw away the *I*, which God always loves, but the fault, the sin, which God does not love in me, and which causes me harm.

3. But we are living in a world which, even visibly, seems to be completely "under the power of the evil one" (1 Jn 5:19). How do we preserve optimism? Certainly not by refusing to lift a finger, but by doing everything possible, having faith in Him who said "Take courage, I have overcome the world" (Jn 16:33), and by not wasting our time complaining. Bonomelli wrote: Invectives against the times in which we live are useless and harmful. Useless, because they complained in the same way in the times of Solomon,

Aristophanes and Horace; there is nothing more common and nothing less effective than this kind of whining. They are harmful, because they annoy some people who do not want to see tears all the time, and they paralyze others with fear. Our age has its troubles, and great ones. But it has its advantages, which we must know how to use properly; it has its merits, which it is right to recognize.

4. I return to the *I*, which is composed of spirit, sensibility, and body. The spirit is the center of culture, which people talk about so muchtoday. It can be humanistic culture, an expression of *homo sapiens*, that is, knowledge of letters, arts and sciences; it can be the culture of *homo faber*, completely taken up by work and dynamic action, that is, by a way of living, enjoying yourself, working, expressing yourself, dressing, praying, eating, etc. Some people have written that in the past the Church was against culture. I would say: some in the Church were against it; they were usually exaggerated spirits like Tertullian, who wrote: "What is there in common between Jerusalem and Athens? Between the Academy and the Church? We no longer have any need to speculate after Jesus Christ, nor to research now that we have the Gospel."[3] A more recent case is that of Gaume, who in 1852 wrote the book *The Worm Eating Away at Modern Society*, where "worm" indicates the study of the classics. Dupanloup and others immediately rose up against the book, and Pius IX published the brief *Inter multiplices* (1853), in which he asserted that the classics, read in the proper spirit, are very useful. Other Catholics, although favorable to culture, like St. Augustine, were carried away in the heat of discussion, and used a few isolated pessimistic expressions.

But the Catholic Church, on the whole, has always appreciated culture and condemned the exaggerations of the zealots. It is usually believed that it was the fifteenth-century humanists who were the first to think that knowledge of the Greek and Roman classics ennobled human life. But Servatus Lupus, a Benedictine abbot, lived in the 9th century; he not only knew the Latin classics perfectly, quoting them constantly in his many letters, but approved the thought of the priest Probus, a friend of his from Mainz, who removed both Cicero and Virgil from hell in order to place them in heaven. That's how much he admired them! It is only one case among many. Already Clement of Alexandria, in the 3rd century, believed secular culture to be an indispensable preparation (*propaideia*) for the formation of the religious soul. Other Fathers began the legend of a Socrates enlightened by the Word and Plato as a tributary of the Bible. Didn't Eusebius of Caesarea write that "Plato is a Greek Moses?" St. Basil, St. Gregory Nazianzen, and St. John Chrysostom also showed great appreciation for the "worldly" poets. St. Peter Damian, at first an austere monk, and then a cardinal, would feel nostalgia for the time when "*mihi Tullius indulcescebat* when Cicero delighted me." As you can see, classical culture is often appreciated by churchmen for its own sake, and not only because it is helpful to religion. Pope Nicholas V would give money to Lorenzo Valla and Poggio Bracciolini because they cultivated the classics, though he knew that their minds were against the Church. St. Francis de Sales, the founding father of "devout humanism," would write that culture does indeed help devotion: he would add however, that devotion, in turn, helps culture.[4]

5. Human sensibility regards the heart and its emotions. "Either God or man" some people have said. "If I take God seriously, the rest must be nothing to me." Blessed Angela of Foligno, a great mystic, who expressed with unheard-of vehemence the tragedy of a Christian life crucified with Christ, desired to belong completely and solely to God. After losing first her mother, then her husband and children, she wrote: "I had begged God to rid me of them all; their death was a great consolation to me."[5] These are extremely harsh expressions, perhaps they are good for some exceptional souls, but they are not to be imitated. The same Blessed Angela showed herself more moderate and practical when it came to giving advice to a group of devout people who had gathered around her. The correct

expression, therefore, is not "Either God or man," but: "Both God and man," man to be loved as God wants, in a manner subordinated to divine love.

Let's take an example from the Bible. It calls Jacob holy (Dn 3:35) and loved by God (Mal 1:3; Rom 9:13). And yet he worked seven years to win Rachel as his wife, "and they seemed to him but a few days," says the Bible, "because of the love he had for her" (cf. Gn 29:20). Francis de Sales comments on this and writes: "Jacob loves Rachel with all his might, and he loves God with all his might; but he does not therefore love Rachel as God nor God as Rachel. He loves God as his God, above all things and more than himself; he loves Rachel as his wife, above all other women and as himself. He loves God with absolutely and totally supreme love and Rachel with supreme marital love; one love is not contrary to the other, because love for Rachel does not violate the supreme prerogatives of love for God."[6] In other words, love for God excludes only those loves which would be against God or more than God; other loves are sometimes enjoined, sometimes permitted, with the one condition that the love of God predominates. I must love my parents, my wife, my husband, my children; I can love art, books, entertainment. It is enough that I do not love anything against God, or more than God.

6. As for the body, some pious authors have presented it solely as a holocaust to be offered to God: Then God would be a God who expects only the immolation of this body. This is exaggerated. The body is an instrument. God has given it to us and wants it to serve us, on our part, we must take care of it, preserve it and use it well. The Lord at times during His mortal life had His body undergo fasting and vigils. Ordinarily, however, He did not treat it as "Brother Ass." Jesus slept and ate like the Apostles; His penances were first of all his everyday manual work; then the journeys, speaking at length, receiving people of all kinds, patiently bearing the criticisms of his enemies and the faults of his apostles, adapting himself to whatever food and lodgings there were when traveling to

preach. Our ordinary penance is the "daily tragedy": the ordinary actions of every day sometimes become tragic through their constant repetition with the monotony of actions, of surroundings, of people. In order to face this "tragedy," the body must not be weak, but strong. If you do not sleep at night and if you eat too little, it is difficult to succeed in accomplishing your work properly during the day. St. Francis de Sales said: "In two instances deer run badly; when they are weighted down by eating too much, and when they are too thin through lack of food." He added, "health and holiness go together." And to the very austere Mother Angelique Arnauld, the abbess of Port Royal, he wrote: "Don't burden yourselves with too many vigils and fasts . . . you enter the Royal Gate of religious life through the royal road of love of God and your neighbor, humility and kindness."[7]

All this concerns the body in its principal aspects. There are the secondary ones: entertainment, dress, neatness and personal appearance, etc. Here there also comes on the scene the virtue of *eutrapelia*, which we never hear about. But St. Thomas, recommended it. Be eutrapelic, he said, that is, capable of turning the things you hear and see into laughter, in the appropriate way and measure.[8] *Eutrapelus*, he explained, is someone who *bene convertit aliqua dicta vel facta in solacium* [turns everything said or done into solace].[9] St. Philip Neri, a eutrapelic saint par excellence, once said to Pope Clement VIII: "May they kill you!" All those present held their breath, but Philip continued, "For faith in Jesus Christ!" They all let out their breath and laughed. It is all right to hope a Pope may die a martyr. Being a comedian, St. Thomas adds, is not something illicit in itself, since it tends to amuse people.[10] Mark Twain, with his newspapers and humorous books; Chaplin with his farces, brilliant and human at the same time; and Goldoni with his comedies, could have become saints, according to St. Thomas, if they had added to their art and their genius the right intention and the practice of the other Christian virtues. We would have had in them attractive, smiling patron saints, to teach Christians how they can and should laugh. There seems to be a need for it. Considering all the vulgarity that exists today, what Tommaseo said is still valid: "The Italians are like toothless old women: they don't know how to laugh without spitting." St. Thomas goes even farther and states that boorishness, or excessive seriousness, can be a sin: "Those who do not participate in jokes, who say nothing to cause laughter are committing a sin; they annoy those who are speaking, because they do not react properly to moderate jokes. *Tales vitiosi sunt, et dicuntur duri et agrestes* [Such people are defective and they are called crude and boorish]."11

The Christian and the *homo ludens*, therefore, go well together. A Christian and a well-dressed person are also in harmony, if St. Francis de Sales could write: "I would like my devout man and my devout women to always be the best dressed at a gathering."12 In other words, Christianity and a healthy humanism, Christianity and optimism, are closer than is usually believed.

With Paul VI the Christian makes his the words of Terence *"Homo sum et humani nil alienum a me esse puto:* I am a man, and I think nothing that is human strange to me," and of Shakespeare: "How beauteous mankind is."13 I then compare these words with the words of Psalm 8: "What is man, [O God] . . . You have made him a little less than the angels and crowned him with glory and honor . . . putting all things under his feet" (Ps 8:57). I conclude from this: our religion encourages man to beautiful things, to progress, to advancement: it really does not want inertia and stagnation; in it a just "human advancement" is actually a part of evangelization.

Notes

1 *Opera* 8:26-31.

2 *Memorie biografiche*, XVIII, pp. 806ff.

3 *De praescriptione* 7.

4 Cf. *Teotimo*, 1, 6.

5 *Le livre des visions de la b. Angèle de Foligno* (Paris, 1910), pp. 47-48.

6 *Teotimo,* 1, 4.

7 *Oeuvres*, XVIII, p. 390.

8 *Commentario all Etica di Nicomaco* (Turin-Rome, 1949), p. 235ff.

9 *Summa* 22, q. 168, a. 2.

10 *Summa* 22, q. 168, a. 3 ad 3.

11 *Summa* 22, q. 168, a. 4.

12 *Filotea*, 3, 25.

13 *The Tempest*, v. 1. 183.—Trans.

Fra Claudio Granzotto: Artist and Saint

Opening of the Informative Diocesan Process[1]
December 16, 1959

In St. Peter's basilica, at the end of the apse, there is an altar called the altar of the cathedra; high above it, there is an oval space surrounded by rays: the famous "Gloria" of Bernini.

To arrive up there, canonized, with your head surrounded by the halo of the saints, is the greatest honor that can come to a child of the Church. The greatest honor and also the end of an extraordinary flight, one that can only be accomplished on two wings: the testimony of God and human testimony. The testimony of God, or the miracles, the human testimony, or the sworn deposition of witnesses. Both of these testimonies must be submitted to a most diligent examination, to processes that can last for years and even centuries. It is at the beginning of one of these processes that you have been present this evening.

It happened like this. The Order of Friars Minor, through the Postulator General, used this line of reasoning with me, the bishop: "We Franciscans have seen hundreds and hundreds of our own rise up there, in the "glory" of Bernini, from St. Francis, St. Anthony and St. Bonaventure down to the last, who is St. Carlo da Sezze.[2] We also now have under study hundreds of subjects, who we consider fit to rise, to take flight for the same post: among them, Excellency, there is one who is truly a flower that blossomed in your diocese: Fra Claudio, in the world Riccardo Granzotto.[3] From what we have been able to observe, the two wings are already working; on one hand, people are asserting that many graces have been received from the Lord through the intercession of this servant of God; on the other, people are saying more and more that he is a saint, an authentic saint. Will you agree, Excellency, to set in motion the machinery of the processes and the examinations?" With all simplicity, I said, "Yes!"

To be more precise, I must say that this evening we are beginning two processes: the one of the writings and the informative one. It is called informative because its aim is not declaring whether or not Fra Claudio is a saint, but gathering the sworn statements from the witnesses about his life, his virtues and the miracles claimed. When these two processes are finished in Vittorio Veneto, the bishop will not make any judgment, but will close and seal everything and send it under seal to Rome. It will then be up to the postulator of the order to see to it that they open these two packages in Rome, and that they study and properly examine them to see if this is really something solid.

If everything goes well, as we hope and wish, the Pope will emit the decree *De introducenda causa*: we will then be at the true introduction of the cause. And to introduce means to begin again, because the Holy See will give an order to redo this process from beginning to end here in Vittorio Veneto, which will be the first step on a new, very long iter, which it is not my intention to explain here. Here I only want to add this: I willingly agreed that the process should be begun because I hope and trust that Fra Claudio has a message to deliver.

You will say: "It is a message for the diocese of Vittorio Veneto!" No! Of course, the diocese of Vittorio Veneto feels honored that one of its children gives hope of being raised to the heights of the saints. And a possible canonization will turn out to be very beneficial, because saints never pass in vain through our parts.

You will say: "Then it is for the Franciscan order!" Not that either! The brothers in religion of the servant of God, especially, the little brothers of Chiampo (the Fratini), who you see here and the fathers of the convent in Vittorio Veneto, will rejoice if Providence decrees that Fra Claudio is to rise to the honors of the altars, but they have hundreds and hundreds of Franciscan saints from whom they can draw light, encouragement and guidance.

What then? The message is for the class of artists. Fra Claudio was an artist! And he has something to say to the art world.

And first of all, he can help artists understand that art is subject to the moral law. Not all artists are convinced of this. At the movies I have observed more than once the logo of Metro-Goldwyn-Mayer: a lion comes out roaring; then there appears the writing: Ars gratia artis [art for art's sake], then a second lion stretching out its claws and opening its jaws wide in a new roar, as though to say: "Art for art's sake! We artists are independent and we will defend this independence like lions!" And they really seem like lions! For them, art is superior to moral laws: an artist, while he is making a work of art, is obedient to no one; outside of this, while he is not making art, perhaps he will observe the commandments, but while he is making art, he is independent, he is in a parentheses, which is closed off, outside and above moral laws! Therefore you have this kind of claim of the artist, of saying: "Once I am an artist I am a godlike being, someone superior. I will not submit myself." And it is difficult to persuade them. If you present yourself to them as a bishop, a priest, anyone who offers exhortations, they roar at you: "You are not an artist! You don't understand anything! Don't meddle here!"

Let Fra Claudio come! Frau Claudio can present himself to these people and say: "I am an artist! I studied six years at the Academy in Venice, I graduated with the highest marks, I received congratulations from the greatest professors of that time, I loved art. I refused to become a Benedictine because they did not guarantee that I would be able to continue to be an artist. I have seen and caressed my masterpieces, like creatures of my own, quivering with life; what you feel I have felt too. But I never dreamed that because of this I had the right to set myself apart from the law of God. Art yes, is an elevated thing, but not above everything. I compared my masterpieces with other things and I said (these are his own words), 'to serve one Mass is worth more than all the sculptures in this world.' And while I was chiseling away at my Wildtian works,[4] I asked the Lord to be chiseled in turn. And I said: "O Lord, make of me your masterpiece!"

What a voice this will be for artists! The lion will answer the lions.

Fra Claudio could bring a second, more specific warning to those who work in the field of sacred art. Sacred art today, in fact, finds few people who will understand it and treating as they should: when they enter a church, these blessed artists find it difficult to enter with their heads bowed, and instead they think like this: "We are artists, therefore masters." And they do not understand that in church they are guests, never masters. When they entered to work for the churches, Raphael and Michelangelo graciously asked the advice of theologians, they even beat their breasts, out of compunction. It seems that this was done in vain for certain artists, who are not yet persuaded that in order to make a work sacred, you must first feel it and study it as sacred! To the repeated admonitions of the ecclesiastical authorities, they continue to answer: "You are not an artist, you don't understand!" Who knows what will happen with Frau Claudio? What if he presents himself to them as an artist and as a saint at the same time? As one who knows these things, who has very recently lived them?

Eight hours he sometimes spent in church praying, eight hours at a time! When they saw him kneeling, the peasants and pious people, they left the church on tiptoe, saying, "We don't want to disturb a prayer so filled with the Lord!"

Frau Claudio first remained in contemplation, he first heated his heart in the furnace of divine love; then, when he was well heated and had truly contemplated, only then did he set his hand to his masterpiece, and when his masterpiece was finished, he returned to contemplate and tried to bring what he had sculpted to life again. It is a powerful teaching, and one that we should truly hope becomes a teaching for artists.

I have nothing else to say.

You have heard the names of those making up the tribunal. They have been chosen by the bishop, they have the bishop's trust; to them I express the hope that they may proceed in their work, quickly and successfully. It will not be the result that is the reward for their labor, because here the road is full of unknown factors; here we have to apply the words of St. Paul: *Non volentis neque currentis, sed miserentis est Dei* [it depends not upon a person's will or exertion, but upon God, who shows mercy] (Rom 9:16).

If this cause that is beginning today reaches port, it will be due in part to the good will, care, attention, diligence and zeal of all those who have had a hand in it; but above all it will be due to the mercy of the Lord, who, only because it has pleased him, chooses who he wills from the group of so many chosen souls, the one that he decrees should be set on the candelabrum of the holy Church.[5]

Notes

[1] *Opera* 2:60-63.

[2] He had just recently been beatified, on April 12, 1959.—Trans.

[3] Born to a peasant family in Santa Lucia del Piave in Treviso on August 23, 1900, Riccardo Granzotto graduated from the Academy of Fine Arts in Venice in 1929. He joined the Franciscan order in 1933, where as Fra Claudio, he remained a lay brother. He was known as much for his intense prayer and work for the poor as for his religious sculptures. But his life was soon cut short by a brain tumor, when he was only 46, on August 15, 1947.—Trans.

[4] Adolfo Wildt (1868-1931) was an Italian sculptor, and Fra Claudio was in a sense of his school.—Trans.

[5] Luciani's hopes for Fra Claudio's cause were fulfilled, though he didn't live to see it. Pope John Paul II, who shared Luciani's belief in the importance of the vocation of the artist in Christian life, beatified Fra Claudio on November 20, 1994. At the beatification Mass, he said: "He knew how to express the contemplation of the infinite Divine beauty in the art of sculpture, of which he was a master."—Trans.

Prayers

A Prayer For The Beatification

Of Pope John Paul 1

Lord Jesus,

You Who gave to us the great joy of venerating
Pope John Paul I as Your Vicar on earth,
and then in Your inscrutable designs,
gave us the immense sorrow of his unexpected departure,
grant us the graces that we ask of You . . . so that,
sure of his intercession with You,
we may one day venerate him on the altars;
then his goodness and humility presented as an example
to the faithful, will be a perpetual invitation
to translate his teaching into life and to spread serenity and love.
      Amen

         † Maffeo Ducoli, Bishop of
         Belluno-Feltre

Call to Prayer by Bl. John Paul II

Let us pray to good Pope John Paul I,
especially for the Church so greatly loved by him,
That he may obtain for us the grace of unity and sanctity.

To the people gathered at Castel Gandolfo for the Angelus,
August 26, 1981.

Prayer for the Intercession of John Paul 1

Triune God, Cenacle of Love
From whose benevolence
life has its origins
And in whose will
our happiness grows

We ask you to exalt among us
the work of your love
As we recognize the original holiness
of your servant Albino Luciani,
Pope John Paul I.

In our needs, we invoke his intercession
In order to obtain the grace we need.
Grant it to us that we may imitate
His serene abandonment in You.

May we be sustained by that example of prayer
through which during his life
he opened his whole heart to You,
And now in your glory,
he praises You. Amen

† Vincenzo Savio
Bishop of Belluno-Feltre (†2004)

About the Translator

Lori Pieper received her BA in the Humanities and MA in History from the University of Northern Iowa and her PhD in Medieval History from Fordham University. Her historical books include *The Greatest of These is Love: the Life of St. Elizabeth of Hungary* (2007). She has had articles published in many periodicals, including *Our Sunday Visitor*, *The Catholic Digest* and *L'Osservatore Romano*. She has also worked for some years as a professional translator. Since 1990, she has contributed translations of John Paul I's writings to the journal *Humilitas*; some of these appeared in *The Smiling Pope: The Life and Teaching of Pope John Paul I*, published by Our Sunday Visitor in 2004. She is also working on an upcoming biography of this Pope. A member of the Secular Franciscan Order, she lives and works in the Bronx, New York.

Available from Tau Cross Books and Media:

A Woman for Our Time: St. Elizabeth of Hungary (DVD)

A Passionate Adventure: Living the Catholic Faith Today by Pope John Paul I (e-book and paperback)

The Greatest of These is Love: The Life of St. Elizabeth of Hungary (2nd rev ed) by Lori Pieper (e-book; paperback coming soon).

www.taucrossbooks.com

Tau Cross Books and Media
30 W. 190th St., Apt. 6N
Bronx, NY 10468-2553
(646) 938-0432